(A WRITTEN INTERVENTION)

BY W. P. IRISH

FOREWORD

To give up smoking for good there is only one technique. This technique is called giving up smoking for good and it is done using the stop fucking smoking method. This method is a written intervention which tells you exactly why you need to stop making excuses and get on with it. It is the no nonsense approach to using your lungs to breathe air. The tools for this method are common sense and Willpower. It is different to any type of smoking book you may have read previously because it will speak to you in a way that many don't like being spoken to. My intention in writing this book is to stop you from killing yourself through smoking and nothing else. It is written as a straight forward no nonsense approach without the usual bullshit techniques, strategies and celebratory back slapping. I do not require you to read the book in its entirety as I believe those who are serious about quitting will get the message after the first 100 pages. If you feel the need to finish the book and still continue to smoke afterwards, then you are a selfish idiot who will die a smoker and that's a promise.

This is not a threat. This is a medical and statistical fact. I typically rant and rave about things which irritate me or that I'm passionate about. As you can see from the title, this filthy addiction is something I'm not too fond of. When I started writing, I initially planned on writing a couple of pages that I would give to family and friends after listening to the same bullshit excuses over and over again as to why or when or how they couldn't quit smoking. This was to be my gift of intervention to their self-pitying plight. I understand this through my own addiction to this poisonous shit. I spent many years talking the same bullshit and feeling sorry for myself coming up with any excuse to go back for one last drag. Many books you will read on this subject will string you along until the end to find out the secret ingredient, magic trick or some other shit, but I'll just tell you how I personally did it from the first page. It was simple in theory and hard in practice but it worked for me. This was to be the last time I ever placed a cancer stick in my mouth and I never will again.

It is just over 13 years ago that I decided to put down a box that contained 20 poisonous cancer sticks and replaced it with a 24 pack of breakfast biscuits (Weetabix) cereal. And that's it. Instead of having a smoke, I ate a dry biscuit with a swig of water. I kept this up for 21 days as I used 21 days as my detox period. In my mind, if I decided to smoke after that, then I was a fucking idiot who deserved whatever happened to him. I'll talk about that later on but just so you know, there was no magic cure for my many failed attempts only a willingness to live. Get this clear from the very start. My thoughts during this detox and since then are all contained in the words you are now reading and are not pleasant. No scaremongering, just truth. These are some of the things you probably don't ever give a second thought to whilst trying to quit, but that you most certainly need to hear.

I didn't pen this originally to become a book. It just so turned out that the more I wrote, the more nicotine and the addiction to smoking irritated me, so I kept going off on the rant you now hold in your hands. The two pages I originally planned to write quickly turned into over 200. It was not written to cater to weak self-pitying individuals. You will not read 'please' or 'thank you' directed at you. The book is an intervention and should be treated no differently. It is written to intervene in your dangerous stupidity. The discussion in the book is no different than a conversation with a family member who genuinely gives a shit about you being around. It rants and it raves unapologetically and its tangents will leave you trying to catch your breath. Many of you will wheeze whilst trying to keep up with its pace. But this is the beauty of the whole book. If you do wish to complete it and take its advice, then taking a breath is something you won't have to worry about from now on. I hope common sense prevails and you get a grip on the reality of what you are doing to yourself. Enjoy reading this book because I most certainly enjoyed writing it, as much as a fucking idiot it made me realise I actually was for putting this shit near my body in the first place.

W. P. IRISH 2016

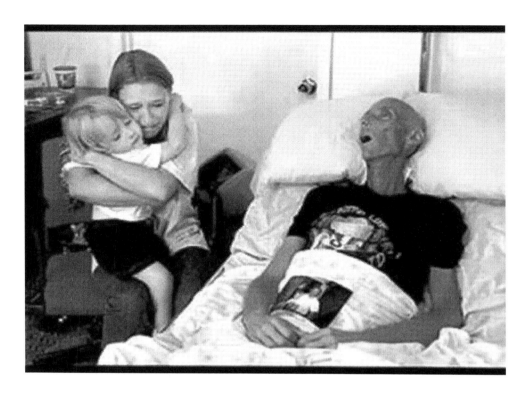

BRYAN CURTIS LAYS DYING, SURROUNDED BY HIS YOUNG FAMILY

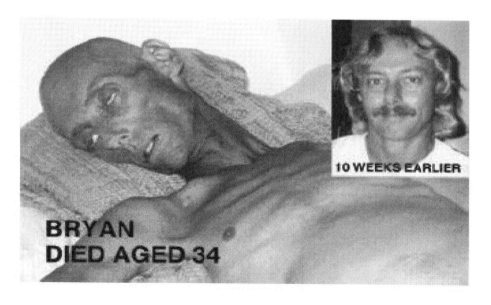

A YOUNG LIFE TAKEN THROUGH AN ADDICTION TO NICOTINE....

Contents

INTRODUCTION		p 1
1	In memory of Bryan Curtis	p 5
2	On borrowed time	p 10
3	The Unimmaculate Conception	p 17
4	Shit talk, (because shit sticks)	p 25
5	Born again smokers	p 27
6	The gambler who joined the 50/50 club	p 32
7	A dirty habit or a filthy disgusting addiction?	p 37
8	In denial, in deep shit	p 43
9	No smoke without fire	p 49
10	Shitting on your own doorstep	p 54
11	"My family means everything to me" and other bullshit	p 60
12	The devolution of the nicotine addict	p 67
13	Births, deaths, marriages and the any excuse, excuse!	p 70
14	Do my lungs look black in this?	p 73
15	The best sex you've never had	p 81
16	Your breath smells like shit	p 86
17	Woe is me	p 89
18	Smoke signals	p 95
19	Putting your money where your mouth is	p 102
20	Simon Cowell (1959-2025) REST IN PEACE	p 108
21	Hollywood and the blame game	p 114
22	My kingdom for a hearse	p 124
23	Quit the shit, and the bullshit	p 129
24	Smoke and mirrors	p 135
25	A friend in need and an enemy indeed	p 141
26	Who or what the fuck is Willpower?	p 148
27	No ifs or butts	p 155
28	Saying no to the yes men	p 161
29	I want to live	p 167
30	The 10 commandments of the ex-smoker	p 175
31	Joe versus the volcano	p 182
32	21 days of hell for a lifetime of heavenly health	p 189
33	The conversation on a poisonous past	p 193

INTRODUCTION.

Let's be very clear from the start that this book is not going to be pleasant for everyone and this is by design. An intervention for those not in the know is not about telling you how wonderful you are. Interventions take place when a person affects everyone around them with their addiction or reckless behaviour. Some may see their addiction to nicotine as a harmless habit or that the only person being harmed "is myself" and this is an ignorant contradiction. This is undoubtedly the biggest health issue you currently face. If ignorance is bliss then smoking will ensure that you probably die in ignorance and bliss doesn't come in the same sentence as a premature cancer related death. If you are soft or weak then stop reading and keep smoking the poison which is almost certain to kill you on short notice. If on the other hand you have someone or something to live for then read on to see if the words you read are as offensive to your ears as the 4000 chemicals(in every cancer stick) that your body is offended by, every time you force it to inhale toxic poisonous shit. This book was written for one purpose and that is to intervene in the lives of those who are cutting their lives short. It was written by more of a street scoundrel and not a scholar or saint, so don't expect any Pulitzer type language of the gods. It was not written for academic debate, drama or for controversy and if it happens to get discussed because of either or because of all three, then good. Oscar Wilde famously wrote "the only thing that's worse than being talked about is not being talked about" and public perception on this filthy addiction needs to be discussed urgently. It's not making any apologies or taking any softly softly approaches and doesn't really give a fuck for critics. Referencing, citations and all that crap can be found in journals and this is not a journal, dictionary or text book, so go back to the library if proper grammar and literary perfection is your thing. Let's not fall out over spelling mistakes and misplaced commas. The message this book wishes to convey is very simple and it's written on the cover for everyone to see. Those who have tried every conceivable way of quitting this poisonous shit will benefit if they manage to read the book from the first page to the last (if needed), without flinging their rattler out of the playpen. Don't expect any bullshit self-help, hypnotic; breathe easy type of book you've read previously as this book wasn't written to enlighten your soul, but to open your eyes and your lungs.

We must make it clear from the beginning that what you are doing to your body is butchering it with poisonous chemicals, and this book will not congratulate anything less than full abstinence from inhaling poisonous shit. You are killing yourself and you are not taking it seriously. You're listening to loved ones begging you to stop and you are not taking it seriously. You are struggling to run far, (or for some), walk up a stairs and you are not taking it seriously.... and sadly, (for all of you) you are dying prematurely, without taking it seriously. This does not make you the lovable fool who laughs in the face of danger type of moron. This is the fucking idiot who is inconsiderate and idiotic enough to believe it will never happen to them, and then whinges and whines uncontrollably when told that they have a smoking related terminal disease or cancer. It is this ridiculous bravado which leaves your husband, wife, children, family or friends mourning your passing and all because you decided to ignore the scientific and medical facts, that 1 in 2 smokers will die of cancer or of a premature death. This doesn't make you a hero. It makes you a smoking related cancer statistic. A sad, needless and unavoidable waste because you whinged for your cancer sticks until you got your own way and the disease to go with it. This is a mess you are in, that only you can get yourself out of. You created this mess by starting to inhale this shit and only you can clean it up by putting air in your lungs instead of addictive poisonous chemicals.

For far too long now, many addicts of this poisonous shit throw tantrums or use excuses to get their way. You will not get that in an intervention. You sit still and listen for a change. Life and everything in between is no longer going to be held accountable as reason or as logic to destroy every cell in your body with addictive poisonous chemicals. The blame in this dangerous game stops firmly with you. Remember that no one pointed a gun at your head and demanded you inhale your first cigarette, so stop thinking back to the workmate or the old school friend who offered you a smoke when you were twelve and pointing the brown stained finger of blame. You may have started as a child but now it is time to behave like an adult and take control of your health, your pocket, and more importantly your life. The blame game is something every addict of nicotine plays, along with using the any excuse (type of excuse), which we will elaborate more on in further chapters. The best way to prepare yourself from the very get go is to acknowledge that your addiction is exactly that ..."**your addiction**", and is not to be mistaken with the first person who got you hooked, your spouse or just because you see some insensitive celebrity prick endorsing its poisonous use. Excuses as you will learn, are for the feeble and the weak and have no place in conquering an addiction like nicotine for good. If you are killing yourself just because "they do it in Hollywood", then you fit into this feeble or weak category and need to harden the fuck up, because back in the real world, your biological clock is counting down quicker than nature intended. If you think the occasional smoke isn't that bad, then it is this misguided fools belief that we must tackle as soon as possible. Sympathy as you will see, isn't going to be in abundance for anyone who puts this poisonous shit into their lungs, bloodstream, heart and brain and thinks that this isn't a bad thing. I abused my own body for years with this cancerous poison and considered myself one of these indestructible heroes and I'll elaborate more about my own addictive credentials as we progress. Let it be known that I'm not a campaigner of any sort. What you are doing to your body in the privacy of your own home is your own business and I don't give a fuck whether you read this book or fuck it into the fire. Whichever you choose to do will tell a lot about how determined you actually are. What I do care about is anyone, be it the stranger at the bus stop or your children in the car, your long suffering spouse, elderly parent, basically anyone for that matter, who has to inhale this poisonous cancerous shit against their will because of your stupidity or the ignorance of others.

A strong individual will quickly acknowledge mistakes made and will try making amends by moving on through making changes to their offending behaviour. A weak individual will make excuses and point at everyone but themselves and fall back into the same habits. They will sulk without ever progressing, always feeling sorry for themselves. Which one are you? I know which one I was when I blamed everyone and everything around me. I also know who I became, and how liberated I felt when I took responsibility for the damage I was doing to my body and to those I forced to inhale the shitty fumes from my poisonous addiction. It has since left me with a horrible taste in my mouth when I see the damage caused by a poisonous product that has no place in society and most certainly not the human body. This could I suppose, be classed as my own personal hate and has given rise to my distain with anything nicotine or smoking related.

What led me to write this book was reading an article written in an American paper about the man on the images you have just looked at inside this book. The skeletal man in the pictures were for me, shocking to say the least, but it was the fact that we had so much in common and the manner in which he died, that led me to start writing this. We were both the same age, worked in construction, had a young family and I too had smoked for many years. I was blessed to stop when I did and looking at these pictures made me more grateful that I had. I showed these images to many friends and family, many of whom glanced briefly and reacted by turning away horrified and refusing to look at them. This to me was offensive as it meant that the man in the picture had died in vain which is something he didn't want. He wanted people to look long and hard and to **stop fucking smoking**.

That man was Bryan Curtis and just like me, his story will be very similar to many of your own. I would like to think that by reading this book and understanding the message that he wished to convey to the smokers (or would be smokers of the world), that his death wasn't in vain. Bryan didn't expect to die and he wanted people to acknowledge that this horrible suffering can await any smoker. There are people (and I firmly believe this) who turn the television off, or turn away when they see advertisements on starving children or other suffering human beings. I believe this is because it's a stark factual reality of the shitty world in which we live and many can't handle this because it involves the truth about how things really are. To not have to view the horrors of the world or the situations we prefer not to deal with, many of us choose to turn away in denial. Those who turn away may do so because it hurts them to see the truth or because a starving child puts them off the pizza they just happen to be eating at that particular moment, or they simply may feel a sense of guilt. There are many reasons and every one of us will react differently. Then there are those who force themselves to watch it and react angrily and decide to contribute or donate so they take action to make a difference or change. How did you react when you looked at the dying man in the pictures you just looked at? If you quickly turned away, then look again. This was the hope of the dying Bryan Curtis. This is what many of you have already done. Some of you glanced at the pictures and quickly flicked the page or closed the book. Others showed it straight away to a family member or friend for shock purposes and some of you are still staring at it in disbelief because the reality of the addiction you keep trying to conquer, has hit you straight in the face hard just like Bryan Curtis would have wanted. His goal was for you to take heed. I personally believe that every human being wants to leave a mark on the world and this is what Bryan Curtis done with his own life, in the short months he had left. Let's talk a little more about the man in the photos who inspired me to put pen to the paper, which became this book..........

IN MEMORY OF BRYAN CURTIS.

You do not have to stare at the images of Bryan Curtis in order to see that he doesn't have much time left to live. A glance at his pictures is enough for any person to see that this is a human being in distress. It is not a case of telling someone to have a long hard look just to add to the shock value as a glance is what most smokers will give anyway. This picture simply is what it is and unfortunately it is the last photograph to be taken of Bryan Curtis alive. These photos, as graphic as they may seem are used on cigarette packages as a warning to smokers (or would be smokers) of the dangers involved, when inhaling their poisonous carcinogenic (cancer causing chemicals) toxic fumes. The image you see above is the same man only eight weeks before his untimely death, taken with his two year old son, smiling and completely oblivious to the fact that the end of his life was only months away. Pictures may paint a thousand words but this graphic image says only three and again, the title of this book is a clue. The following few pages will give you an account of Bryan Curtis's life and tragic demise.

Like many smokers worldwide Bryan Curtis started young. He was 13 when he had his first cigarette and was smoking two packs a day when he was diagnosed with his terminal illness. Call it habit, addiction or stupidity, Bryan continued to smoke right up until he no longer had the strength in his body to inhale any more. From the first cigarette he smoked to the last puff he inhaled, it was his choice and he paid for this choice with his life. Little was he to know when he did at first light up, that in the short space of 21 years, he would no longer walk the earth. Working as a roofer in the construction sector, Bryan was as able bodied and as physically fit as any other young 33 year old. As a mechanic he also worked on cars and machinery and like any young healthy person reading this, could never have imagined he would get cancer, let alone a terminal cancer.

This is the first misconception amongst many of the world's smokers; they forget that cancer doesn't discriminate. It kills young, old, the infirm, healthy weak and strong and cancer doesn't recognise race, skin colour sex or gender. After attending his local hospital following severe abdominal pain on the second of April, Bryan was to soon learn that the stomach ache he was having was caused by oat cell lung cancer which had spread to his liver. He did not have it very long but the disease, also known as small cell lung cancer was a very aggressive type of cancer known to be a killer that usually gave its sufferers only months to live. Doctor Jeffrey Paonessa, the oncologist who treated Bryan was not surprised by his diagnosis as he was seeing more and more young people presenting themselves to the hospital with the same condition. Chemotherapy which can sometimes slow the progression in certain cases was tried but unfortunately for Bryan, this had no effect as it had already started spreading to the vital organs of his body.

I believe that it doesn't matter how well a person's coping mechanism is or how strong a person believes themselves to be mentally. When you are given the news that all efforts have failed, and all hope is lost, it is completely natural to feel a sense of utter shock, sadness and I suppose betrayal to an extent, to know that your body has given up and is telling you that it's now time to go. Nothing can prepare a person for such news and if you are a 33 year old father of 2 children, then it is all the more devastating. Bryan Curtis took the horrible blow that was dealt to him and he made a decision. His death would not be in vain he decided. Some good has to come out of such a tragedy and it did. He wanted to get his story told and he wanted to get the message across that "this is what smoking does". "Look at what it did to me" is what he wanted to say.

One can only imagine the thoughts which consumed his mind. I did not expect to die. I didn't have life insurance because I didn't think I needed it. I'm 34 next month and I won't get to see my 34th birthday. I have to leave my partner to raise my two children on her own. I won't get to play ball with my son or watch my daughter get married. I'll never get to see my grandchildren. There is no more holding hands while walking on a beach for me or growing old with my wife and all because of a filthy disgusting addiction. Bryan Curtis spent his last days at home struggling to sum up the strength to get his affairs in order and arranging his funeral service. Anytime he ventured outside and got stared at on the streets by young kids he would warn them "this is what happens when you smoke". The kids would react shocked which is what Bryan hoped to see. Bryans mother Louise Curtis called newspapers, radio and television networks searching for someone who was willing to tell Bryans story. This was his last wish before he died. Because Bryan was given such a short time to live, he didn't get the message that he wished to convey to all the smokers he wanted to reach everywhere.

He did not realise however, he would be leaving behind such a legacy. In his final weeks he got to marry his childhood sweetheart Bobbie and to see out one more birthday turning 34 on the 10th of May. When the end finally came, it was a sad day, not only for the Curtis family but for his many friends, colleagues and the people of his community who had lost a young hard working family man. The man who had spent most of his time worrying about others finally passed away surrounded by his family on the 3rd of June at 11:56 in the morning. The last thing he whispered to his mother at 9 am that morning was "I'm too skinny, I can't fight anymore". In his hands lay a picture of himself with his young son, Bryan JR. Unfortunately; because of an addiction that eventually killed him, Bryan Curtis would hold his wife or children no more.

Now for anyone who is a smoker, regardless of sex, age or background, I would ask you a very simple question? What impact did the last few pages of Bryan's life have on you? I know as an ex-smoker, that in my uneducated, ignorant and careless smoking days, I would have answered "None, no affect whatsoever" or "such is life" or "Shit happens" or some other laid back, take no responsibility, brash bullshit type of statement. I state the above because I know that this is the response that many of you will give. To those of you I will say "continue to read on". You are my target audience, the challenge, the ones who have "tried it all" to give this poisonous shit up by patch, gum, e cig, and hypnotherapy and still congregate outside in the smoking sheds at work or in pubs, clubs or restaurants. The real die hards!

For those of you who felt Bryans story or the images of him in his illness or death was enough to make you think twice about lighting up, I salute you, but just read on to ensure you keep the cancer causing poisons out of your vocabulary, your body and your life. And for any type of smoker out there, be it the social smoker, the occasional smoker, the stressful times only smoker, the passive smoker (although you may not be to blame), the one a day smoker, the 60 a day chain smoker, basically anyone who inhales nicotine's poisonous fumes; I, like Bryan Curtis want to tell you something and it's something you already instinctively know, but have been waiting until you picked up this book to hear. These are the same words every ounce and every cell of your body has been screaming at you since the very first cancer stick you ever put to your lips. They are the very words on the lips of your doctor every time you walk into his or her office coughing spluttering wheezing and whinging about your chest pains, your cough or low immune system. The professional code of conduct and ethics by which your doctor follows the guidelines, stops them from doing and saying that which they really want to say or do. Every doctor wants to reach over to grab you by the shoulders, shake you roughly, look you in the eye and shout **"STOP FUCKING SMOKING"**.

The same doctor, ever ready to assist his or her patient, will help you in whatever way they can to alleviate your suffering or help you with your self-inflicted ailment. They will offer you the guidance and their expertise only to watch it wasted, as you falsely nod in agreement, knowing they are also wasting their time in talking to you yet again, (about an ailment that has reoccurred), because of your poisonous addiction. Unfortunately both of you know that as soon as you walk out of their office, straight out the door biting your fingernails with cravings for nicotine (after a 15 minute stint in the waiting room) you will inevitably light up before you even get to the car. Your medical practitioner can only do so much. They know you have a problem with addiction to nicotine and they know that the majority of a smokers health problems are smoking related. You are already aware that the acknowledgement to any type of problem is the first step in the action to tackle it. This acknowledgement must also be made by and taken very seriously by you. No room for shit talk and empty promises here.

Now although that statement to some of you might sound like the words of a counsellor or spiritual guru or life coach, I can assure you it's not. It is a common sense statement by a normal Joe soap who happens to be an ex-smoker. Here are some of my credentials. I first used nicotine (of my own accord) when I was 11 years of age and I stopped when I was 23. I have had my fair share of ups and downs in life and all the drama in between both as a smoker and an ex-smoker. When I inhaled this poisoned filth, I was reckless and didn't realise that I was a fucking idiot for doing so. I needed someone to say stop fucking smoking, but it was at a time when smoking was considered almost as normal as breathing, so I had to learn by many trial and error attempts. Interventions were not to be found in a house where all are sinners. I needed confirmation that what I was doing was wrong but I never got it and never wanted to hear anything about my stupidity anyway because like many of you I chose ignorance. This is all about to change in your poisonous regard. By the time you are finished reading this book you will feel like an idiot for ever smoking this poisonous shit in the first place and not only because I say so or because of the death of Bryan Curtis, but because you will realise that the message he wished to convey is aimed directly at you, and your demise like his, will be for no reason other than addiction. It is important from the outset that you understand that all smokers wear invisible manacles. Addiction has you chained and is beating you with every breath you take.

Circumstances of life won't be accepted as reasons or feeble excuses as to what you are doing to your body. As you will read later on, even smokers who live in castles are slaves. You will understand this statement before you get to the last page. From the next chapter onwards, I will highlight any relevant words in **bold** so as to remind you throughout this book key words and points to emphasise exactly what you need to remember about what you are actually putting in your body. I will do the same when talking about anything I think is relevant for you to remember specifically such as money which can be saved or longevity of life etc. All at the cost of tedious typing time, but I know it will be worth it for those who actually give a shit and who will follow the task of reading (which some of you may complete), right through to the end. The following text in the next 200 odd pages is what your Doctor, son, daughter, husband, wife, loved ones, significant other, your inner voice and body has been screaming at you since you first lit up and every dreaded day since. We will now move on to the next chapter because you my friend, just like Bryan Curtis and any smoker for that matter, are living on borrowed time whether you care to believe it, or not.

ON BORROWED TIME.

On borrowed time, the definition being thus: 'Time during which death or another inevitable event is postponed temporarily'. Although we don't have to go back over Bryan Curtis, his life and early death, I will from time to time use his circumstances as a reminder that there is no difference in his situation to that of any other smoker. Of course there are those who will argue the whole height, weight, race, sex, gender and lifestyle issue such as the "yes, but I run 3 times a week or the "I only smoke when I'm having a drink", and you are the same type of people living in the very dim and far removed from reality bubble, who will also argue that alcohol is quite good for the liver. To those people I will say, keep turning the pages. If you inhale poisonous nicotine into the lungs that were designed for the fresh air to keep you alive, then you have a problem, especially if you fail to realise this, make silly excuses, or see a combination of strenuous exercise and pushing tar filled blood through a struggling damaged heart as acceptable. I was raised to respect the opinions of others but if any person who claims to think logically, attempts to debate that smoking isn't harmful or that it has any type of benefit, then my respect for one's opinion very quickly falters. Never attempt to defend a thing that is stealing your time and your life in equal measure.

Back to the chapter title. Now can we all agree that nothing lasts forever in the biological human sense? And can we all agree, smokers or not, that the human body can only take so much before it packs in, shuts down, wears out, whichever analogy you wish to use. Can we also agree that as a biological working wonder, the human body and everything it allows us to do, see, hear, touch, taste, smell, walk and run, is absolutely and without doubt the finest piece of machinery we will ever possess? How any person can agree but also continue to pollute this remarkable piece of clockwork with poison is, (if you really think about it), not only stupid or ignorant, but both. If a person who thinks that 'ignorance is bliss' applies to not being fully aware of the damage being done to the body they possess, or if there are those who don't really care what their filthy addiction is doing to them, then fuck them, as I'm not here to change the world. I'm not concerned about their chosen ignorance, but again, I am concerned for the ignorance shown to the health of the innocents who don't have the voice to speak up for themselves, when forced to breathe in the toxic poison of theses selfish fucks.

The human body which is constantly running like clockwork and this chapter called 'On borrowed time' all tie into each other and have much in common. The body like the clock has many parts that need to be maintained in order for the wheels and cogs to run smoothly. The body, if well-oiled and maintained will run like clockwork. At some stage in life, we will have all seen or may be familiar with the mechanics of a watch or a grandfather clock. Open the door or take the back off a watch if you haven't done so before and look at its intricacy. Every cog you see runs in synchronisation with one another, moving in a perpetual perfect motion. We know if you stay silent enough, you can hear the tick… tick… tick, of the seconds of a clock as every wheel and cog run perfectly in unison to allow this almost mathematical perfection, which is time running over and over again without failing. For as long as this time piece is maintained, it will run smoothly and continue to do its job, time and time again.

Now, what would happen if we were to take the back off a watch and look at the cogs and wheels in motion in all their glory? Only this time, if I were to take a small burning candle and allow a drop of wax fall onto the wheels and cogs? Let's look at what happens. The first thing you will notice is that the tick… tick… tick sound will quickly become tick…tick as it slows down because the hot wax will hit the clockworks and begin to slow down the movement as the cogs fight with all their strength to push and turn through this sticky mucus like substance. The clock always designed to work at its own pace is now struggling to cope with something it is not designed to cope with, and it strains to push past something which is forcing it to use all of its energy to breathe, to move freely at the pace which it was designed to move at. The cogs, the wheels, the clockwork, now work together to fight against this invasion of privacy only to stop, very abruptly and very suddenly, as the wax hardens and the watch and its very essence, which is time, stops dead in its tracks.

I am not writing this for the penny drops type of reaction or in the hope that someone says "wow, so true". It is obvious that a 4 year old child could grasp what I'm saying, but it's written in the hope that those who do understand it truly get its meaning, and that they make a decision to use this analogy and compare it to what they do to their body every time they pump it full of poisonous chemicals. For those still struggling to grasp what you've just read, what I meant was this… The wheels, the cogs symbolises the organs of the body, the heart lungs, arteries, blood veins etc., the watch meaning the body itself. Take the wax and swap it with tar and there you have it, it's not rocket science, but simplicity. Wax has no business in a clock and tar has no business in a body.

This book will feature a lot of analogies and simplicity and if you are a smoker who feels somewhat stupid whilst reading the simplified structure, then good stuff, because you are stupid for smoking in the first place. "Tough love" is the expression used meaning being blatantly or brutally direct with someone who is of concern to somebody else, but refuses to listen to or to take advice and it is tough love you are going to get. To love someone enough to care about their wellbeing is completely natural. Unfortunately for most smokers, their families have come to accept that their filthy disgusting addiction is naturally a part of who they are, when in fact, their filthy disgusting addiction has nothing natural about it. You will hear me repeat on numerous occasions throughout this book, 'air, pure air, pure fresh walking on the beach, or freshly cut grass air and lots of it'. This is what your lungs are designed to breathe in and out and not thousands of poisonous chemicals. If you are in a family or in a relationship where lighting up in the presence of younger siblings has become the norm, then you need to quite literally step back, take some much needed deep breaths and take a break from the your misguided version of the norm. Smoking and all of the misery that comes with it is very far from normal.

Science and medicine has come on in leaps and bounds in the last number of years and something that was once seen to be cool and sexy in the earlier part of the 20th century, is now thought by many people to be a filthy, disgusting addiction and proven to be deadly dangerous. You and/or your loved one as a smoker (or smokers) have serious health issues ahead of you, along with a very low immune system to tackle the same issues. Due to your filthy disgusting addiction you are living **on borrowed time** and this is a fact.

I will repeat certain questions throughout this book also, to drive certain points into your skull so we will start by getting you to ask yourself this…And please, answer it honestly or you may as well close the book. If told by a doctor tomorrow that if you inhaled one more cancer stick, that you would be dead, would you still inhale that filthy smoke? Now, think carefully. If you have a family who loves and depends on you and you have answered "yes, I would take a drag", then you have zero respect for yourself or the family you like to tell yourself and others, you claim to really care about. Back in the real world, a man or a woman who bring offspring into this world are blessed by whatever god they worship to have the gift of children in their existence. It is their duty on this planet to raise those children to the best of their ability and to keep them safe in a warm and loving environment in preparation for the big bad world around them. If by keeping them warm and safe, you allow them to sit in the same breathing space, be it a room or a car whilst lighting up with 4000 poisonous chemicals first second and third hand smoke, then you are uneducated, ignorant, and unfit to be a parent. Nature can be cruel and my heart bleeds for the millions of people worldwide who struggle, stress and pray to conceive a child together as a couple. Some people paying thousands to have a child to call their own without success, while some undeserved shit bags sit there and blow smoky poisonous fumes into the faces of the innocent children, whose only choice is to sit and breathe in and out this poisonous toxic cancerous waste.

If any persons would like to disagree with what's written or for raising this issue, which is something done quite often in this book, then go ahead and argue your point. All I will say is this… I think you are disgusting and should be ashamed of yourself. If you feel the need to justify smoking a cancer causing piece of dangerous weed in the presence of a non-smoker, especially a child or a little baby, then you don't have a leg to stand on. It is wrong on all levels and is filthy and as far as I'm concerned, should be treated or viewed as no different from a form of child abuse that should be dealt with in a court. **Degenerate** is a word I'll use frequently throughout to describe such individuals. The only people who will be offended by being called a **degenerate** are **degenerates**, and if you smoke this shit in the presence of a **defenceless young child**, **baby** or **non-smoker**, then you are a **degenerate.** If you are now offended, it is because although you know what you are doing is wrong, you still continue to do so. Society (as I will regularly point out) accepts smoking but thankfully not in the presence of non-smokers. If you are someone who forces their shit on their children, you probably don't play by these rules. Even though what society views as disgusting or as morally wrong, makes no difference to you whatsoever. You may be able to feed and clothe your children but this doesn't make someone parent of the year. If they are born addicted to nicotine because you couldn't give up your **filthy disgusting addiction** whilst they were developing in the womb, then (as studies have shown), they too will also be very likely to repeat your foolish mistakes and take up the same **filthy disgusting addiction,** because they've tasted it in the same blood you've shared as they grew in your womb. A great legacy and a great family tradition, which statistically you won't get to see, since your addiction has already taken **15 years off your already short existence**.

If you allow this legacy of cancerous smoke filled misery to continue, then again shame on you. The most important thing any person can teach their children is respect and everything that goes with it. Respect covers all aspects they will encounter in life and is more valuable to a child than any sum of money or trivial material wealth. Respect for their parents, their surroundings, their family, their life partners, the planet, themselves, but most importantly, respect for life and what it represents. Life is living, living is breathing. Only when a person respects life, can they show complete respect for themselves, enabling them to handle what life has to throw at them. It gives them the strength, character and it makes them resilient to the many negative aspects we all encounter at some stage in the growth of life. To **respect life is to respect yourself** and to **respect yourself is to respect all life represents**. All you have to do is to **take a deep breath** to understand this. If your child is walking around aged 12 or 13 with **a cancer stick** hanging out of their mouth, then go back and revise your parenting skills. I'm not saying this not because I think you're a bad parent. We all know that teenage hormones bring about rebellion and an experimentation phase, but look at how you've approached the issues in their lives so far. Set an example and lead by this example. If you have addressed the need to show the highest regard for your children and their health in such a way that they can refuse the offer or point blank refuse to bow down to peer pressure, then you've succeeded. The words smoking, **cancer sticks**, **smokers cough** and **smoking cancer** won't be a part of their daily vocabulary.

If on the other hand, you are a parent who **smokes poisonous shit with their children** or worse again, started your children off **inhaling this dirt**, I would say that although you probably won't get this message (because id imagine reading books is not your thing), but here goes my thoughts on you anyway. You and your children are living **on borrowed time**. If you are lucky enough to one day read and understand this statement and have decided you need to make urgent changes to your life and the life of your children or family, then there is a shred of decency somewhere in your poisonous DNA. Redemption is a great thing. If the word goes over your smoke filled head then look up its meaning and apply it to your **filthy disgusting addiction** for the sake of you and your children. If not and you couldn't give a fuck, then stick on some more daytime television, open up a can of beer, enjoy your **limited shitty life** and keep up the foolish pretence that it's the good life. The saddest thing about this is the amount of people who either don't fully understand or who are not willing to take in or to dissect the meaning of the words **"on borrowed time"**.

The great apple co-founder and CEO Steve Jobs who was responsible for much of today's modern computer technology, understood the meaning of this when he learned of his impending demise. Before his early death he said, "Time is limited so don't waste it living someone else's life. Don't be trapped by dogma, which is living with the results of other people's thinking and don't let the noise of other people's opinions drown out your inner voice" Steve Jobs truly understood the meaning of **living on borrowed time**. If you decide, either for yourself, or for the sake of your loved ones, (and the ones who need you around), to listen to your inner voice, the one that says **"enough is enough"**, then you have a shot at success over this poisonous shit. Do not give your precious time to those who offer their unwanted opinions about your decision **to quit inhaling shit** and who tell you not to be ridiculous and to have a smoke. Use time wisely to give back to the body which has so far taken care of you to this day.

Someone once wrote, "Be nice to the body because you have to live there, and this is a very true statement. Make a declaration to, either yourself or out loud and be as vocal as you feel you need to be. If that means looking into the nearest mirror and saying **"Fuck it!! Todays the day, no more poison"**, then by all means do so. Whatever you feel works well for you. Freedom from the chains of addiction is what you seek. This is the ugly truth of the matter. From the day you bought your first 20 pack up until this moment you have been a slave who has **obeyed every command of your master** every time a craving comes asking you **to beg to be fed your poison**. Nicotine is the boss who calls the shots and abuses your feeble attempts to say no. **A poisonous pesticide is responsible for putting you on borrowed time**. It's time to take time back. It's time to **throw the poison in the bin** or in the fire where it belongs and for good this time. In order for you to gain control of your health and your life, you must first take full and complete control of your poisoned addicted thoughts. This involves you setting your own deadlines to your own future existence and in your own time, without the control of addiction. A deadline in this case can have two meanings. "I won't smoke by 12 o clock tomorrow" is a good deadline to set whereas, "the chances are these smokes will kill me in the next 5 years" is a bad one (if you don't listen to your words and act upon them), simple!

Make sure that those deadlines don't involve **addiction to a poison** that will turn your **cells cancerous and kill you eventually.** The moment you do, then you are no longer in charge and lose your power which **puts poison back in charge,** and puts you straight back **on borrowed time.** This **poison has brought you to your knees** and will continue to do so until you decide to stop doing it. **Stop fucking smoking, take your life back** and learn to stand on your own two feet again. Live a life where you are in control and start doing it today…**Fuck it, start doing it now.** There is no time like the present as they say and especially not when the present time is borrowed. A happy time in life can quickly become a time of sadness through a **smoking related illness, cancer or death.** This in turn unnecessarily leads to a time to say goodbye, and no one wants to have to do this prematurely and permanently. The older we get, the faster we start to see the hands of the clock turn. Many of us become aware of our mortality in our thirties or forties. We start to realise that we won't be around forever. Nicotine will ensure these hands move quicker than you could ever imagine and this is not bullshit, but the truth. **Cigarettes, fags smokes, cancer sticks, coffin nails**, whatever you want to call them, they're bad news. Fuck them into the bin. The clock is ticking and the countdown begun when you **first picked this filthy shit up**. Put them down and stop racing the clock, or at least slow it down and **hang around for an extra fifteen years**. Everything moves and our biological clock stops as we know when the ticker stops. The one thing we can't stop is the time but we can choose how we spend our time and what we choose to do with it. Choosing **to fill your body with poi-**

sonous tar is not using your time wisely and by bullshitting yourself that you enjoy it makes you an even bigger **idiot**. Take control of your limited time and **stop fucking smoking**.

THE UNIMMACULATE CONCEPTION.

I am an ex-smoker. What gives me the right to say this is that I used to smoke but now I no longer do. Because I haven't smoked in over 13 years, I feel I have the right to use the expression **"no thanks, I don't smoke"** when a person who still smokes offers me a cigarette. This doesn't make me a saint or give me special status of any kind. This just means that I no longer do something I used to do. I won't give you some bullshit inspirational speech or a philosophical quotation about how wonderful my life is since I've had the courage to say no because firstly, it's too early in the book for that and secondly, I wasn't always that quick to refuse the offer of **addictive nicotine.** Again, I am not qualified in philosophy or inspirational speaking. If I'm being completely honest, my relationship with nicotine goes back a lot further than the first time I put a lit cigarette to my lips. Being born in the 1970s, I was unlucky to be born into a time of ignorance as well as bad fashion. This ignorance allowed my parents who both smoked heavily before, during and after my conception and birth, to continue blowing this shit into my face without realising the impact of their actions. Although they would often playfully remind me on numerous occasions growing up that I wasn't planned, this was by no means an immaculate conception. Immaculate, the word meaning, 'not defiled' could not be applied with the word conception if this biological marvel called pregnancy was laced with **over 4000 poisonous chemicals.** This information we have today as common knowledge (we will touch on this often in this book) but back then, people were ignorant. Some were unaware and others oblivious to the fact that **every single cigarette contains over 4000 chemicals**. Does it seem fair or unfair to say that after beating 300 million other sperm in a race to the golden egg with the odds already stacked against me, that my prize for first place was a one way ticket to nicotine town?

When I said that the odds were stacked against me, please bear in mind that because medicine and science has advanced at an alarming rate, we now know that men who smoke have a much lower sperm count than those who don't and their chances of impregnating a woman are **43% less than that of a man** who **is not dependant on nicotine.** The same can be said for a woman who is trying to conceive. Her chances of conceiving greatly diminish if she is dependent on nicotine. **Her chances are 63% less** than that of a healthy woman and if she manages to conceive, then the chances or risks of having a miscarriage, underweight, or unhealthy baby are **greatly increased by her addiction to nicotine.** This to me only suggests that the odds against a baby of two parents that smoke are always firmly against them. To get back to my own conception, birth and newly arranged marriage to nicotine; I (like many hundreds of millions of babies before and since then) unfortunately spent 9 months in the one place where a growing foetus should feel most safe…in a womb, whose placenta was feeding me, not only nutrients from what my mother digested, but also any of **the poisonous chemicals from the thousands of cancer sticks** either ingested or inhaled through direct or **passive smoking**. What went into my mother's bloodstream went directly into my fragile growing foetal body. By the time I finally made my entrance into the world, I was already a fully-fledged **underweight nicotine addicted baby**. My parents would put the fact that I cried nonstop for the first month down as a sign of a healthy baby who just whinged a bit more than others. If they had taken note that my siblings cried nonstop for the first month also, they may have realised that we were probably screaming out for the nicotine that our addicted bodies were craving. We were **born strung out to a poison** we had become **addicted to in the womb**. This is a **medical fact**. Just as my siblings were born crying out for a fix, I also would not have to wait long for what I cried out for. My **withdrawal symptoms** would be addressed as soon as I was discharged from the hospital as my mother enjoyed **a hard earned cancer stick** along with my father who drove me home in a **smoke filled car**, to a **smoke filled** celebratory welcome home party. They frequently told this story and with embarrassment, my father still speaks of it today. Any photographs of my grandparents, aunts or uncles holding me, shows them cradling me, the latest family edition, with **a cancer stick either between their lips or their fingers**. This wasn't done with the notion that ignorance is bliss you understand. It was done through ignorance, plain and simple. Cigarettes and holding the baby was a global norm in the 1970's.

This was how the generation I was born into viewed smoking, a harmless pastime that almost everyone did. It was the same in my parents' generation and my grandparents before them. For some reading this, the events I've described will be all too familiar as it's also their story and not just mine. It is not my intention to allow the readers, regardless of how they themselves are raised, to think of what's written as some sort of Oliver Twist, snot nosed orphan with no shoes kind of written tragic drama. It's not for violins and tears nor is it told through my remarkable memory or dramatic recollection of the event! It is just how it was back then. I want for you, the reader, to feel an affinity with myself who personally understands how someone can be affected by nicotine and smoking. I'm not drawing comparisons with people who have suffered greatly, either physically or mentally but stating what I now view as a form of child abuse. I want people to see that nicotine and poisonous chemicals have no place in the human body and most certainly not in the body of a growing foetus or a child.

When I think back on it now, I can only ever recall two people in my family who didn't smoke in a very large extended family. Besides that, everyone I knew or can recall always had a pack of smokes. My mother, my father, my aunts, uncles and grandparents all smoked. I can even recall my schoolteachers smoking as a young child. It is actually harder for me to remember those who didn't smoke to be quite honest because they were few and far in between. It seems that smokers seem to bunk with smokers in this addictive like attracts like. In retrospect it kind of makes sense to see how a person can become addicted to a substance without wanting to become addicted to a substance. Let me explain. If you grew up in a house with alcoholics and every time they took a swig of whiskey, they poured a drop into your bottle of milk as a baby, do you think you would become addicted to alcohol? As the years went by, do you think your body which was still developing would be affected by alcohol with a high percentage of alcoholic spirit as your body struggled to build up a resistance to the chemicals it is being forced to endure at such a critical stage of growth and development? As well as the physical effects of the alcohol, how do you think you'd be affected mentally? If you were to watch your parents, the ones who created you, gave birth to you and raised you, consume alcohol without relent, do you believe it would be a case of monkey see monkey do?

As of today, the year 2016, scientists and doctors through extensive years of research on patients treated for smoking related illness and smoking related cancers and deaths, have concluded that 97% of patients have come from homes where **one or more parents were addicted to nicotine**. I was raised as I've said, surrounded by **poisonous addictive chemicals.** Every time that they lit up, which was together usually, it was my siblings and I who were forced to inhale their first, second and third hand smoke. It was our developing bodies that were forced to inhale thousands of toxic chemicals every time **nicotine came knocking**. It was our **lungs, hearts and organs which struggled to grow** due to the ignorance of our parents, and it was the sins of the father and in this case the mother also, which to this day, has given my siblings and I, **an uncertainty in regards to our future health**. Whatever the doctors or scientists discovered in their studies into **nicotine addiction through imitation,** I like many of you, think that I am living proof of such studies, because as soon as I turned 11 years of age, I had already smoked **my first cigarette**. This took place because I had been conditioned to do so. It quite simply was done in a complete copy cat routine or as I said earlier, monkey see, monkey do. As a kid of that age, like many other things we weren't supposed to do, it was fun, and the risk of getting caught made the danger of what we were doing more attractive to us. By the time I was 12, I was purchasing or stealing smokes from my parents and by the time I was ready for secondary school, I had a small summer job which ensured I had the money for a fresh 10 pack every morning. By the time I was 14, I was smoking openly with my mother, (she caught me and I swore her to secrecy) and like many of the other kids at the school, we had all the tricks not to get caught or sniffed out, using mints, chewing gum, toothpaste etc. This poisonous relationship, which like my parents I considered to be quite normal, lasted until I turned 23 years of age. Up until then, I tried every technique known to man or woman in order to quit.

The simple fact of the matter and you need to hear this (if you previously have or are **still struggling with nicotine addiction**) is that you will only quit when the time is right. This is not a cliché. Believe me, there will come a time when after many attempts, finality comes when it is supposed to. There is nothing I haven't tried, tested, read, eaten, or stuck to my body in my efforts to finally give my body back to itself, not to be controlled by addiction and to allow it for the first time do what it was designed and born to do, which is to breathe. I used to tell people who asked me, 'how long did I smoke for?', that I smoked for 13 years from when I was about 12(that's when I started to purchase packs for myself) up until I was 23 years of age. But this is not a full or honest answer. The simple truth as you've already read is that I was **conceived in this poisonous struggle to survive**. And this is what a growing foetus does. It struggles to grow and survive under the wrong conditions and thrives in the right conditions. I was quite literally given a baptism of fire (or maybe smoke).**I was born addicted to nicotine**. I was raised to grow in a house where nicotine was **one of the many toxic chemicals out of the thousands which filled my air space**. I was being far too polite in my previous answer that I only smoked for 13 years. Yes, sure enough I had smoked for 13 years by choice, but in reality, and on the other hand, what choice did **a foetus, baby, toddler, infant or juvenile have in my stages of growth to have poisonous chemicals absorb into my bloodstream**. As I said earlier, I had been conditioned to smoke and that is calling a spade a spade.

I will often repeat throughout this book, that regardless of how it started, only **you can stop it,** but mistakes must be acknowledged before this takes place. Like many of you, I love my parents dearly although only one living parent remains. I have discussed the writing of this with my lone parent, my father who has given his blessing. He acknowledges mistakes made as well as realising the harm done, but also hopes that this book will offer those who read it a chance to realise that ignorance can no longer be used as an excuse. He has asked that I tell it like it is so that is exactly what I'm doing, telling it like it is. For those of you who see my story as your own or are familiar with what's been written so far either through personal experience or through someone they knew (or know of) who grew up in a very similar fashion, I have the following question. Is it wrong that any baby, child or any person for that matter, should be born and raised or **forced to endure the addictive poison of somebody who shows no consideration for someone who doesn't choose to inhale poison**, or who **is unable to defend or protect themselves?** Can we continue to use ignorance as any kind of excuse for such behaviour? Can someone claim ignorance if 80 years ago, **cigarettes were even advertised as a miracle cure for asthma**(yes it's true!) or that 50 years ago, celebrities weren't seen or photographed without a cigarette, or even that 30 years ago, they were endorsed, promoted and sponsored at worldwide sporting events. Many could argue that maybe in the 1920s, 30s, 40s, 50s, 60s, 70 and 80s, that 'they didn't know any better' could cover a wide variety of things once considered normal. There are many things which we now view as truly shocking, unbelievable, downright dangerous or just plain stupid from back in the day.

Regardless, be it a lack of education, poor advertising standards, stone age communication systems or even because the world was different back then and humble folk just tolerated it, we now as of today 2016 (and for the last 10 years especially), have absolutely no reason whatsoever to allow any person, no exceptions, to force any other human being to endure even one breath of another person's **poisonous and toxic chemical filled smoke**. Personally, I am resigned to the fact that my generation knew no different and like the many people of my age, understand that those who forced us to endure their **poisonous second hand smoke** didn't do so out of carelessness, just ignorance.

Although I consider myself to be a calm individual, I still find myself getting to a level of anger I find hard to control when I see people today, who are only too aware of the dangers of their **filthy addiction,** yet still continue to do so in the **presence of an infant or child.** I struggle to contain myself from not grabbing the **cancer stick** from their mouth and crushing it on the ground, especially if the poor misfortunate forced to inhale this poisonous shit, is stuck in a room or a car with some inconsiderate prick that understands the danger and continues to do so. To avoid confrontation, I usually manage to refrain and restrain myself as hard as it is. Seeing how these types of incidents are so common and I have no say over how parents treat their offspring, I will instead write the following about what I think of any person or persons, who force anybody, but especially an unborn child, a young baby, a toddler, or elderly person to **endure deadly poisons**. I mentioned the word **degenerate** earlier and to save you some time flicking through a dictionary to understand the true meaning of the word, I have already done the homework for you. After researching, I believe that this is quite apt to describe any individual who forces their own unborn, new born, toddler or child in our modern time of 2016, to purposely or carelessly inhale their **first, second and third hand poisonous toxic smoke** and the term could not be more fitting, once we apply its meaning….

DEGENERATE….Word explained: **degenerate:** pronounced **de-gen-er-ate, ADJECTIVE:** having lost the physical, mental or moral qualities considered normal and desirable, showing evidence of decline, **NOUN:** An immoral or corrupt person, **VERB:** decline or deteriorate, physically, mentally, or morally. I believe this to be quite fitting, wouldn't you agree? For anyone reading this who is livid, boiling with rage and is asking "is he talking about me?" Is he calling me or my husband or wife **a degenerate?** Well, to answer your question, like a politician, I will have to answer your question with a question. Do you force your children or someone else's children to breathe in **your filthy poisonous fumes?** Do you consider the health of others every time you take out **a cancer stick** and light it whilst standing close to someone who chooses not to breathe in toxic chemicals? Do you light up in the same airspace of an elderly person with breathing difficulties? If you answered yes to the above, then in answer to your question, **YES, you** or your husband/wife, or anyone for that matter who lights a cancerous cigarette that **contains 4000 dangerous poisonous chemicals** and over **100 cancer causing carcinogenic** that allows anyone, especially a child or your unborn to inhale or absorb it against their will, **is a degenerate**. It is the only term I could find that came close to **piece of shit** but **degenerate** has every angle of that covered so we'll stick with it. And in case you haven't taken that in yet, I'll repeat it for you again, "**You are a degenerate**".

It could be seen as fair enough if one chooses to go outside into the open air to poison their body, although still doing a disservice to their health, as they still have an issue with addiction which needs to be resolved (as it will eventually harm their family when they are no longer around), but at least this person has the respect not to force their **miserable poison** in or around other human beings. Those of you who still need to quit but have an awareness of the dangers to those around you don't fit into the category of **a degenerate,** as only someone whose attitude is a selfish "fuck everyone else" including their own children/family, is truly deserved of this title. For anybody who feels somewhat victimized or singled out, I should say at this point that if my own parents had recently given birth to me and continued to **inhale cancerous poisons** with the knowledge we have by today's standards, then they would fit into this **degenerate/piece of shit category** also.

As this book is being written, I am delighted to read that new laws are now being introduced to make it an offence to smoke in a car with a child which is a great step forward in tackling **this modern day scourge**. Hate is a very powerful word and I try my best never to use it, but to see children or babies in a smoke filled car drives me crazy. Or a pregnant woman sucking on a cancer stick. I have far too many times, (like some of you I'm sure), seen a woman whose pregnancy is full term and who is fit to burst, with a **filthy cancer stick** hanging from her mouth. This infuriates me as this is **blatant child abuse** and no one seems to call it out for what it is. **It's vile, disgusting and any piece of shit who smokes poisonous chemicals whilst carrying a baby is not fit to be a mother, full stop.** No laws will ever punish anyone who commits this vile act hard enough, and it is in my opinion a form of **child neglect or abuse** which should result in the social services becoming involved as soon as the person is reported. If you witnessed someone injecting poison into a baby on the street, would you report them to the relevant authorities? Of course you would and you would hope the perpetrator was locked away for their horrific crime so what's different about this? To force something so small and fragile to share your poisonous blood is something that says you have a long way to come before you can call yourself a civilised human being. Whilst researching other terms for these individuals, I also tried to find words to describe the **"dirty habit"** we seem to have picked up or is often used to describe "smoking". This is a word I find far too polite to describe the damage these disgusting cancer causing pieces of paper actually inflict. Because the dictionary is too polite, I have decided on street slang and a combination of different expressions we should all be familiar with, to describe what I believe to be the **filthiest scourge of a person's health** amongst the civilised world. I am swapping the term smoking for **filthy disgusting addiction** and will highlight this also and believe me; you won't see it any differently than this by the time you get to the last page. Cigarettes will be referred to as **coffin nails** or **cancer sticks**, a slang term familiar with many of us that gives a wonderful description for what they actually are. Several other words associated with **this foul addiction** will also be used and given different titles also highlighted to make you aware throughout the book. This is not only to enhance the words. It is again by design. By the time you have finished this book and successfully come to your senses, you will label these **poisons** and anything associated with them and recognise them by burning into your brain what they actually are, instead of using or listening to polite terms or words that go in one ear and out the other. Polite terms make the addiction almost sound acceptable which it most certainly is not.

If you are one of the **degenerates** who has reluctantly or ashamedly admitted to themselves that they have made mistakes and you continue to read even though it pains you to do so, there could be something in this for you. Remember that our society teaches there is redemption for anyone of us who makes mistakes, acknowledges these mistakes and learns from them. If you decide you want to change and to give your family and yourself another chance, then do it now. Turn the page and read on. But be warned. This book contains a lot of home truths and may not sit comfortably with those easily offended and possibly even those with the thickest of skin. We will repeat the old expression that "The truth may hurt but it can also set you free" throughout this book because you need to hear it until you find your freedom from addiction and return to your senses. I'm not going to fall out with anyone over words, but selfish actions as I've said before, that affect those unable to defend themselves infuriate me, especially when it's unnecessary and feeble excuses are used as a ridiculous defence. This to me is shit talk.

SHIT TALK
(because shit sticks)

Smoking is filthy I'm sure we can agree. Everything about it **is dirty**. From your **"shitty breath"** to the filthy ashtray and from the **brown stains on your teeth** to the **brown stains on your fingers**. Be honest with yourself…is this you? If you're not sure, then look at your fingers or your teeth in the mirror. Are they stained yellow or brown because of your addiction? Look at the whites of your eyes, bloodshot and tinted slightly yellow. This is because the waste products like tar and toxic chemicals that go into your everyday pack of smokes **contain poisonous shit** and as we know **"shit sticks"**. **This filthy poison** (we will discuss in greater detail as we progress) is doing your insides and your outsides absolutely no favours whatsoever. You may think to yourself that **"you look the shit"** on a night out when in fact, you actually **"look like shit"** and **"smell like shit"** and probably also **"feel like shit"**, and this is why you need to **"clean your shit up"** or **"get your shit together"** because **"this poisonous shit" is killing you** whether you choose to believe it or not. This is not **"shit talk"** but stating facts. **"Shit talk"** is when you tell everybody including yourself that you will **"quit smoking this shit tomorrow"** when deep down you know that this is **"bullshit talk"**. Can we agree that nobody likes being **"In deep shit** or **"up shit creek"** as it denotes we are in a spot of bother? This is one place that statistically, 1 in 2 inhalers of this **"poisonous shit"** is going to end up eventually. When **"the shit hits the fan"** regarding an illness or disease associated with **"smoking this shit"**, then it is often a case of no turning back and **"dealing with this shit head on"** when if you stopped **"talking shit"** and **"cleaned your shit up"** then all of this **"shit talk"** could be avoided. If you are diagnosed with an illness because of **"inhaling this shit"**, then you now have the **"shitty task"** of explaining to your loved ones that you may not be around for much longer and because of this you have **"left them in the shit"**. Your family now face a future of uncertainty and being **"scared shitless"** because you couldn't put down your **"addictive shit"** and left them **"facing the shit storm"** If you **gave a shit about your family**, you would not **"leave them in the shit"** by **"treating them like shit"**. This is what you do when you **choose poisonous shit before those you are supposed to care about.** Again there are **"shit talkers"** who will say "I love my family but I also love smoking"… So fucking choose! **Which is more important; family or shit?** If you choose **smoking this shit before family**, you are risking your health, your wealth and most importantly the life and the very limited time we have on this planet, over a poisonous addictive chemical made by billion dollar companies who couldn't give **"two shits"** about you or your family. That's **enough shit talk.**

It's time to get stuck into this because the sooner you **"stop talking shit"** about **"inhaling shit",** the quicker we can **get you to "give this shit" up for good.** Now I want you to try reading the same page again but imagine we are talking about water or a piece of fruit instead of **shitty chemicals**… Actually don't waste your time. Fruit is fruit, and water is water… its healthy and designed to be eaten or drank by humans. Water is designed to be hydrate us and to keep us alive. Our bodies are designed to get rid of chemical waste but you are using your shitty addiction to do the exact opposite. **Inhaling toxic shit** is exactly that…**shit? It's shitty, its waste, it's disgusting and it's wrong.** You are **putting this shit** into **every organ of the body including your bloodstream**. If someone threw **shit in your face** would you be offended? Of course you would. But you expect no backlash when you do it to your own body? **The shit is hitting the fan** and you are too stupid to see it coming. If you don't **give a shit** then you are weak. Close the book; you are a weak failure who **only gives a shit about their cravings** for **poisonous smoke** in their long suffering body. If on the other hand you are tired of **feeling like shit**, then keep turning the pages until **you give this shit up** for good. We will continue our discussion further on when we return to the topic of smokers and **bullshit excuses** later on. My aim for you at that stage is to be able to **see this shit for what it truly is**.

BORN AGAIN SMOKERS.

To become a born again smoker is very easy and the chances are that if you are reading this right now, then you probably are one. It may be a religious enlightenment to become born again in any other way but there is no "hallelujah praise the lord!" moment associated with becoming a born again smoker. The person who understands what it means to be a born again smoker, is the one who has tried time and time again to tackle their poisonous addiction to toxic nicotine and failed. In many attempts to finally conquer my own **chemical addiction,** I have fallen into the born again category more times that I care to remember. The foolish mistake made by those who struggle/d (including myself) is that when you first take **this filthy addiction** on board, you foolishly allow yourself to think that stopping it is just as quick or as easy as starting it, or that putting them down, is just as easy as picking them up. You have sadly learned that this is not the case. As with any addiction (food, alcohol, drugs sex), casual use quickly turns to habit and then to addiction, (we will discuss this further on), and addiction to something can never easily be put down. The born again smoker may not realise that they have an addiction until it is too late. This indicator usually happens when after giving up for the tenth time, you meet someone you know who says **"Oh, I see you're back on the smokes"**. Some of you will have made your quit smoking pledge to anyone willing to listen and may then feel embarrassed when the person(s) whom you made your pledge to, catches you out **having a sneaky smoke**. However this **embarrassment of being caught** out is usually quickly overridden by the **poisonous** bitter sweet nicotine as it creeps back **into your lungs and your blood stream** putting that craving at ease, and leaving you not really giving a shit about someone pointing out your broken declaration.

This is when addiction has overridden a feeble cautioned attempt and you no longer care. There are over a billion people on this planet at this moment in time **addicted to nicotine**. Out of this billion or so there are those who have never even contemplated quitting and there are the **born again smokers** who attempt to quit every day of the week. Then there are the other types, those who can quit by just stopping using the strength of discipline and **Willpower**, to achieve complete **abstinence from their addiction**. There are also those who foolishly believe that reducing their intake of **20 coffin nails** to 10 a day is cutting back or a genuine attempt at quitting. The **born again smoker** will realise and fully acknowledge that they are a **born again smoker** when they have tried, tested, worn, researched or read every available product, gimmick, medicine or miracle on the market, in order to finally walk away from **the poisonous shackles** that **this disgusting addiction** forces them to wear and has failed miserably every time. As I said earlier, like many of you I also tried, tested and failed with several of these products. I now believe that the majority of these **expensive gimmicks and treatments take advantage of a person who is addicted to a substance more addictive than heroin** and strings them along using false promises of success in overcoming **their disgusting dependency**. Although I realise that certain products can help those with an **addiction to nicotine,** I have also found that the same products only seem to work for the period of time that the person uses them, say for example with a patch or with gum. A person chewing gum may do so for months at a time, replacing **nicotine in a cigarette form** to **nicotine in chewing gum form**. For those who wish to argue that the chewing gum form is a lot safer than inhaling poisonous smoke, I'd like to remind you that you are still paying an extortionate amount of money for a packet of chewing gum that doesn't really work and is **dosing poison into your bloodstream through your saliva**.

I will often repeat this throughout, but the chances are; that if you are reading this book, then the gum hasn't worked for you. Remember folks, its **nicotine in another form** and **nicotine is deadly dangerous.** It's a **pesticide used to kill** and is **dangerous, deadly and lethal,** no matter what title or form it is marketed in, or how colourful it is packaged or advertised. Anything sold warning you of danger to your health is dangerous to your health! The withdrawal of nicotine from the body and the **other poisons which give the addict withdrawal symptoms** takes 24 hours to leave **the addicts** system. After which, the **addictive element** has left and all that needs to be done is to tackle the habits you have picked up with this addiction, such as using your hands to **hold a coffin nail** or reaching for a pack of poison whenever you falsely feel you need a coping mechanism.

There are techniques and strategies you will devise to help you cope with withdrawal from nicotine and the other thousands of chemicals in your body but this withdrawal will pass very quickly. You must be able to convince yourself and not just tell yourself, that you want to quit. You can only convince yourself once you listen to the truth and that's what you are doing by reading this book. No gimmicks, no nonsense, no bullshit. For as long as you remain addicted to nicotine, there will be a market for smokers, and as long as there is a market for smokers, there are those who see a gap in the market to deter those from using nicotine, by using products containing nicotine to keep you addicted to nicotine. This is a cruel circle you must walk away from. Don't replace inhaling nicotine with ingesting it or sticking it to your arm with a plaster or patch. Be strong and not weak. It is just another form of using nicotine to stave off your addiction and don't listen to this shit about taking the edge off. The companies that supply these products understand that you are addicted and they claim that gradual withdrawal with their product is the only way to quit for good. I have no problem in acknowledging that this may work for some but these people are very few in numbers.

If you are to look at how many born again smokers you've encountered in your life you will realise this. The argument here is that someone reading this may get confused with quitting smoking temporarily and **quitting this filthy addiction permanently**. If you are one of the people who say "well patches worked great for me because I stayed off them for 6 months after using them" then you automatically fall into the category of born again smoker or someone who has merely quit temporarily. What this means is that you have slowly drained your body of the poisonous nicotine that you used to inhale and replaced it with lower doses in mg of chemicals in the form of a patch or gum or e cig and used them for 6 months while you still **screamed out for nicotine** in the **cancer stick form**. Now that you are **back inhaling poisonous shit,** you are also back to square one and reading a book about how to quit smoking, all the while telling fellow smokers that you found the nicotine patches to be great, or the gum wonderful in attempting to give up something that you have never really given up at all. So.... let's cut the bullshit. We all know that the only way to give up poisoning ourselves is to **STOP FUCKING SMOKING**, period. Anything else is only prolonging the inevitable. What is your opinion of a heroin addict who is staying off heroin but is taking methadone as a substitute? Would you consider them a success in overcoming their addiction? No, you wouldn't…and the reason is that, not being dependant on a drug means abstaining from another drug as a substitute. Addiction is addiction by any other name and **nicotine** like heroin is a **lethal and highly addictive dangerous substance**. This is where the term "I'm clean" is used by a recovered or ex addict who is tested for a substance. It means that their body is cleansed from a toxic substance and that they aren't dependant on anything chemical anymore. With nicotine, wearing a patch or chewing gum, may be considered the lesser of two evils but it also means you are still **feeding your body with a poisonous chemical** to get by. And believe me; you don't need to waste your money.

What is really laughable nowadays is the amount of people I see on a daily basis, standing outside in smoking sheds, outside a bar or the workplace, **smoking E cigarettes** while others stand beside them **smoking real cigarettes.** I could have very easily been one of these people. They **stand outside inhaling nicotine electronically amongst the second hand smoke of others** and discuss the new flavour of nicotine they just bought such as strawberry, banana or coconut flavour. Someone might be out in the shed because they forgot their charger or **never plugged in their E cig overnight**, so they go out to the smoking shed to **bum a real smoke until their E cig charges or whatever**. This is fucking craziness! I spent a number of years in a hospital environment and this involved testing water for Legionella. For those of you who haven't heard of this, it's basically a bacteria found in water which can be inhaled into the lungs in tiny water droplets (such as the vapour or mist you may see whilst taking a shower). It is usually found to affect people over 45 years of age, smoker's, heavy drinkers and those with respiratory problems, lung or heart disease or those with low immune systems. It is rare but there are occasions where outbreaks have killed individuals or groups. Now, whilst I don't make claims to be an expert on this condition or even on E cigarettes for that matter, I can tell you of the grave concerns of the physicians and the World health Organisation, (WHO) in regards to the inhaling of a vapour which **contains poisonous chemicals**. They have openly voiced their concerns about the lack of knowledge on the short and long term effects on a human's body, with some claiming that the effects may even be as bad as or worse than the damage caused by the **deadly toxic smoke of a real cancer stick.** This is not scaremongering. It's like the trial of a successful new drug that is hailed as the next best thing until someone drops dead taking it. The biggest issue or concern amongst the medical world is the production, storage and shipping of these products made in sweat shops in countries like China or Indonesia and the number of **unlicensed premises** and online shops which sell them as a healthy option to inhaling poison without any scientific or medical backup.

Listen again carefully, read and then repeat… **STOP FUCKING SMOKING**. This is how you **avoid all this bullshit** and E cigs and patches and other crappy gimmickry. That is how you claim your life back. Do this without the aid of anything that contains **deadly dangerous nicotine.** Do not prolong this any longer than you have to. If your withdrawal takes hours or days then stick it out. If you can suffer the few days now, then the rest of your years won't involve **constant ills, sickness and suffering**. Cut all ties with these **shitty poisonous chemicals** completely. Stay away from gimmicks or books that promise you overnight success in any aspect of your life and try to think about it this way. Gimmickry is the promise of quality or success that is often impossible in the time frame it promises. Devices of gimmickry never deliver on such promises. When told that it's too good to be true then it usually is. We see this often with literature such as 'become a millionaire overnight' or 'instant weight loss'. The only book that can make you a millionaire overnight is a book which contains the following weekend's lottery numbers and liposuction reduces body fat instantly paired with a rigorous exercise regime not sitting down reading about it. It is the same with a hypnotherapist who claims to be able to stop a 30 year addiction to nicotine in a one hour session. Forget about it. **It's bullshit and a waste of money.**

And, as for theses E cigs! These ridiculous looking devices will be the stuff of embarrassing photographs in ten years' time, just like when you look back at pictures of yourself with a bad haircut you now regret, clothes you wouldn't be seen dead in and a device that looks like Robocop's dick hanging out of your mouth. Ditch these **ridiculous looking dangerous devices** as soon as possible and don't ever, I repeat, don't ever, be suckered into believing such ridiculous advertising for some of their **poisonous products** such as "become a healthy smoker" or "try new mango flavoured nicotine drops". This is dangerous drivel and only attracts young teenagers and children by enticing them to the same flavours as candy or soft drinks. Several of these devices have **also exploded** as you probably see on the news on a daily basis globally and are notorious for catching fire, maiming or even killing those who use them. Do your own internet research or check out the footage of the damage these things can do when they explode and prepare to be shocked. **This dangerous threat is unavoidable** and this is not propaganda against E cigs. The truth remember, speaks for itself. Check it out for yourselves, they are not properly researched and badly constructed.

If I told you there was a brand new **fruit flavoured rat poison available to smoke**, you wouldn't purchase it, and a product containing nicotine is just as lethal, even if it does taste like wine gums. Inhaling anything but fresh air regardless of whether you use an electronic device or a **real cancer stick** means you are a **born again smoker.** You may foolishly think that this fancy new **electronic gimmick** you have in your mouth means that you now only inhale vapour and not **poisonous chemicals** which **cancer sticks are laced** with, but you are still **ingesting the most dangerous, most addictive substance of them all** and it doesn't matter because you are **ingesting nicotine into your bloodstream by inhaling this shit deep into your lungs and airways**. A smoker by any name is still a smoker. E cigs for almost every smoker is a fad, believe me. They are a gadget, a gimmick to try **out of desperation** because some other **born again smoker** has recommended or sworn by it. Look around you. How many have gone back to **using real cancer sticks** as soon as the novelty wore out or the charger broke or some other bullshit excuse like the vapour shop was closed. A ridiculous and dangerous trend that I predict will leave many suffering in its wake. Do yourself a favour and stay the fuck away from electronic cigs, real cigs, or anything for that matter that requires you to **inhale poison into your lungs**. Instead of becoming a born again smoker, breathe in the air as much as possible and become a full time non-smoker. You know it makes sense. Common sense!

THE SMOKER WHO JOINED CLUB 50/50.

With or without realising it, anyone who takes the **horrible addiction**, has signed up to join a club that in the last century was responsible for the **untimely deaths of over 100 million people.** All of these people and your good selves have subscribed to this club unknowingly. As of today, the year being 2016, the World Health Organisation, along with doctors and scientists globally have published their confirmed data report, which they had already been quite aware of or at least suspected. This report concludes that **1 in 2 smokers will die prematurely** from a **smoking related illness**. Those are some deadly certain odds. Let's inspect this a bit closer to bring home some realistic horrible truths. **1 in 2** or **50/50** is a club you have joined whether or not you have signed to become a member. This club has over a billion members globally and it makes no difference what your age, colour, creed, race, religion or nationality is. A man addicted to nicotine in Pakistan is no different to a woman addicted to nicotine in Paris, and regardless of their back ground, **addiction is addiction**. The benefits of being a member of this club is that **there are no benefits**, regardless of what part of the world you inhabit, only addiction and a **1 in 2 chance of death**. Every member is treated the same.

The only differences between any of these members if we are to look for one is that **50% of them will die prematurely** from the use of their daily prescription, whilst the other **50% will linger on in poor health** constantly suffering problems with their **poisoned bodies**. The shitty thing about being a member of **club 50/50** is that you never know which of these many illnesses will eventually cut you down in your prime. It is not a case of taking your pick of a **heart attack, stroke, liver, throat, lung, or stomach cancer.** Like addiction to any **poisonous substance,** the **chemicals that cause cancerous cells to thrive** will seek out and **destroy the body** without mercy or relent. Now, to bring it a little closer to home. If you and your husband or your wife inhales this **poisonous shit** together, that means that either you or your partner will leave this planet early because of your **addiction to inhaling toxic chemicals.** This is terrible for any person to lose their other half, but sadly even more so, when it could so easily have been avoided. **Club 50/50 has simple rules. Either you will, or you won't.** Do you or your significant other already have any **existing health issues?** Do you imagine that club 50/50 sympathises with your distress or illness? That your wellbeing is the clubs priority?

Let's say you were signed up to have a magazine delivered but you no longer wished to read it… how would you go about stopping the magazine from being delivered to your front door? Yes… You would unsubscribe. Walking away from poisonous addiction might seem a lot harder but it's no different. To stop yourself from becoming a **statistic with club 50/50**, choose to walk away… unsubscribe. Give yourself a fighting chance at least. Presently, you are playing with a **1 in 2, or 50/50 chances of dying** and these are odds far too great when it comes to **throwing a bet on your life.** Your chances of surviving Russian roulette are 1 in 6 but very few of us would put a loaded revolver to our temples even if we were playing for a million dollars. There are no prizes associated by being a member of **club 50/50,** only **illness and death,** all courtesy of your hard earned money. If life is a gamble, then it is wise to remember that it is the one who plays their cards wisely who has the odds in their favour. The great Kenny Rogers famously sang in the worldwide hit 'The gambler', the following words of wisdom that I always think of as it reminds me of making the right decisions in life. He wrote,

"And when he finished speakin

He turned back toward the window

Crushed out his cigarette

And faded off to sleep

But somewhere in the darkness

The gambler he broke even

But in his final words I found

An ace that I could keep"

Now, I'm sure the great Kenny Rogers didn't have **quitting inhaling poisonous chemicals** in mind when he penned 'The gambler', but I think the lyrics are quite apt for this particular chapter and to those who take a gamble every time they light up. Play the game of life wisely.

Far too many people today will suffer because of **this filthy addiction** and will do so needlessly. I say **fuck the billion dollar tobacco companies and their poisonous products.** You have already given them too much of your time health and hard earned money. **Walk away from club 50/50 now.** Don't suffer any longer. Remember, **1 in 2 people who inhale this poisonous shit will die prematurely,** so quit together and do it as a couple if it works better for you both. If not do it with a fellow smoker or do it on your own, but most importantly, the bottom line is to just do it. You have far too much to lose if you continue to **poison every organ in your body**. Whilst on the subject of gambling, **50/50,** betting odds, chances and statistics, it may be interesting for you to think about this. Hopefully it offers you a different perspective, regarding **the filthy shit you put into your lungs**.

How many of you do the lottery every week? Let's just say for arguments sake, most of us. Well if you do this religiously every week and without fail, you probably do so because deep down in your heart, you hope there may be a tiny little chance that all 6 of your numbers might just pop up in your favour. Most of us do this, sometimes even twice a week and cling on to the hope, even though the odds may be 1 in 6 million of a win. Now try look at it this way. The lottery chiefs are telling you that you have a 1 in 6 million chance of hitting the jackpot and you cling to the hope that it might just be you. You imagine that if you just cross your fingers hard enough and pray, you may have a chance, whereas your doctors, cancer researchers, scientists and medical professionals are telling you that your chances of a sudden death or a painful or slow agonising death from cancer is a 1 in 2 certainty, and you walk about hoping it might not be you! Read this again in case it doesn't sink in because deep down your heart is begging you to. Take heed, these are not the odds created by the book keepers or lottery chiefs. These are the well-studied and researched statistical and medical facts analysed and presented to the world by the WHO's foremost leading experts on cancer research. This includes global oncologists, doctors, scientists and professors. These are specialists and experts on cancers and diseases presenting these odds through many years of study and research.

These odds are as real as it gets. You see, we all want to believe we can win the lottery because it fills us with hope. We live thinking about the big win and how one day it will be our turn. We do the exact opposite with our health. Many of us believe we will be around forever and because of this, our health takes the brunt of this false awareness about how fragile the human body actually is. If the odds are quite clear to you now, you will understand the point I'm trying to make. It simply says **1 in 2 cancers and certain death** and even this won't be enough for some people to absorb the reality of **their filthy addiction.** This is the false hold that nicotine has on the individual, and it allows them to choose ignorance and blindness over reality and the bigger picture. The reality is cancer and the bigger picture is suffering and death. In one year there are 52 weeks. That means that there will be 52 millionaires at the end of the year in whatever country the lottery is held. How many deaths from a smoking related cancer will there be every year? Hundreds of thousands in your country and millions across the world. You are eventually going to be one of these 50/50 statistics. Not if but when is the odds in your early demise.

Before we finish up on this chapter, I would like to ask your honest opinion on an experiment that I'd like you to take part in. If I was a complete stranger who approached you on the street and told you that I had in my possession, a thousand dollars that I would give you no questions asked for your troubles, if you would perform a very simple task…how many of you would do it. "Well", you may ask yourself, it depends on what kind of a task it is". I tell you that "it's very simple". Taking a small box out if my pocket and I hand it to you and tell you "I would like you to take the contents of this little box and swallow it". "Ok" you say, "sounds easy, but what is it", you ask. "It's a pill" I tell you. You open the box and look at the pill and it has a skull and cross bones on it. "Hold up one minute" you ask, looking concerned, "why has this got a skull and cross bones on it?" "It's because", I tell you, "It contains 4000 poisonous chemicals, many of which are cancer causing carcinogenic and others that will clog your arteries and bloodstream. Feeling suspiciously alerted you now ask, "And will this pill injure or harm me in any way?" "I'm not sure I tell you, all I do know is that there is a 1 in 2 chance that it will cause a stroke, heart attack, cancer, or painful death". "So then", you ask me, "I will or will not die, is that what you're saying to me?"… I tell you that "even if you don't die, you are never going to be the same after taking it"… "In what way you ask me?". "Well for starters, you will lose 15 years of your life and between now and the day you finally meet your demise, you will always suffer from poor health because your body will be damaged by this permanent dose of poison". "Hold on a minute" you say, stepping back away from me. "Now let me get this straight", " You want me to put 4000 chemicals in my body that may or may not kill me suddenly, with the prospect of ill health, suffering pain or cancer even if I don't die and you want to offer me 1000 dollars for my troubles!!?" "Well basically… yes" I tell you, "that's basically it". "FUCK OFF", I think is the answer I would get from most of you. "Ok then", I tell you, "how much money would it take me to offer you in order to get you to swallow this pill?". "I wouldn't take it for a million dollars" you tell me abruptly, walking away laughing and thinking I was crazy.

The chances are as a member of **club 50/50**, that after this scenario, you would then walk into the nearest shop and **purchase 20 cancer sticks,** light one up and **inhale 4000 of the poisonous chemicals** you turned down a 1000 dollars for only moments before, and without realising it, you have swallowed the pill you were just offered and along with billions of others, you will digest 20 maybe 30 (some even more) of these **poisonous pills**, hour after hour, day after day, and year after year. Because you are the idiot addicted to these poisons, it is you who spends on average 3000 dollars a year to poison yourself and it is **the billion dollar cigarette companies who laugh at the stupidity of those** who refuse to believe the cold hard **facts that smoking is killing you.**

If you have a feeling that you may just win the lottery this week, just bear in mind that your chances of **dying or being diagnosed with cancer or emphysema** are far greater than the 6 numbers bouncing out in the order of your favour. If you wish to win the lottery, continue doing the lottery. **If you have a death wish, continue smoking shitty toxic chemicals** because inhaling this dirt is a **dead cert** every time. You or your partner may or may not ever strike it rich or win the lottery, but one or both of you has a **50/50 chance of dying a painful death from your filthy disgusting addiction.** It is this that separates the dreams in our minds from the reality of cancer in the body. Wake up and smell the roses before you are rudely awoken with terrible news that no one should ever unnecessarily have to hear.

A DIRTY LITTLE HABIT OR A FILTHY DISGUSTING ADDICTION?

Let's clarify something from the very start of this chapter so as not to allow ourselves to become confused. This is what, through my own research on what is considered a habit, or an addiction (and what are the differences), have found. Both addiction and habit are learned behaviours and both can become unlearned or unrecognised by the person who owns them. The fundamental differences are that addictions have a biological basis (meaning the chemistry of the brain changes and the source of the addiction becomes a necessity). An addiction will also interfere with at least one of life's social functions, such as home life, relationships, work or school environment etc. A bad habit on the other hand, or a habit of any kind although it may feel compulsive, has no effect on the chemical change of the brain whatsoever and whilst annoying, doesn't actually interfere substantially in any of life's functions. The definition of the word habit is described as 'a regular or settled tendency or practice, especially one that is hard to give up', (Whilst reading this please note the words hard to give up denotes that it's possible and not impossible-just hard!).

There are many things in life that may be hard to give up or to part with, but with perseverance, we somehow always manage it. The definition of the word Addiction is described as 'being physically dependant on a particular substance'. Now although some idiots may choose to use names such as "pastime" or even hobby to describe forcing their body to do something unnatural, there is still a vast majority of those who (even though **addicted to poisonous nicotine)** will still choose to convince or tell others in a truly heartfelt (a very fitting word) way, that what they are doing to their body and to the bodies of those around them is just **a dirty little habit** that they will give up eventually. This is a feeble and weak attempt to **bullshit yourself** and those around you, which as you will read later on, you cannot possibly do. No my dear friend, what you have is far from **a dirty little habit**, but something far more **sinister, deadly, dangerous and disgusting** than you have ever allowed yourself to believe. Let's have a look at how you've been confused, blinded and stupid, by giving you examples of how you may be one of the many who has gotten their

habits and addictions mixed up. We will also look at what many of you may actually perceive **an addict** to be.

How many of you have been scolded as a child or even scolded a child yourself or an adult for that matter, to stop picking their nose? You tell them "Stop that, **that's a filthy habit",** or when you tell someone not to speak with their mouth full, another **dirty habit** we frown upon? Then another, (probably the most common of habits) which is biting of the nails. The three examples I've just given are common habits which some of us may have, but most of us are familiar with. They also allow us to see that any of the three, be it nose picking, talking with your mouth full or biting your nails (although fairly common habits) are still only that, habits. We had them, then we were scolded so much about doing it, that we stopped. Or maybe they no longer served us a purpose or we just grew out of them, and we simply stopped picking or biting. We managed to do so and to do so relatively easily because as habits, they had not **affected the chemical balance of our brains.**

We know this because we didn't climb the walls in anxiety and because our moods weren't altered in any way, because there were no poisons **or addictive substances** to drain from our bodies over a period of time, leaving us in an uncomfortable state of withdrawal. Obviously there are those reading this who may still prefer to use the term **habit** as opposed to **addiction.** This is because they see the term addiction and withdrawal best used when describing a **junkie drug addict** and **substance abuser** and not someone who enjoys their 'little ol ciggies'. If this is how you view **your own addiction** as harmless just because society accepts it, then you are very much mistaken. It is the wise smoker (if there is such a thing!) who understands and can admit to themselves that they share many of the traits of a **drug addict** (or junkie if you prefer). If you haven't started to view it this way, then it is time for you to inhale a dose of reality rather than the **highly addictive nicotine fix.** It is time for you to discover **why you and the junkie** may be very different people, but are in many ways on the same wavelength. For those of you, who upon reading this, are now asking themselves horrified "Surely, he's not going to compare me to some crack whore who sells her baby for a fix, or to a smack head who will steal from his own grandmother to score some heroin?", and I will have to say no, I won't. I will however be drawing comparisons, so listen up.

There are several parallels between any **persons addicted to a substance.** They share so much in common that it is completely wrong for any person who depends on a **substance,** to be allowed say that they may only have a habit whilst saying the other had an addiction. Again, the nail biter has a habit whereas the addict feels fucked up without their substance. If you were to speak to a **drug**

addict who told you that they **had a drug habit,** would you feel obliged to correct them and to let them know that it was an **addiction** they actually had and not a **habit?** If someone was to say to you perhaps, that they had a silly old habit of putting crack in a glass pipe and smoking it, or that they couldn't break that dirty little habit of inhaling crystal meth off a piece of tinfoil, you would see them as extremely misguided and that they were trying to kid themselves.

But then again, maybe they are genuinely foolish enough to think, or to even believe that their bloodstream was designed to carry heroin, or that **those poisonous chemicals** such as crystal meth, is **what the lungs** really need and not air! Now then, when it comes to your own **personal substance abuse,** (because yes, that's what it really is, **abuse of a substance**, namely tobacco/nicotine) are you foolish enough to try and convince yourself and others around you, that your fix is still only a little habit? Even though every single coffin nail you put to your lips and ignite **contains 4000 individual poisonous chemicals,** which are not only **used as pesticides,** but as a **method of execution in the US?** And if so, can you also acknowledge that your habit **contains deadly carcinogenic**, anyone of which can trigger cancer at any time when it clings to the **very DNA strands of your body?** If you're answering yes whilst using the term habit then you have a problem my friend.

You see, modern society sees itself as exactly that, modern, when in actual fact we are no nearer a civilised society than we were 200 years ago. Society, any society that is, that allows a man or woman be penalised, jailed or even killed in some parts of the world for using freedom of speech or nudity as an expression or symbol of protest, whilst still legally allowing people to **inhale toxic poisonous chemicals** into **their own lungs or exhale it** into the faces of **innocent defenceless children,** cannot allow themselves to be classed as a **civilised society.** If this is the case, then as a civilised society we have gotten it **all wrong**. If you, up until now, believed that **forcing your lungs and body to endure poisons**, was "only a habit", just like picking your nose or biting your nails, then you, like society has gotten it all wrong. What you did when you first picked up a **cancer stick** and lit it, was to carry out a **dangerous experiment** without even realising it. You may have been a 13 year old inexperienced teen looking to fit in and to impress others or you could put it down to peer pressure. Or maybe you were in your 30s when you took your **first drag of poison** whilst trying to be sociable with colleagues or friends out in the smoking shed in college or outside the workplace. Whenever, wherever and whatever the reason, anyone who now has **this poisoned addiction** didn't become a **full blown nicotine addict** whilst fumbling around with the first **cancer stick** learning to hold it properly.

Any person who has taken up this **poisonous addiction** is also aware that before you can learn the techniques of inhaling properly you have **to suck that poisonous smoke deep down into your lungs** for the full effect. I know this from first-hand experience after being teased by friends that if I didn't inhale it into my lungs, then I wasn't **a real smoker** because I wasn't doing it properly. This particular **exercise in death** is only mastered after much **coughing, spluttering,** and is followed by **bouts of choking.** When you have finally mastered the technique of **inhaling poisonous chemicals deep into your lungs**, you have passed this **filthy rite of passage** and instead of being presented with a certificate of qualification, you now (if you choose to continue your new found "passion"), get to buy your very own 20 box of **cancer sticks** to symbolise how experienced you actually are. For any readers who understand this as their own story of how they started, I'd like to remind you of the following. While some may use peer pressure as an excuse or social gatherings or even stress as a reason as to why they **began inhaling poisonous chemicals,** it would serve you well to remember at this point, that even if you were held down and forced to **inhale the offensive second hand smoke of others** back then, that to personally pick up **a cancer stick**, light it and inhale it now, is done by choice. And that's exactly what it is, choice. To do so, if it is your choice is obviously, entirely up to you and if you are someone who **chooses to blame your addiction today on others**, then I will remind you that the buck of blame stops firmly with you.

The first **coffin nail** you lit up as an experiment became a bit of a habit and the habit you so quickly became used to, became a need which turned to dependency and that rapidly **turned to addiction** and **that addiction** (whether or not you care to agree with), has more control over your life and your future than you may ever realise. To allow it to be called **an addiction** on its own, almost gives it an everyday status or a medical term as if **addiction** is a term that makes it sound acceptable for a person to have. You see, your **addiction** is not **just** merely the words **'an addiction'** when it's actually broken down and it is wrong to make something so harmful sound so harmless. The onus of responsibility is taken away when you claim **your addiction** makes you do it. "The bad poison made me do it!!" It puts it almost in the same category as of the dirty little habit you couldn't shift and makes it sound almost acceptable. It's **an addiction by choice** if you continue to do it. When the cravings are conquered, you are 90% of the way there. Anything after that is just feeble excuses and weak minds .This is a tough one or two days there's no doubt, but that's all it takes. It's uncomfortable in the chemical comedown sense, but clean air versus a filthy set of lungs wins every time for those who desire to live long.

What we will do from here on out is call it for what it actually is and that's a **filthy disgusting addiction** to **poisonous chemicals.** Allow me to break it down for you and elaborate on the words as follows: **FILTHY**= the smoke that clings to every piece of clothing, even your skin and hair, ash trays beside a bed or on a table full and overflowing with a foul smelling **toxic stench**. The yellow or brown stains on a person's fingers or teeth that's almost impossible to scrub off. **DISGUSTING,** = the **green, brown,** or **yellow phlegm** that becomes **lodged in the lungs, throat and arteries of a smoker's body**. To cough up this **foul poisonous looking hard piece of jelly** that has come directly from your lungs, has been forced up your throat, because your **lungs are rejecting it** and are instead begging for the **fresh air they were designed to breathe**. Your bloodstream is also struggling to cope under pressure and pumps blood around your body which is also competing against **the tar in your veins**. This is **no difference to the tar used on our roads,** it's actually the same product. We will elaborate more on this later but that so far covers **the filthy disgusting** part of **your addiction** and finally **addiction itself. ADDICTION,** = yours in particular. The main instigator in all of this and out of all of the **4000 different chemicals** that go into **every cancer stick,** is the **highly addictive substance nicotine**. This is the name which you laugh with other addicts about being hooked on that is eventually going to stop your heart from beating. There's fuck all funny about this.

In a nutshell, I will give you the basic information needed and will only refer to it when possible by its purest name or form which is indeed **poison** and is exactly **what nicotine was originally used for**. This **poison you spend your money on** breathing into **your lungs is a pesticide**. If you're not familiar with the term pesticide, **it is a poisonous chemical used to kill**, repel or control certain forms of plants or animal life that is considered to be a pest, hence the name **pesticide,** like **homicide,** only for pests. It is known to be as **addictive as heroin** or **cocaine** in its hold over the addict themselves. It is, (along **with 4000 other poisonous chemicals**) forced into your body through your airways and against your body's wishes and there it fucks around with the natural chemicals of your body and your brain, sending confusing messages to both, in the form of **confused addiction**. To **force your body to endure such trauma** over and over again is quite literally breath-taking, as the body strives to recover with fresh oxygen in between breaths only to be punished for its efforts by the **inhalation of another 4000 more poisonous chemicals,** as you start all over again. What is just as breath-taking or perhaps even more startling is that even after reading this or even though most **poisonous nicotine addicts** already know this, they still don't love either themselves or those around them enough, to realise **how tragic the life** of a **nicotine addict actually** is. When inhaling poison becomes the norm then your twisted version of the norm is truly warped. What's more warped is casually admitting this but denying addiction.

When you purposely inhale a poisonous substance, even though you are fully aware of the consequences to the **health of your body** and you do so for fear of withdrawal, then **you are an addict**. The **addict** who is afraid of the comedown because of the unpleasant symptoms should realise that even the admission of not being able to cope without **inhaling poison chemicals,** is not only a cry for help from you, but also a cry for help from your body and your inner voice pleading "**no more please, no more**". Your body will forgive you for putting it through withdrawal symptoms, believe me; it has been through a lot worse up until this point. **Admitting you have a filthy disgusting addiction is a good start.** It shows **intent to stop** and if it contains **self-belief,** then you are already on **the road to recovery** from **addiction.** Just remember to keep repeating the more you read on, to affirm to yourself in an honest fashion that **you no longer wish to be addicted to a filthy poison,** every time you feel the urge to light up.

The greedy actions of the tobacco companies who have **taken your hard earned money in exchange for your health,** your wellbeing and **your very limited time on this planet** should hang their heads in shame but they don't because **they don't give a fuck about you in the same way a drug dealer doesn't give a fuck about a junkie and only cares about the dollar.** You are one of the pests that their **pesticides** are **killing off.** This of course may not be how you view yourself, but this is how they view you. You are no more than a cockroach to these people, a pest, and when you are finally laid to rest, when you meet your demise, the tobacco companies which sold you the poison that put you in the ground will have a new 12 year old, **up and coming addict** ready to take your place in being **hooked on a poison** so readily available, just as it was to you. I challenge anybody to tell me that their cigarette company really cares about them. In fact, don't even bother. Anyone who attempts to try justifying such bullshit is deluded and not playing with a full deck. **Everything about this addiction is filthy and disgusting**; from the production line that **sprays the tobacco with poisonous chemicals,** right down to **the stains on the teeth** and the tar in the lungs and **bloodstream of the addict.** Take your habit if you still believe you have one and carefully revise it. You have **a filthy disgusting addiction** and I want you to remember this so we can move on with the task at hand, which is to **STOP FUCKING SMOKING.**

IN DENIAL,
IN DEEP SHIT.

In denial can cover a varied group of things in one's life regarding our health, our happiness or our overall wellbeing. We can be in denial for any number of reasons, either mentally, physically or both, which can be disastrous especially when the denial can lead to a dreaded realisation and quite often realisation can come too late. I can remember being told as a child that you can never lie to yourself and scratching my head wondering what it actually meant, thinking all the while "of course I can lie to myself". It didn't make sense to me then, but now, like many things said, or warnings given to me as a child, I understand them completely. To help you understand me, I'll ask you to look at it this way. If for example, you were born Tom or Mary and you bumped into a complete stranger in the street who asked you your name, you could choose to tell them that your name is John or Sarah or whatever, be it harmless fun or simply through a type of mischief. They (the stranger) would be none the wiser. Now verbally, with words, you just told a lie about your real name, so unbeknownst to the unsuspecting stranger, you have just lied to them by speaking an untruth.

Now, because you told them a lie in regards to your name, the stranger now knows you as John or Sarah, when in actual fact, you are still Tom or Mary. This makes no difference to the stranger except for you instinctively know the truth and that your own name Tom or Mary, as your birth name is your real name, simple as. You could if you wished, try to convince yourself that your name is actually John or Sarah but not even then will your brain allow you to accept this. When a person lays in bed at night and closes their eyes, the voice in your head knows the real truth, the real you. You cannot lie to yourself! To look at another way, you may also tell a work colleague that life is great when in fact you struggle every day to look in the mirror without breaking into tears. You may tell a friend that your happy marriage or relationship is glued firmly together when in actual fact its falling apart day by day and you can tell yourself "one more cigarette won't kill me" or "I'll give them up after Christmas" with the utmost of intent, but again, when you lay down in your bed at night and run through your day and your life in your mind as we all do, you cannot, no matter how hard you try, lie to yourself. If you are unhappy, the mind knows. If the body is unhappy or unhealthy, you cannot lie to yourself and the inner voice we all have inside of us will communicate telling only truth, (remember, you cannot lie to yourself) as hard as you may try.

When attempts are made at this in regards to smoking this poisonous shit, most addicts will apply the ostrich effect as a strategy of denial. This is classical amongst many individuals who turn a chosen blind eye to the damage caused to their health, much to the upset of those forced to witness the often rapid decline of the ostrich that chooses to keep its head buried in the sand. This takes place in many aspects of an individual's lives and every day we witness people who need to be told the truth about issues they choose to remain blind to, by attempting to be dishonest with themselves.

When a person is overweight, it may only be by a few pounds, (or to a point to where it affects their daily lives), it becomes apparent to the people around them that they may have a problem because of their physical appearance. Weight gain can be seen. When a person has a problem with eating food such as a disorder which makes them unable to keep food down or a psychological condition such as anorexia nervosa which makes it hard for them to the see damage they are doing to their bodies, then the family, friends, doctors etc., will step in at some time and say "listen, we notice that you're not eating properly", or again, in the case of obesity "you are overeating and we can see the damage you're doing to your health. These examples are of people who, because of a combination of physical and/or mental health issues, the people around them, loved ones, friends' colleagues, etc., take notice and offer to assist them in their recovery, through their genuine concern. The overeating of food can be caused by comfort eating which is recognised as a psychological condition. The effects of overeating can have disastrous effects on the person's physical wellbeing and can be fatal if not addressed in the correct manner and on time. The same can be said by the undereating of foods. A person who purges (self-induced vomiting), after forcing themselves to eat food, usually has had an event or trauma in their life which affects them on a psychological level and also affects their physical wellbeing, that like overeating, if not addressed properly will lead to suffering, death or both. These examples of conditions, are classic scenarios where the person doesn't always see the damage that they are doing to themselves because of mixed signals from the brain, a personal trauma or what is also sometimes referred to as a chemical imbalance.

There are smokers out there (we all know someone who fits into this category) who genuinely don't believe or fail to see the extent of the damage they are doing to themselves. It is those around them who witness the barbaric onslaught of the damage caused by their poisonous addiction. Sadly for the ones who don't see this, they foolishly believe that they are the ones in total control. With any **addiction to a substance**, knowing who calls the shots is extremely important. Denial is often found when a person fails to understand the control they actually possess. It's almost like choosing to be stupid to a clear and present danger.

Now, as most smokers are aware or maybe don't care, here's is a basic rundown on how nicotine wears the trousers in the filthy relationship you both share. Nicotine, given its name after the 16th century French diplomat Jean Nicot, is like a politician, absolutely useless, full of shit and of no use to anyone it encounters! It is as we have already established, **highly addictive just like heroin**. No matter what any person may say to sugar coat their use of an **addictive substance such** as **"I only use occasionally"** or the old **"I've got a handle on it"**. Listen to me…**Addiction means it's got a handle on you** regardless of how you view it. If something makes you feel uneasy when you don't have access to it, **chances are you're an addict**. As **an ex-smoker of this poisonous shit**, I can remember that I have often bitten my nails into the skin of my fingers and paced the floors whenever I was deprived of **my master's fix**. If I'm painting a bleak or bad picture of myself then good, that is my intention. Those who agree with what I'm saying will also be familiar with the ridiculous expressions we use such as **"I'm hanging for a smoke"** or **"I'd kill for** a cigarette now". How often have you wanted to murder a bottle of water? Have you ever had a hanging or longing for a bowl of brown rice or an apple perhaps? Probably not, and the reason is this. You have trained your body and your mind by **starting a filthy fad,** slowly building pace to develop into a habit. Your body became accustomed to this habit of the **occasional cancer stick after dinner** or lunchbreak and before you knew it has blown into a **fully blown addiction to nicotine**. Now, in order to get the **poisonous nicotine** into the **bloodstream,** it must also allow in **another 3999 chemicals** with every single, **stinking cancer stick you inhale**. Your body, always at your beck and call has allowed you to build up a tolerance to **this poisonous addictive substance**, and now that it has become used to it, the **mind tricked by toxic chemicals** screams out for it at any given moment, whenever or wherever it needs a fix. The brain screams yes but the body begs no. To take a serious look at what in denial is, we don't have to look very far.

With all of the media we have access to today and taking into account, that the different age groups from different decades are reading this material, let's boil this down to what it really is. **Ignorance**- first off, 'a lack of knowledge or misinformation'. Unfortunately for some, ignorance is bliss, (or they'd just prefer not to know). Then there's **stupidity**, which is given the definition- 'a poor ability to understand or to profit from experience'. **Do you as an addict who inhales 4000 different poisonous chemicals per cancer stick,** fit into one or both of these categories. If you answered "I might be ignorant, but you don't know the trouble I've been through, my husband left me **alone with two children and I need cigarettes to help me cope**", then you are both **ignorant**

and stupid. Keep reading, if you want to **feel sorry for yourself**, I've written a chapter for you up ahead.

Being in denial is to have someone state the obvious for your attention, right in front of you saying, "here's what you need to see" or "here's what you need to know" or do, and refusing to point blank to open your eyes or pin back your ears. A person can be **in denial** for any number of reasons but if this involves finally being made aware through the **diagnosis of a life changing illness**, then I seriously hope you are already starting to turn your back on **denial** and get ready to listen up good.

The world has been in denial about many things since we started to take notes as humans on our historical stupidity. It wasn't so long ago that humanity believed that the world was flat. Since then, we have sailed around it. We never believed that man could fly. We have since put a man on the moon and have at this moment in time, a buggy collecting rock samples on mars. We used to communicate by pen, paper, and horseback, now we push buttons to see what's happening live, thousands of miles away. And finally, we used to have a life expectancy of 25 as Neanderthal cavemen, which as of today, has risen to 75 for men and 84 for women in the western world. All of which (both biologically and technologically) is evolution at its finest. When we evolve, remember, (evolution meaning the gradual development of something)…development, growth, progress, we move forward. Why do you think men and women are living longer these days? Is it the science and medicine, or is it that they are becoming more aware of what is right and what is wrong in regards to their bodies, their health and **their mortality?** Are they starting to look at what keeps them safe and what **does them harm?** What makes them feel good and what makes them feel bad?

The man or woman who watches what they put in their body, be it food, drink or vitamins, does so because they realise that their body is the house they have to live in. To maintain this remarkable piece of machinery is their primary goal. These are the people who realise that they are forever evolving. They are the ones who realise that they will get out of their bodies what they put in and if they take care of the body, then the body will take care of the mind. These people understand that you cannot lie to yourself. When they suffer from a common cold, they can turn to each other and say "there's a bug going around, I must have caught it in work" and believe it to be true because they don't have to make excuses as to why they have a dose of the sniffles or a constant cough. Those who care about their health and wellbeing will treat themselves with a Lemsip or double up on cod liver oil to boost their immune system, repairing or strengthening the body they care about. How many times has the man or woman with a **filthy disgusting addiction** walked into a doctor's surgery and complained about or **moaned to their doctor about being breathless** walking up the stairs, or not being able to shift that **reoccurring cough** or **congested chest** only to be asked " do you smoke" or **"are you still smoking"**? If the person answers yes, when all the while being previously told by their doctor to quit and continues to do so, then I have zero sympathy for them, when even the pleas of their medical professionals are ignored.

To **live in denial** is **to die in ignorance** as far as I'm concerned. **Billions of dollars** are spent worldwide on the treatment and repairing of the damage done to humanity by **poisoning themselves** with **toxic self-inflicted chemicals. Cancer causing nicotine infested poison** is **responsible for up to 4 million deaths globally per year.** That is a **cold hard fact**, and if you fit into any of the categories of one of the **many millions who will die of a poisonous inhaled illness** because you choose to be **ignorant to all the signs** you have been given, then **your denial will sound your demise. Your denial** will cause you to leave your family prematurely and you will become a **cigarette caused cancer statistic.** Great way to be remembered no matter how cherished a memory your family has of you. It must really pain medical professionals to see repeat offenders walk into their offices with the same complaints and the same reoccurring issues regarding their **chesty coughs, wheezing, low immune systems**, or **a far more sinister illness**. It must also pain them to have to waste their precious time and even paper to write out a prescription hoping to cure or fix the same self-inflicted ailment. All the while knowing that in reality, that the medication given for that sore throat or **to shift that mucus and tar on your lungs**, is only wasted when they are quite literally **washed down with smoke,** as soon as the patient gets back into their car.

It would be more humane to prescribe a bullet to a person who slowly and regularly forces their body to defend itself against this **constant toxic chemical attack.** If anyone reading finds this to be a harsh statement, id challenge you, if you haven't already had the misfortune to witness a young **child with cystic fibrosis who struggles and gasps to breathe** and to **rid their lungs of a build-up of phlegm and mucus.** Or to witness a healthy adult who has taken care of their body throughout their life, waste away within weeks of **being diagnosed with a terminal cancer or illness**. There are people out there as we speak, who realise that time is precious and very limited in human terms and they may not have very much of it left. While they **struggle to breathe, struggle to live and inhale whatever fresh air they can into their bodies** because they know it may be their last, you do the exact opposite. You complain about your skin, your complexion, your health and then without hesitation, take a lighter, put **a filthy poisonous piece of paper to your lips and light it**, only to **breathe in**

4000 different poisonous chemicals straight into your bloodstream, heart and lungs. You have no consideration for your wellbeing whatsoever and to argue that you do is **bullshit**. Numbskull is a fitting word. **In denial** is what you truly are. The warning signs you see on your box and all **the red lights** that have flashed before you in the form of your **yellow and brown stained teeth and fingers** are some of the outside damage. Inside, your organs tell a different story altogether. You may say to yourself that "this is not new to me" or that you "already know all this" and this is a classic case of being in denial. You may indeed think you have heard all this before but keep reading, remember, **there is no smoke without fire.**

NO SMOKE WITHOUT FIRE.

What you know about smoking and what you think you know about smoking are two completely different things. As we covered in our last chapter, we are aware that most people who have **a filthy disgusting addiction** don't see it for what it actually is or choose to remain blind by attempting to live untruths about their addiction. This is because of the way that **addiction** is presented globally. The **poisonous cigarette companies** for well over a hundred years were quite **literally getting away with murder.** I'm talking about the **murder of hundreds of millions** and not only because of their **miserable products,** but the endorsements and advertising campaigns which allowed the ignorance of the time believe they were actually good for a person's health. They have survived for many years living lavishly on the now **trillions of dollars made globally on the misery of every man, woman and child** who has ever **succumbed to their filthy products**. Any book you have ever picked up will give you cover to cover of medical and scientific jargon on the statistics of **smoking this poisonous shit.** The following pages will tell you everything you need to know in a nutshell and skips all the irrelevant bullshit.

The tobacco companies from where you buy **your filthy disgusting addiction,** is only worth the trillions of dollars it has amassed, because of you and **other pitiful addicts.** You can name the **brand of poison you place to** your lips every day because you see yourself as **addicted** to that particular brand. The companies that take on average between **3 and 5000 dollars from you per year** don't know your name **and don't want to know your name**. All they want to know is that you will **keep putting your hand in your pocket to purchase the poison** they have you **hooked on,** and it's that simple. Even the man who sells you a life insurance at a premium of 5 dollars a week knows your name and will shake your hand before you sign a contract, as this is considered good business. To shake the hand of a person to which you give money during a transaction is a common global gesture as we are all aware. This is not however the case with the tobacco companies who take **your thousands per annum** as they will do no such thing. They don't shake because there is no need and they don't care because they don't have to. They are not in the caring business, and even now, by law, they have to warn their **addicted customers** that their **products are killing them** and they still have no shortage of customers on a global scale, lining up to **purchase more and more of their poison** day in and day out. These addicts flock like sheep unaware they are being led to a slaughter house.

They have hundreds of millions of slaves worldwide with new members joining every day. The world health organisation (WHO) has recorded that in 2004, **over 5.4 million deaths** were reported globally and noted as dying of a direct result of smoking or a death registered as smoking related. For those of you who had to do a double take, I'll give you that figure again. **That's over 5.4 million people** worldwide who left this planet early because of **a filthy disgusting addiction,** or poor innocent passive smokers who perished because they were **forced to inhale the poisonous fumes** from the second hand smoke of some ignorant fuck. That's the population of a country like Ireland, in one year! And for all those die hards (a word all smokers will eventually become aware of in one way or another) who say, "That's not much" or "I thought there'd be more", then you are more of an idiot than initially thought. If one death from inhaling poisonous fumes can affect a whole family or community, can you imagine the devastation felt by the deaths of **5.4 million people's families**, friends and colleagues worldwide? That is **5.4 million men women and children** who have **all died prematurely** from one of **the most preventable causes of death** on the planet. Now although I don't want to sound like a missionary, but preventable deaths that number **5.4 million** is pretty fucked up, am I right? If those figures have made some of you take note and question the accuracy, then do your research and check it out. And if the figure **of 5.4 million** drew gasps of disbelief then again consider this; over **100 million deaths, from smoking have been recorded in the 20th century alone and this number is ever growing**.

What does that say to any human being with even the slightest bit of common sense? Does it say **inhaling poisonous fumes** from **cancer sticks** is a good thing? No it does not. Does it say **smoking shitty toxic chemicals** adds years to your life? No it does not. What it actually does say in short, is that smoking (or **inhaling poisonous chemicals)** is **deadly dangerous** and the cause of **suffering and misery** to **hundreds of millions of people** since the first fucking idiot decided it was a good pastime, right up until today and until people realise the **damage they are doing**, will continue long into the future also. "Your body is a temple" as the old saying goes and if you decide to treat it as **the temple of doom**, then you are at a much lower level of awareness than those who respect their bodies. Those who I see as being on a higher level of awareness are those who decide that they want to change and start looking after themselves properly. They are the ones who are aware that the bodies they possess are robust, yet fragile. Our bodies are intricate and perfect in design and those with this knowledge and awareness understand how to treat the body as it should be treated. Sticking with knowledge and awareness, let's take a little bit of a science lesson for a minute. We as humans are born as individuals. We all have our own stamp our own fingerprints and our very own genetic code or DNA.

This DNA (or deoxyribonucleic acid) is also known as the building block of life. If you haven't seen what it actually looks like or are unfamiliar with the term, it is the genetic make up of any living biological form. It resembles a ladder, a sort of spiral shaped ladder which is found in all of us. It is often referred to as the double helix. One DNA strand is found in every cell in our body, so one drop of blood or one human hair can contain billions of DNA samples. This gene is so perfect in its creation, astounding scientist's, doctors and people from all around the world with its intricacy and perfection. This same little marvel which like a snowflake is so magnificent in its structure, can be pulled down, torn apart or mutated by every single poisonous chemical found in **every single cancer stick.** Their **poisonous tars** and **toxins** bind to the DNA strand and don't allow it to function in the way it was designed to operate and this **genetic mutation** is responsible for thousands of illness and cancers as the DNA strands of the body are forced into hard labour by working overtime to ward off the chemicals that wrap around them. Your DNA strands are now faced with a battle of survival as it struggles in its natural environment to fight against **4000 of the most unnatural poisonous chemicals with every cancer stick** you light up. You are literally forcing nature to turn on itself by doing something so **horrifically unnatural** (**inhaling poison**) to something so natural (your body and DNA).Remember…the same **poisonous chemicals** you force upon your body, your blood, your DNA, your very genetic makeup, includes the chemical hydrogen cyanide, which again, is used to execute people on death row by lethal injection. Just to give you a quick rundown of **some of the shit you are forcing your body to deal with**, I will name some of the **poisonous chemicals** and their actual uses and please bear in mind, that these are only the first few ingredients.

Firstly, in alphabetical order, **ACETIC ACID,** This is a very powerful acid which is extremely corrosive. Vinegar you use on your food is considered a very watered down version of this particular acid. **AMMONIA**, this is what adds flavour to your cancer stick. **This chemical is found in over 90% of all household cleaning products** and is also found **in dog shit.** It is known to cause lung cancer and in large amounts can cause blindness and **irreversible damage** to your skin and your heart. **ARSENIC**, this is used in rat poison to kill vermin. It is known to cause untold damage to the organs of the body including the heart and is a poisonous chemical which is known to kill humans by its very name. When someone hears arsenic we immediately think of murder or death by poisoning. **BENZENE,** this is **a flammable poisonous liquid** which is found in the fumes of petrol. **CADMIUM**, A highly toxic metal found in batteries. Once inhaled, this can stay in the body for up to 22 years and if the levels of this chemical builds up like this over a period of years, it becomes resistant to treatment and becomes strong enough to cause irreversible damage to the liver, kidney and the brain. **CARBON MONOXIDE**, This is the complete opposite of what our lungs were designed for. This is the poisonous gas that stops the body from getting the oxygen it needs to live and to repair itself. It also thickens the blood making it hard work for the heart to pump it around the body, and is a known cause of heart attacks. This poison can be found coming from boilers and car exhaust fumes and is also known as the silent killer. **CARBON TETRACHLORIDE**, A chemical that was used in cleaning fluid until it was realised to be hazardous to the health of the user and banned for use in cleaning products. **D.D.T,** this is a chemical insecticide which is now banned in the UK because it is known to have **carcinogenic** (cancer causing) properties. **FORMALDEHYDE**, A chemical used to preserve dead animals, dead humans and body parts. This chemical can cause untold damage to the eyes nose and throat of any person who handles it incorrectly and can cause severe irritation as well as irreversible damage to human skin. **LEAD**, this was also added to petrol for many years and to paint before it was banned for its lethal affects including poisoning of the blood and severe breathing problems within the respiratory system. It is also believed to be responsible for stunted growth in adolescents. **METHANOL**, this is a solvent and also used as a fuel. How many of you have heard of solvent abuse? This is what they are talking about. **NICOTINE**, This disgusting little gem is as we know is powerful and as addictive as heroin or cocaine. This increases the heart rate and the blood pressure, forcing the body to work overtime, all of the time. This same disgusting poison is also a pesticide and if you were two drops of it to fall onto your tongue in its liquid form, it would stop your heart before your body hit the ground when you swallowed it. **NITRIC ACID**, This chemical is used in many industrial businesses as a cleaning and dissolving properties and has extremely strong corrosive properties. **SULPHURIC ACID**, A dense and corrosive oily liquid that is used in fertilizers and in explosives. **TAR**, found on the roads worldwide, this is known for its cancer causing properties as well as causing massive damage to the heart, lungs and bloodstream of the body. It clings to the teeth, gums and fingers of the addict and if you ever tried to pick tar up of the road with your fingers, you'll see how stuck to the road it actually is. The lungs have the same job in trying to shift tar that has settled in your arteries and ventricles and capillaries and this is why smokers are always breathless. **TOULINE** is used as a solvent in the manufacturing of dyes and explosives…. should I continue?

OK, I've just named **17 different poisonous chemicals** and I'm fairly disgusted with myself at this stage for allowing myself to pollute my body and those around me for far too long, during my own years of **inhaling dirty poisonous shit**. Remember that I have mentioned only 17 chemical poisons out of 4000 that are found in every single cancer stick. That leaves you, the reader, the option of looking up the remaining 3983, just in case you are one of the smartass idiots who already knew about the 17 I've just named. It truly is a fucking idiot who has read the details of this poisonous filth and continues to inhale this shit whilst still feeling sorry for themselves, whenever a smoking related illness upsets their life.

Any single one of the 17 poisons named above is a good reason stop killing yourself if you have an ounce of logic or even self-respect in your body. I am not expecting readers to gasp in shock in reading this as most addicts of nicotine are aware of the damage they are doing, but even if you don't care about the damage you are doing to yourself, then have some consideration for others around you. They are the ones who depend on you; the ones who need you and who want you around for as long as possible. To continue inhaling poisonous chemicals, whilst ignoring their pleas for you to give up or to stop, is yet again to be found in denial, and to live in denial as we've already stated is dealing in death, especially when you factor in the **daily inhalation of thousands of poisonous chemicals.** No smoke without fire doesn't require any more elaboration. You already know that you are killing yourself and it's time for you to stop this madness and to **stop fucking smoking.**

SHITTING ON YOUR OWN DOORSTEP.

Our bodies, your body, my body, their bodies, are our addresses, the places we have to live and I need for you to recognise this. Remember at all times that you live here .Your body is the shell which contains whatever it is that "you" may actually be. If you respect the place in which you live, then your body will return the favour by allowing you to enjoy life itself to the very best of your ability. And best of all, the body doesn't charge you rent for staying there. All that your body asks in return for living here and for its wonderful use is that you maintain it and treat it well while you stay there. It isn't much different than being told by a landlord or house owner that you can stay in their property for as long as you wish once you maintain your accommodation and treat it with respect. This could be considered a fair deal and one that we couldn't really argue with. "Staying in a property once we treat it with respect with a possible eviction if we don't" seems a quite simple agreement. If you agree with your new landlord, that you, as their new tenant will adhere to the terms and conditions they have laid out before you, then how long you remain in this property is entirely up to you.

As a human being, there has been no change, (whether you realise it or not) in the pact made between you and your body, which was sealed by the doctor who slapped your backside to make you cry, on your naked arrival onto this crazy planet of ours. The terms and conditions signed by both you and your body agreed that your body will live for only as long as you give it life, and not a minute longer. This for many of us is the start of a wonderful friendship and for others not so much so. Your first gasp of air as a new-born is your gift or confirmation to your body, that you will uphold your end of the bargain as a symbol of life and a promise of keeping it alive. It's almost like a declaration by the self to protect it with every breath in your body. Think about this. If you didn't take a breath as a baby then you wouldn't be reading this book. Your first breath of air is the very essence of life. It is you keeping up your end of the bargain. Your first cry as you inhaled this fresh air and your eyes opening is your body's acknowledgement of this gift of air, and it is at this moment that the deal to work as a team has been struck. The unwritten contract is now between you both, simply stating for as long as you look after me, maintain me, you can stay with me without fear of eviction. This agreement or pact will be made by us all but as we know, unfortunately, most of us will not keep up our end of the bargain.

Sometimes protection will be outside of our control with unavoidable illnesses, diseases, or accidents. Other times that our bodies may have to suffer is because of our lifestyle choices or environments. Often our bodies will have to suffer needlessly because we haven't upheld our end of the deal, making us completely responsible for not adhering to the terms and conditions of caring for the body which at the moment of our birth, we agreed to. The body can be quite forgiving, just like the landlord and may be willing to turn a blind eye or forgive a few faults that we may be responsible for, but what happens when we push it so far that these minor faults become major issues? Is eviction not a possibility? And what if these major issues become persistent? Is this not bringing trouble to your front door? Are you not shitting on your own doorstep? Will this lack of respect lead to the eventual breakdown of communication and a certain notice of termination? There may be those of you who, on reading this will think "It's my body and I'll do what I damn well please with it." That, first and foremost is a foolish thought pattern used by someone who is weak willed and who has missed out on the true meaning to this life. Not just the word "life" but the motion of life or living itself. Life and its very essence, the main ingredients of which are "breathing and living." The opposite of which is dying. To die is to no longer live and to force oneself to die unnaturally is no different to vandalism of the body. Vandalism in the biological sense of the self is a form of self-harm.

Many of us if asked the definition of self-harm would describe someone who cuts themselves. We stereotypically will imagine an angst ridden teenage Goth girl with depression and body image issues, or a young man struggling to come to terms with his sexuality who constantly thinks about suicide and who cuts their own flesh to release the pain or sorrow. These are stereotyped self-harmers and we cannot see it any differently in society to look past our ignorance and acknowledge that a depressed teen with a razor blade is not the only form of self-harm out there. Shitting on your own doorstep is a term we use to describe bringing trouble to your own front door and bringing trouble to your own front door is bringing trouble to where you live. Bringing trouble to where you live is unnecessary, it is unneeded grief and feeling aggrieved is what we feel, when someone or something has done us wrong. When the harm is done by the self, to oneself, the only term suitable if the harm is done repeatedly and knowingly, is self-harm, is it not? If you happen at this point to ask yourself, "is he saying what I think he's saying?" Then if you think what I'm saying is that "I believe those who inhale poisons into their lungs when they realise it is harming or even killing their bodies is self-harm", then yes, that's exactly what I'm saying.

This may be hard or even impossible for you to accept, but allow me to help you to understand how I have come to what I see as this very obvious conclusion. After watching a documentary about a 16 year old British girl who fought since birth with cystic fibrosis, I found it hard not to feel emotional to watch how tirelessly she campaigned for more research to be carried out worldwide on her illness, so that another child would never have to endure the suffering she was going through on a daily basis. This crippling illness caused her endless pain and I watched as her family pleaded for more to be done to help their young daughter. Her disease caused restriction of her breathing where her lungs were constantly filling with mucus and phlegm. The only comfort this girl had was fresh air and her parents gave her as much of it as possible by driving her to open aired grassy hilltops and into fresh aired forests where she could breathe as deeply as her restricted lungs allowed. This show ended with her meeting a celebrity she had always wanted to meet and although it was obvious that she was extremely unwell, it was still an unexpected and sad moment to see her name, age and with the words rest in peace, come up on the screen as the credits rolled at the end of the show. Although I am well aware that there are those who also watched this show or who on reading will again say "such is life", or that "we all have it coming", and this is your opinion no matter how ridiculous I personally view it. But it had quite the opposite effect on me. I began to think of how society has gotten it all messed up in regard to what we perceive to be acceptable and/or unacceptable. This TV show didn't awaken any campaign in me or come as any kind of defining epiphany. It wasn't a "what have I been doing to my health" type of moment, as I had given up my **poisonous addiction** long before this stage. What it did do however, was to make me think of how ungrateful I had been to have been born with a set of lungs, designed to breathe in air, **only to fill them with poisonous smoke**. What struck me, not just then, but even now thinking about it, is, like many things unjust on this planet, was that here was a young girl whose **whole life consisted of a battle to breathe**, (something humanity takes for granted, but also something we deem to be a god given right) and who used most of the energy given to her fragile body by the small gasps of air she could barely inhale, to campaign for better research for this illness, all whilst people like myself and any other **nicotine addicts** emptied our pockets daily to **purchase a poisonous product which polluted our airways and organs.**

The parallels which struck me was that this young girl found comfort and therapy when sitting on a hillside or in a forest, where her lungs were given a little respite by opening up a little bit more, to free up the congestion which caused her discomfort. "This fresh air" she cried, works better than any man made medication she was taking. Here was a child so **grateful for the air that I had often taken for granted** and the time she knew was very limited of which I took no notice of, or wasted on things not worthy of my own limited time. These are things everyone takes for granted. Again, this is not written to tug on your heartstrings or as some type of guilt trip or sad violin type tale. It is something I felt inside and something I'm sharing with the reader. I'm not looking for a show of emotion. Whether you choose to laugh, cry or neither is entirely up to you. On a human level, we all view things differently but if you are affected in a positive way by what you are reading then you will realise there is an element of your own life that needs adjusting or completely changed, in regard to an addiction. I didn't realise it at the time but as someone who has been **addicted to nicotine**, I now see very clearly that **the suffering or misery inflicted** on my body was all done by myself and to myself. This is not a defining moment or grand admission of guilt. As we now know, most people who **inhale poisonous chemicals** such as nicotine frequently use expressions such as "I know they're no good for me but…..", but nothing; but maybe, how many of these people are actually listening to the **bullshit words** that are coming out of their mouths? **I mean really listening** and repeating these words back to themselves.

This is where I believe society has gotten it wrong by allowing this **highly addictive and lethal poison** to be viewed as something almost normal or acceptable. You are **addicted to a drug that is killing you** and those around you that is deemed acceptable and this is what's unacceptable about it! To give you an example of how **ridiculous this filthy disgusting addiction** is seen by society try to imagine this: Two men sitting on a park bench, one eating an apple and the other **smoking a cancer stick**. You may read this and say "ok, sure, so what's wrong with that?, You might even add, "we live in a free world, these are two grown men, one chooses to be healthy and eat an apple and one chooses to **smoke a deadly cigarette,** they're both adults, they can make their own choices, so what's the problem?" The answer to this is in your question, "what's the problem", as this is where the problem lies. It's the fact that seeing two people, one of which is digesting an apple, a piece of nature's fruit in a natural way. His body has asked for this piece of fruit through a natural bodily reaction to hunger. Watching him digest a piece of fruit in the natural way as his body works in sync and allows him to swallow as nature has intended him to is normal. All whilst the other man **forces his body to do something unnaturally.** Because of his confused thought pattern, (through the **horrific mind fuck of addiction** to a **poison**) his brain has screamed at his body to ease the longing for this nicotine by lighting up a cancer stick. While this man's brain is screaming yes, yes, yes, his body, his lungs, heart, blood, and the rest of his DNA are screaming no, no, no as the natural air in his lungs is **polluted and replaced with over 4000 poisonous addictive chemicals and smoke** which clings to every cell in his body. This man's heartrate will increase alarmingly and his body will immediately go on the defensive to fight and to counteract the **unnatural poisonous chemicals it is forced to endure**. When this onslaught of his cells finally stops as he stubs out **his heart stopping cancer stick** and **inhales his last plume of poisonous smoke**, his cells will immediately begin to regroup, bury their dead and begin to repair and prepare themselves for the next attack, by the very person supposed to be protecting them. They will not have long to wait as **addiction has no concept of time**, just like the man who is unaware that his **biological clock is diminishing faster than he could ever possibly imagine**. This is unnatural and just wrong, wrong, wrong on so many levels and viewing it as normal is very abnormal.

When you are at a stage that you can say to yourself or anybody else who is interested **"I'm going to stop smoking these things because their killing me"** and you genuinely understand the declaration you just made as not simply, "words" without meaning, then you have a will to live. This is useless if you speak these same words just to make conversation with someone whilst out in the smoking shed having a **cancer stick** and it holds no intention or will whatsoever. It will be then and only then my Smoky friend, that for the first time in the years (or since you began this **poisonous addiction,**) will you stop talking out of your backside and take direct and intentional action on your statement. Realise something very important at this point and accept not only that you have a problem, but that you have a big problem. It's a big problem because of the **knock on effects and the consequences.** Your life and everything it involves including your family, your home, your work, will, (if they haven't already been **affected by this addiction**) suffer terribly. Allow yourself to see that what you are doing is indeed a **form of self-harm.** There is no better way of dealing with something by putting a label on it and owning it. There is no shame in this whatsoever and the only time you should use the word shame is **if you continue to allow your addictive master to control you**. Then shame on you will be a deserved title. By allowing yourself to recognise what you are doing is **self-harm** pure and simple, (it is harm caused to your body through self-infliction) then your admission of truth and **responsibility** is **your admission** of **understanding** and your **acceptance** that shit needs to be done differently.

People need to be aware not only of **the damage to their own bodies,** but that of **those forced to inhale their 1st, 2nd, and 3rd hand smoke** (smoke and chemicals that settles in dust). A person **who inhales poison designed to kill** has to begin to acknowledge that their actions are actions of **self-harm** and that children should be made aware of the dangers of harming themselves and to keep away from this **poisonous addictive scourge.** Shitting on your own doorstep must now come to an end. When **this disgusting addiction** is recognised for what it is and that is a **filthy disgusting and deadly act of self-harm** ....only then will people start to realise that the body is the most important thing they will ever possess. By **polluting it with it with poisonous toxins** like the **4000 chemicals** that go into every **cancerous heart stopping coffin nail,** you **are shortening a life** very much worth living. if you would only start using it for what it was actually for, to be maintained properly, to be lived and **to breathe air.** If you do **continue to pollute your body, your lungs, your airwaves** and the place you have to live, then remember this, by deciding that you wish to **continue shitting on your own doorstep**, it is only a matter of time before the landlord, tired of taking your shitty treatment, will tear up the contract and evict you from your premises for good. **Getting evicted from the body means death!** When this happens, there is no going back.

"MY FAMILY MEAN EVERYTHING TO ME" and OTHER BULLSHIT.

It is only natural for a parent to use the expression "I'd die for my kids" or for someone to say "I'd do anything for my family". This is a way for many of telling someone that you would rather see your own life end, before you would allow any harm come to those you love and cherish. If you are **one of the many millions who inhale toxic chemicals** whilst making this same declaration, **then dying for your family** is a dead certainty except it won't be as flippant as your statement and it promises to be either **slow and painful** or if your very lucky a quick **sudden heart attack to finish you quickly**. This is where the real debate starts, with readers who find themselves slightly offended or perhaps angry as fuck by this chapter title and the literary truths which follow. To be honest, I really don't give a fuck because it is what it is. I would like to challenge anyone of you to read on and please feel free to disagree with what's written, as I see it as the obvious and blatant truth. Any human being with **an addiction to a substance** which is **harming either themselves** or those around them, talk's pure and utter bullshit, when it comes to how much they love their families.

Those who have addictions to substances such as nicotine, alcohol, or heroin will at all costs put their **poisonous substances** before their so called loved ones. In regards to a person's **addiction to nicotine,** let me ask you this? If you are a parent to a child, or you are a brother, a sister, husband, wife, grandparent, who has been asked more than once by that family member to, "please try and quit your habit" and have refused to do so, then that means that you have automatically chosen **your poisonous addictive substance** over the pleas of concern from your "loved one", and it's because you find it too hard to say you will do it. Through your own stupidity and ignorance, you will automatically jump on the defensive and angrily shout "But that doesn't mean that I don't love my family", so please, allow me to continue, and again, feel free to disagree but read carefully and think, before you decide to react or over react. Stop, breathe, relax and think on this for a moment…Why has your family, the ones you live for, the ones you love, **asked you to stop smoking?** Why does a 5 year old or a 10 year old ask their mother to stop? Is it because your family know instinctively that **your addiction is harming either you, them or both,** or is it because they have taken heed from doctors, the world's media, and even the common knowledge from the dog on the street, about the dangers and the repercussions of your **filthy actions?** How many times have you been asked by your family to give up eating oranges or drinking water? The answer is an obvious never, because again, your family knows that unless you choke on an orange or submerge your head under water for too long, the chances are you will not come to any harm! Your family asks you **to quit your addiction** out of concern, and by being concerned in regard to **the poisonous smoking addiction** you now have, it gives them the perfect right to be so.

If you are the type of person who laughs off these remarks, then you are more ignorant than when you first begun to read this book. If you laugh at the pleas of your loved ones every time you place a **coffin nail** in your mouth then you will quickly learn, as time goes by, to see your laid back humour turned from black comedy to Greek tragedy. For anyone **addicted to a substance** (in this case nicotine) , who has been told over and over again that their inability to say no will take on average, **15 years off their life** and still continues to allow it to fall on deaf ears is **putting poison before proper parenting.** I challenge anyone to tell me any different. It is not only our right as human beings to watch our children grow but also to watch them become parents and to see their children become parents if we look after ourselves properly. To allow oneself **through stupidity and feeble excuses** such as stress, a coping mechanism or false enjoyment as to a pathetic reason why we won't be around to see this happen, is a lame and a loveless act. To put **dependency on poison,** before your given right to grow old gracefully and with an entitlement to die peacefully, having made sure that your family is at peace with your passing, is a privilege far too many smokers decide to scoff at or take for granted. To say you would do anything for your family whilst still lighting and **inhaling 4000 poisonous chemicals** is an insult, both to your body, your family and to yourself. It is gone well past fun and games. This is where the expression **"as serious as a heart attack"** takes on a completely serious tone. This is where "as real as it gets" gets exactly that, and that is "as real as it gets" folks.

If you try to tell me that you as a parent, whose children want for nothing and have the best of food, the best of clothes and the best gold fillings that money can buy, then it seems that all they are missing is the best of parenting, because **if you choose poisonous chemicals** over their right to watch you, their parent or parents attend **(remember 1 in 2 will die of a smoking related death or illness)** their college graduation ceremony or wedding, then you take from them what money cannot buy, and again, that is the precious commodity of your time. If I asked you what is it that goes through your mind, every time a loved one has asked you to quit smoking?, (and again, think seriously on this before you answer).Does it feel as though they are pestering you? Is it an annoyance? Don't they understand that it's not as easy as they think? If you are nodding whilst reading in agreement and thinking "yes exactly, that's exactly how I feel", then I will ask you to consider (if you can do so genuinely) the following.. **Why do they want you to quit?** What is their mission, their agenda? Why are they constantly on your case? How would they cope/survive financially, emotionally and as a family unit if you were to **get a life threatening illness, a cancer or death?** Because this **disgusting addiction carries a 1 in 2 risk of cancer, stroke, heart attack, or death**, is your family going to be cared for when you are struck down with this 1 in 2 chance of **fucking misery?** What is the plan you have set in place to help them cope with the months of **medical bills and then funeral costs?** How will they pay the mortgage on the property? Is eviction likely? How will they survive without your support emotionally and financially? How will they cope mentally with the stress of watching **you waste away and die in unnecessary pain and suffering?** How can you avoid all this? How can you, a person who claims that they would do anything for their family, continue to spend their **hard earned money on poisoning** their body with **thousands of dangerous chemicals,** which will eventually or suddenly cause you **great suffering.** How can you choose to end this, for yourself and for your family? How can you choose to live instead of **a self-inflicted miserable death?**

When or if you happen to agree with what's being said, then there is obvious salvation for your health and for the health of those around you, and this involves a promise of intent with nothing else. If, for example a young couple who smoked decided to get married and spend the rest of their lives together, were to **stop inhaling this shit** to literally start fresh together, they could **save 6000 dollars per year** if they both decide to break **this poisonous pact.** By not **self-harming** with **pollutant chemicals** they are giving themselves the opportunity to grow old gracefully and naturally and not die prematurely through **self-harm**, **skin damage,** and **unnatural poisonous toxic smoke.** The same goes for an elderly couple who decide enough is enough. Because your body begins to repair itself the moment it gets the opportunity, make your decision now and allow your body the chance to **make your recovery.** There is never a better time to **decide you wish to live** and it doesn't matter what age you are. Fortunately, as our science and medicine is advancing, we now understand that the reversal effects from **inhaling this poisonous shit** begin as soon as you start to stop. If you are a pensioner, would you prefer to be **out of breath** by chasing your grandkids around playing ball or watching them cry **when you take your last breaths,** as you **struggle to get air into your lungs** from a ventilator which is keeping you alive? You have to earn the right to **say "I'd do anything for my family"** and to win this right by actually doing so. You must mean it instead of just saying it. Any person can just use these words, but only the person who puts their family above all else including **their addiction to nicotine** (or any addictive substance) can truly wear this t shirt because they have earned the right to truly say it. A person who holds their family above everything else shows this by having the utmost **respect for their own health** and in doing so, it reflects on their family, as they love them enough not to jeopardise either their own health (or the health of their loved ones), by not **being able to refuse inhaling a poisonous addictive chemical like nicotine,** to help them cope in the real world.

This is what separates the strong from the weak and it is this act of love for one's family that gives a person the right to say **"I would do anything for my family"**. They have proven or shown this to be true not only with words, but by their actions. They say this because **they would do anything for their loved ones**. If a person was to say **"Well I'd do anything for my family, except give these things up"** whilst taking a **pull from a poisonous nicotine filled addictive cancer stick**, then they fail. If they attempt to wear the "I'd do anything for my family" t shirt, then they will find that this t-shirt doesn't fit. It was only designed to be worn by those who have earned it. Again I will say that anyone who **puts addiction to 4000 poisonous chemicals** before family has nowhere near the same respect over **a person who puts their family first at all costs**. If you **put poisonous paper** and **chemicals over a person** or persons, then that makes you a **weak individual** whose **false pleasure** and **addiction** you put **before your loved ones** and it's that simple.

Another hypothetical question for you now? We touched on this briefly before but absorb it here in its entirety. Read it carefully, and the answer you give to it if it is an honest answer, will tell a lot about you at this point in your life. If whilst sitting in a doctor's office or while standing in the street, somebody told you that **one more cancer stick would kill** you graveyard dead, before you even got to stub it in the ashtray, would you truthfully.. Quit there and then on the spot? Now I know that this type of question may have arisen before in the past and I also know that this scenario has or will happen to many people, but think on it seriously for a moment. Really think on the question and then answer it very honestly, not to me or anybody else but to yourself. One more cigarette and it's over, you lose your life, you lose everything. Your family get the burden of your death, plus your debts/bills and will face a future of sorrow, **uncertainty and endless hardship for that last drag of poisonous nicotine.** The "real honest" answer that you give to this "very realistic" yet hypothetical question will tell a lot about your reaction to the title of this chapter and whether or not its content truly applies to you. Does "I'd do anything for my family" really mean what it says to you, or is it just another empty promise like the ones you make to quit over and over again to yourself, and to the family you keep putting second over your poisonous addiction?

There are those of you who will answer this question without taking the question seriously because they may view it as a "what if" scenario not worthy of an answer, and this is a weak reaction to what can very easily become your reality. It's turning a blind eye to what is obvious in favour of **addiction,** and the choosing of this is **the choosing of nicotine over all else.** Please bear in mind that as indestructible as we all may see ourselves and as sturdy as our bodies may appear, we are very fragile and as we know, there are no certainties in life in regard to our health, so why jeopardise it any further by **killing it with poisons.** We have all faced illness in our lives and we are all aware of someone we've known, be it a friend, colleague or family member **who has succumbed to a disease,** accident, or an **addiction related death**. If you personally know of, or has known someone who has struggled or done their best to **stay alive under the circumstances of addiction** or an illness brought about by **addiction** and has **struggled or fought to stay alive,** can you be so quick to answer the question that was asked? Bearing in mind you are aware of someone who has begged to live and to survive their illness, when you are now having to take time to think about whether or not you would take a **cancerous poisonous dried out toxic chemical laced piece of death** and put it lighting to your lips. If your attitude at this point is "so what", then I wish you and your addiction well, although the two words 'well' and 'addiction' never go hand in hand. These same fools only think that they would do anything for their family, when in actual fact they can't even do anything to help themselves.

To realise that you are making bad choices means you are aware that you need to **change the damage you are doing to your health** and to your body. This means that if **you are a person who has put poisonous chemicals before everything else** including **your health** and **your family**, then it is the time to take the question of "one more cigarette" quite literally and treat the hypothetical scenario with 'As real as it gets'. It is time for you to **put your family and your wellbeing first.** You should be living for your family and not dying for them, but if you don't put every ounce of effort into **tackling your addiction,** then dying for your family will be the inevitable outcome, except it won't be for glory, but **for nothing.**

Whilst on this subject of family and **addiction to nicotine,** allow me to regale you with the results of a recent survey carried out by psychology students In the United kingdom. A study was carried out asking smokers whether they believed smoking makes you a bad parent, has revealed the following statistics: It was discovered that those who are **addicted to nicotine** were shown to feed their children less, buy them smaller birthday presents and with some even raiding their children's money box to **fund their addiction**. There are those who on reading this may say "well, that doesn't apply to me, I'd never do such a thing," and that's all well and good if you are financially abundant enough not to feel the need to do so. But money or not, if you have ever been caught in a situation where it was either the change in your purse for **cancer sticks** in the forecourt of a garage or a drink for your thirsty child, would or could you honestly say that you would sacrifice **the nicotine your body craves?** If you honestly had to choose between the cry for a drink of the parched toddler or the craving for nicotine, what would you genuinely choose? Would your craving be so strong that baby would have to wait until you get home before they can quench their thirst, because **nicotine came knocking** at a time when money wasn't readily available and the choice between proper parenting and poison arose? I can tell you that in times of my own addiction to this poisonous shit, I have made some terrible decisions where nicotine always came first. My own parents would have done the same by admission.

This poll suggested that many smokers admitted to giving into their own cravings before purchasing a drink for the child, in circumstances where this has arisen. It also found that those with a **poisonous smoky addiction** will also go to other sneaky extremes to get a fix. It reports that 7% of people admitted that they have taken money that wasn't theirs or stolen from a friend in order to purchase their poison. 3% admitted to asking a complete stranger for either change or the price of a packet of smokes.12% said they would go without food or lunch money to poison themselves instead and 41% admitted to turning off the heating in the winter months or even wearing extra clothing to stay warm, just so they could afford to **purchase their addictive toxin filled cancer sticks**. What truths are in these surveys? I do not know as I didn't carry them out and to be honest, I really don't care. All it has done is highlight the unnecessary problems that people face by choice because of a **ridiculous poisonous addiction** they have forced and fooled themselves into believing they cannot live without. Even if you truly believe that none of these statistics apply to you, then I guarantee it applies to someone you know. I would have done many of the above as a smoker of this horrible shit and would continue to do so today if I hadn't made a decision that I wasn't going to be **controlled like a slave** by a **poisonous addictive substance.**

If you live alone and you put on clothes to keep warm to save money which **you use to poison yourself,** then you may also be one of those who also feel that this is their life and their entitlement and with this I make no quarrel. I will only say that I believe you are missing out on the bigger picture and that is to live your life for which it was designed. This is sadly not to do with it as you are now doing, which is **killing it**. The bigger picture involves **getting as much**

air as you possibly can into your body so that it can thrive and work toward giving you the best things in life and **not to fill it with poisonous chemicals** so that you can sit back in the cold and **die a slow uncomfortable death.** If you are someone who forces their family to go without in any way, shape or form, just so you can **afford your fix**, then my quarrel with you again, is that you are weak.

Your family, the ones you claim you'd do anything for **is suffering the consequences of your addiction** and even if that is not financially, they will still feel it emotionally when you go into the ground. Your poisonous addiction is killing them physically and eventually emotionally. Your filthy addiction is observed by your loved ones who get to watch you try to get through another daily event, where **your poisonous crutch** takes first place over their pleas to quit. You claim to love your family but you are confusing them every single time you breathe in and out **your lethal poison.** Forget about **your poisonous pastime** and put your family first. Take what you have read on the chin if it has offended you and again, get over your tantrum and stop throwing your rattler out of the pram by having a strop and feeling sorry for yourself. If anything you have read is the truth, then own the truth. I understand this as **I once put nicotine before everything in life,** including my health and more importantly my family. **Stop making excuses,** start taking action. Make a change. **If not for yourself, for your family,** and that is not some bullshit dramatic guilt trip warble. If your family are the most important thing in your life and you would do anything for them, **then stop talking bullshit, stop fucking smoking and prove it.** Life is tough enough. Don't add to it and don't make it any harder for your loved ones for a drag of poisonous shit.

THE DEVOLUTION OF THE NICOTINE ADDICT.

This is very simple. Evolution is basically surviving by adapting to our environment. In order for us to thrive and to grow, **we need to give our bodies oxygen** to allow us to work at our full capacity and greatest potential. The cells in our body including our blood cells work at this level when we **supply them with pure oxygen.** This is why you hear people say **"I've never felt so alive"** whilst hillwalking or after climbing to the top of a mountain. It is because the pure air they now breathe is feeding every living cell in their bodies allowing them to **feel energised and charged.** Breathing in fresh air on a beach or whilst walking through a forest or countryside is something we have all done at one stage of our lives and we all know that feeling of **breathing in the smell of freshly cut grass** or **walking to work on a frosty morning,** whilst inhaling that cold sharp air. There is nothing that feels as good going into your lungs. This is evolution at its finest as we work in harmony with our environment by **breathing in air to feed our cells for stimulation** and growth. This is how we adapt to function and we continue doing so in order to survive.

Your actual DNA is **all about survival** whether or not you realise it. The fact that your children share the same DNA as you and your partner explains this. It is survival of the fittest in its purest form and is all about your lineage and DNAs legacy staying around. There are those who will argue that nothing tastes as good as a smoke first thing in the morning, after dinner or after a sex session and I would have argued this myself at one point. But back then I was **uneducated and ignorant** or thought I **didn't give a fuck** about the effects of inhaling this **poisonous shit.** Every single **cancer stick** you inhale clings to every strand of your DNA as we discussed earlier and is held there by the tar that glues it in place. This tarnished DNA is what you are passing onto your offspring and I can guarantee you that as we are racing forward in our understanding of genetics and technology, we will begin to see that the majority of illnesses suffered by our children today are all **connected to the sins of the mother and the father.** Stillbirths, underweight babies, stunted growth, organ failure, heart defects and lung diseases are all attributed to **inhaling poisonous chemicals into your bloodstream.** If everything is genetic then why would a man or a woman upset the balance of their DNA just to **feed an addiction to a substance** which not only **kills them** but also harms the evolutionary strands of their future DNA? This is devolution. This person is devolving and going backwards instead of producing healthy, fit and strong DNA. This is not science fiction but science fact. It is also common sense. If tar sticks to your DNA and you acknowledge and understand this whilst still continuing to **kill your DNA** or weaken its strain just because an electricity bill comes in through the door or because life is stressful, then you have no respect for the very code that makes you who you are. You may reply "fair enough, I can handle that, I'm an adult", then again, bear in mind that this buck doesn't stop with you and is passed on to your offspring. Can you be so flippant as to say "Yeah Im damaging the cells or DNA of my offspring, and so what?" If you are then you should listen to yourself and book in for a circumcision or a hysterectomy as you are not worthy of such a privilege.

Those with this attitude are the ones who look out their car window at people jogging or heading to the gym and laugh or make snide remarks because they are put out or embarrassed as they are witnessing evolution before their eyes. These people they sneer at walking, running or jogging are doing with their bodies, what their bodies were designed to do. They are evolving and strengthening their bodies and their genes whilst you are sitting there **devolving, inhaling poisonous shit** and talking about the time you used to go to the gym, or the time you will eventually go there. It is not a bad thing to fit into your good jeans with good genes and by looking after your body you can do both. Let's have a brief history lesson on genetics. The eugenics programmes which started at the turn of the last century, may in fact have led to many horrors, as the idea of controlling or creating the perfect genes contributed to what is now known as the holocaust. Since this dark period in human history, scientists and doctors globally have used our knowledge of genetics to push the human race forward. Genetics research has given us cures for cancers and allowed fertility treatments for couples who struggle to conceive children naturally. We are becoming very much aware of the importance of our genetics in our health and our quality of life. Again, at the end of the day we are animals whose survival depends on the structure of our DNA to survive and evolve. This is why when we breed racehorses we don't take a 3 legged nag and pair it with a 20 million dollar thoroughbred Grand National winner. This is not about muscles and testosterone. It means that DNA can be tainted low grade and weak in its strain or strong and healthy.

We all know the old saying that "she's got great genes" or "he's got very strong genes", well this doesn't mean fuck all if they **inhale poisonous shit** because eventually somewhere down the line, that strong gene will become weakened and will break or mutate in one form or another. This is what happens **when a cell becomes cancerous.** It **mutates** and becomes a parasite to other cells feeding off it, **until it eventually kills them by spreading.** The same goes for

the shit that clings to your DNA which is located in the cell nucleus. The **shit you inhale contains 4000 chemicals** which are clung to your DNA with the **same tar** which (as we know) is the same tar you **find on your roads** and is **mutating** the DNA **which allows you to breathe**, walk and talk and yet you continue to do so, and ignore the **damage you are doing**. You can take this information which you are probably already aware of and wake up, or you can roll it up, put it in a pipe and smoke it, it's entirely up to you. What is also entirely up to you is whether or not you want to evolve or devolve. You can move forward or you can go backwards. You can pass on your DNA to **healthy offspring** or watch the consequences of your addiction, as it **slowly dies and disappears** through generations of **bad unhealthy DNA**. The evolution of males and females depend on the care we take of our genes. Go forth and multiply with healthy DNA or **continue to inhale poisonous shit to go back and disappear through devolution.** Anyone who tries to argue that their addiction is good for their DNA is an idiot and is probably better off not pro creating anyway. Your DNA is your stamp on this earth and only you have the choice to feed it what it needs to continue on its journey or poison it, stopping it dead in its tracks. Keep inhaling shit and die or **STOP FUCKING SMOKING** and live.... your call, don't make **a fuck up of your genetics....**

BIRTHS DEATHS MARRAIGES AND THE ANY EXCUSE, EXCUSE!

When a person is addicted to a **substance such as nicotine**, the bullshit they allow themselves to waffle on about can seem like spoken truth when in actual fact it is quite apparent **lies and often drivel**. An alcoholic will look for any excuse to go back on the drink and will celebrate if a dog gives birth to kittens. Falling off the wagon for an alcoholic will usually be backed up with an excuse as to why they felt the need to poison themselves yet again and for the **nicotine addict** it's no different. There is always an excuse or an excuse as to why there's an excuse. **Giving up poisoning your lungs and your body** means giving up **poisoning your lungs and your body** and it's that simple. When you are prepared to give back to your body instead of taking from it, you will understand this. If you look at the **ridiculous excuses** which are most common for **nicotine addicts** as to why they fall off the wagon, or as to why they will wait until next week, month or year to "give them up for good this time", you will begin to understand the meaning of **lame excuses and the any excuse, excuse**. Usually they revolve around the three things in life, which (like taxes) cannot be avoided.

These are **births, deaths and marriages**. We all understand my feelings on those who inhale poisons whilst pregnant so we won't go any further here, but in matters surrounding the birth of a child and the celebration of a baptism or first birthday party, can anyone see how ridiculous it is to set a 'quitting deadline' regarding the joyous occasion of a new life? I have personally known women who although foolish, were thoughtful enough and I suppose in a way, strong enough to give up **inhaling poisonous shit instantly** when they tried to conceive or found out they were pregnant. They then went the full term talking non stop about the anticipation of having a smoke when the baby finally came. The first thing they usually say is that they will give them up after the christening day and this never works out because something stressful happens in between and so they will give them up after the child's first birthday and then an uncle gets sick and the stress is too much to quit now, and then the uncle dies so they will definitely give up after the funeral and before they know it, it's the child's communion day 'and the stress' and then the child's graduation day and wedding and eventually 30 years have passed and so on and on and on and on it goes…

Where is the sense in this? If you happen to be one of these women, can you not see that the child you gave birth to needs you around for as long as is possible? Do not foolishly allow yourself to believe that the **one in two cancers that kills smokers of this poisonous shit** doesn't apply to you. If you doubt this then I will ask you the following again. How many of you are aware of a friend or someone they knew who died young from a **smoking related disease or cancer?** Do you think that this same person believed they would ever **get cancer** so young or would even **die because of it?** No they did not and if they did, they would not have used the any excuse, excuse.

When a **cancer diagnosis** is given because of **self-inflicted poisoning,** all that remains for the sufferer is **sorrow and regret.** Some people will even use the stress of parenthood as an excuse to why they **inhale an addictive substance.** They use words such as **coping** and **stress relief** which are **ridiculous lame excuses** for dealing with family life and life in general. Ask yourself this. Why do you think that you need to **inhale 4000 poisonous chemicals** as a strategy to get by the stress of life when the neighbour next door does not? What separates the both of you? I'm not talking about money or the billionaire lifestyle of one over the other, but the normal Joe on the street that is equal in material wealth or even less well off than you? Why does this person survive his or her daily trials and tribulations by **breathing air,** while you deal with your daily events by **inhaling a cancer causing poisonous coffin nail?** He or she, if **not addicted to a substance,** is coping with life much better than you can because they **don't use dependency as an excuse**. This is not about name calling or blaming but about understanding **that you only believe a substance is needed to cope** when in actual fact **if nicotine had never been invented,** you would not have it to need it, get it?

Start to use this logic and stop making excuses because you are playing a very dangerous game of life and **death unnecessarily.** Sticking with **death again** for the moment. This is another one of the great reasons or excuses used as an excuse to not **quit inhaling poisonous shit.** A loved one who is **terminally ill** and **suffering** or caring for a person **whose health is failing** can often be the reason people hold a **cancer stick** to their lips to help them to cope, get through or to offer some comfort. Think on this for a moment. A person you are related to **is dying** and you are coping by **inhaling a cancer causing piece of dried up addictive weed which contains 4000 highly dangerous and deadly chemicals** just to get you through the day!! Not a walk on a beach to reflect on your thoughts or a stroll in the countryside to gather yourself and **inhale the free fresh air** your body screams out for? And why is this? It's because the **addictive nicotine** which you falsely believe makes you feel better is giving you intermittent relief and will come knocking again and again until you **stop making excuses.** The truth of the matter with this poisonous shit is that like a marriage, in sickness **and 'till death do you part'** is the only way this begins, and the only way **it ends.** There is **no happiness** in this **poisonous marriage** and by walking away from this **chemical relationship** you will find the freedom your body screams out for. Speaking of marriages. Everyone who is **addicted to this shit** has used a wedding as a guideline or as a date to give up **smoking shit.** "I'll just get this wedding out of the way and that's it, I'm done… Its health and fitness all the way for me from here on out" and then you wake up with a hangover and reach for a **cancer stick** and laugh about your attempt to quit which usually only lasts for as long as you were asleep. Excuses, excuses, excuses.

Births deaths and marriages are all intertwined. From the moment of your birth, **you took air into your baby pink lungs** and as we discussed earlier, the reason you cried out is because you gasped for this same air on your arrival. You have since then allowed your body cry out through **addiction to poisonous chemicals which is killing your body**, **blackening your lungs and filling your heart with sticky black tar**. This is a marriage made in hell and nicotine and the other **3999 chemicals in every cancer stick** will send you there without your consent, and leave **grieving family** pick up all the pieces that go with a **premature death.** Try to bear this in mind when you make **bullshit excuses** as to continue **killing yourself.** A new-born baby can be celebrated without **inhaling poisonous chemicals**, the joining of a loved up couple in matrimony can be celebrated **without risking cancer** and the death of a loved one does not mean that **addiction** means you follow them down. **Keep making excuses** as to why you **punish your body** and eventually and usually unexpectedly, your body will come up with its own excuse not to hang around any longer. If you decide to give your heart a reason to say "fuck you", it will do it when you least expect it. Stick to the births and marriages and try stave off the death for as long as possible…stop fucking smoking.

DO MY LUNGS LOOK BLACK IN THIS?

Devastating! This is the only word that can be used to describe the effects that the **4000 poisonous chemicals, found in every cancer stick** has on a person's skin. **Contradiction**! A word describing the saying of one thing whilst doing the complete opposite. This a very fitting word when applied to someone that is **destroying their skin and their looks by inhaling this poisonous shit.** To spend ridiculous money on expensive creams in order to keep your skin looking fresh, young and supple and to store these same creams in amongst a handbag containing **cancer sticks** is a huge contradiction. Chap Stick for your lips and cancer sticks for your lips does this make sense. When a woman keeps her smokes and her skin cream in the same bag, contradiction is what weighs that bag down.

Cool, Chic, sexy and hot are words we can no longer use to describe this **filthy disgusting addiction,** which is a deadly hazard and a **poisonous dangerous scourge to the human body** and the human skin. The days of Marilyn and Audrey were times of ignorance and it is not 1950 anymore. And this doesn't just stop with females either. Men in some of today's societies are taking care of their skin a lot more than they used to and this isn't a bad thing, again only if you don't compromise this skin care with the contradiction of **using nicotine to destroy and wrinkle it.** Women on the other hand have been recorded from the beginning of time using beauty products, (natural and chemical) to keep their skin at its very best. If you inhale poisonous chemicals whilst applying such products, then here's a simple tip to maintain your beauty and youthful wrinkle free skin for as long as is humanly possible. **STOP FUCKING SMOKING!**

If you are a female who **destroys her looks, skin, hair, teeth and health** with this **horrible poisonous shit** then I dedicate this chapter in particular **to any woman who genuinely wants to quit.** Whether you care to label yourself as daddy's little princess, a domestic goddess, an independent strong female, a laddette, a lady of the night, or even none of the above, there is no woman in any part of the world who wants to be known as **saggy Maggie** or **wrinkle tits yes,** (it affects the skin on your body and not just your face), or asked how many grandchildren she has when she's still in her 20s.

When you first took up **your filthy disgusting addiction**, what you probably didn't realise is that; although **inhaling poisonous chemicals** may not have occurred to you at the time as causing any **permanent damage**, it has in fact been working overtime in **destroying every one of your body's cells including your skin cells** since you first started. This is the reason why you run into an old school friend from back in the day and ask her startled "What's your secret" because she looks so damned good every time you see her. Her secret is that **she is not dependent on poisonous chemicals** that kill the **elasticity and collagen** that her body produces naturally. Now, because it is the nature of all women to want to look their very best, it is important to take heed of what helps achieve this and what creates the exact opposite. There is absolutely nothing wrong with wanting **to look great and feel great**. These two things go hand in hand with one always leading to the other. **Looking good and feeling good** or "**looking great, feeling great**" as it goes in the commercials. If any woman chooses to dispute this by saying they'd **prefer to look like shit or feel like shit**, then this chapter isn't for you, nor is this book in fact. I'm not here to argue the feminist issue or talk about wage discrimination but **skin damage** caused by **inhaling poisonous shitty chemicals, i.e. smoking.** If you are affected by this problem, then please read on. If you are not then please kindly fuck off. If you want to avoid cancer of the mouth, throat and tongue or you are tired at looking at the brown shitty hard to remove stains on your teeth and fingers, then please continue.

Now, the only elements of which you have no control over what happens to your skin is gravity, your environment and time so what you must remember here, is this; it is what you do to fill this time which makes all the difference to **the appearance of your skin**. It doesn't for one moment matter what shape, size or colour the body you possess is. Beauty is found in every female and is only taken from her by self-infliction or by allowing outside noise interfere with her self-esteem and confidence. Celebrity bullshit is responsible for endorsing this hot fad crap and is also responsible for turning females against females. One minute the waif stick like insect female is all the rage, next, the hour glass figure or curvaceous hips is a look set by some celebrity or ridiculous magazine article. This nonsense and waste of time should not affect how you feel about yourself. The one aspect of any female in any body shape that will stand out before all else is her skin. People will always remark on the fact that she has **flawless skin**. It doesn't matter whether she's got great genes or she can't fit into those jeans, if a woman has great skin, **she is the envy of the female** who wishes she knew her secret. This is something all females are aware of.

And this ladies, is what separates a woman who can use her brain and the woman who is brainwashed apart. If you text, tweet, email, message, call or bang down the door of your sister, best friend, mother, aunt or daughter because you have just seen the latest commercial or read the latest article in some magazine that claims to have discovered a treatment cream, or a new surgery that can allow you to **stay looking your age**, give you the skin of a 15 year old, or even **reverse the damage done** by **abusing your body** through years of sun damage, **inhaling shitty poisonous smoke** and everyday wear and tear, then you are getting excited about fuck all. This is called hype and as you know, we have all at some stage been caught up in something we believed was going to change or revolutionise our lives in some amazing positive way. This is usually followed by the results we never wanted and a feeling of embarrassment for wasting so much money on hope. This is the skin cream industry, all day every day. Lobster sperm for 2000 dollars or baboon sweat or some other crap to make you look like a 10 year old. They get some skinny celebrity to endorse it and then it must really be true because 'so and so' said so. The fact of the matter is that 'so and so' is a multimillion dollar starlet with an entourage of makeup artists to make them look the way they look. If any real woman was to look at the images of these legendary Hollywood beauties under the microscope at seven o clock in the morning as they rose from slumber, they would not feel so self-conscious about their appearance. A special effects team is often used when a makeup artist is unsuccessful! Hollywood hype and Hollywood bull.

Here's the simple truth of the matter. Over 2000 years ago in Egypt, a woman called Cleopatra was listening to the exact same bullshit. This historical figure, famous for her beauty, brains, balls and **flawless skin**, understood that for her to maintain her youthful looks, she had to **take care of her skin**. I'm sure this beauty regime may have involved crushed scarab beetles applied with camel's milk or some other natural remedy or potion given to her by the latest fad creator at that time and maybe it worked. However, I'm certain she would have turned her nose up at a **poisonous heart stopping cancer stick** if she had the knowledge that it **destroys her flawless complexion.** The point being that even 2000 years ago, women were on record as trying to **maintain their skin** by whatever methods were available, some conceivable and some inconceivable. 2000 years later and people still ponder what these ancient celebrities' beauty secrets actually were. To again save you some time in doing your own research, I can clarify the following for you; the secret to Cleopatra's beauty **wasn't nicotine** or any of the **other 3999 poisons** that go into a **poisonous disgusting cancer stick.** The ancient Egyptians didn't smoke but if they did, maybe Cleopatra would be famous for her wrinkles or remembered for her yellow teeth, brown fingers and the inability to climb the steps of the pyramids without **wheezing or coughing up her lungs.** Even though these people from this ancient civilization didn't have the technology or medicines we have today, they did hold the knowledge that **the skin must be cared for in order for it**

to look its best and that natural remedies could be used to **maintain youthful looks,** but not to reverse it.

I would now like you to please read this simple run down on how to **maintain your skin** by keeping it **fresh looking and supple,** so please absorb the following explanation written so simply, it would be an idiot who doesn't take note and use its advice, as it is meant. **Elastin and collagen** are words which are often heard when talking about the **human skin** and anything skin related with talk of skin wear and tear, **the aging process, wrinkles** etc..... **Elastin and collagen** are basically the **building blocks of your skin.** Well... maybe the blocks and cement which gives it the foundation and stability it needs as a requirement to stay solid, but soft in appearance and to touch. The skin of any human is a complicated organ containing many working structures, but for this chapter, we will concentrate on these two very important elements of this marvel which covers our flesh and bone. **Collagen** is a protein which basically is the strength and support of your skin giving it that firmness... **Elastin**....well the name basically explains itself, is what keeps our skin pulled and wrapped around us tight. Have you ever picked up an old elastic band and tried wrapping it around something and it just snaps because it is so old and worn, well that's the image I want you to hold when thinking about the **elastin of your skin. Collagen** and **elastin** or **firmness** and **tightness** as we will refer to them from here on out, are in fact the main reasons that the beauty and cosmetic industry turns over hundreds of billions of dollars every year globally. Companies try to reproduce elements of nature, that as of yet, cannot be reproduced, with only generic chemically laced unnatural products, with well researched advertising, aimed at billions of the planets desperate women being bought and sold in hope. The truth is that if any human being could invent or devise a treatment that could give permanent **firmness and tightness** in a pill, injection, cream or potion, they would not only make history but also go down in history as a person who possessed or had obtained god like powers. The next step would be immortality because to **stop cells dying** or **aging** would be to defy the natural order of things.

But please remember that because we do not possess the power of immortality today, only means your **exit from this life** is more about what you do with your body within the short timeframe we get to walk upright on this planet. Because we as humanity, and as a civilisation that **regularly abuses its own bodies** are not yet allowed access to the foundation of eternal youth, there are several steps which can be taken to allow **firmness and tightness** stay around for as long as nature allows. The first step in keeping in line with nature **is to not** do **something unnatural** to something **so natural. Inhaling poisonous chemicals** is not natural and this much doesn't need any further explanation.

If you would like an example of how nature harmonises **perfectly in sync with nature,** think of how **your body, your skin** and your wellbeing are affected by any kind of natural treatment, or natural medicine, some expensive, some inexpensive and some free. This could be a spa weekend away with seaweed baths and cucumber face masks, a honey and lemon skin peel or even a brisk walk around a wooded park.

Scientists working around the world with doctors on women's health and the study of the **aging process** are constantly discovering and rediscovering medicines and treatments that contain plant, flower or tree extract as its primary ingredient. The billionaire manufacturers of skin creams and make ups take advantage of these researchers work. This is where expensive gimmickry gets confused with real research and almost anything skin related is believed when the right name or look is put to it. If one of the Kardashians for example was pictured with two mackerels glued under her eyes, every gullible woman on the planet would be walking around smelling like a fishmonger's wife. No one ingredient like the serum from a white albino spider crabs left claw can give you the skin you desire. In the same way that lions and exotic tiger penis is said to give a man a rock hard erection, it has no biological effect or medical significance whatsoever yet these magnificent creatures are butchered needlessly. This is only a slaughter of the innocent to appease the stupidity of the gullible. A combination of natural plant extract and marine life is a different story. The rain forests and oceans of the planet, I have no doubt, will eventually be found to hold the secret to the eternal youth sought by the masses since **keeping the skin supple and young** became important in our cultures and societies. Marine biologists who scour the planets deepest oceans floors are also finding natural cures for whatever ails you on the coral reefs and sea beds. These explorers of the deep, these doctors of dense rain forests and the scientists searching unchartered unexplored territories, are hunting down and discovering the mysterious immortality enhancing beauty treatments and medicines, which are so sought after by the world's inhabitants. How many women reading this can honestly say that after a pampering session of face masks, seaweed and salted baths or even a homemade detox or face mask, have felt like shit afterwards. You couldn't, because to treat your body in the way it deserves to be treated can only **leave your body feeling fit, revitalised, healthy, and glowing**. This feeling of vitality, the feeling of wanting to bounce around regardless of age or condition of the body, is the energy your body now feels as a way of saying "thank you" and we all know this feeling. Has your body ever thanked you for poisoning it with alcohol? No, it has not. In this case it says fuck you, by leaving you feel it's suffering in the form of pounding headaches, nausea, vomiting and tiredness in the form of a hangover which can at times drag on for days.

The body can be very forgiving but can also be treacherous in fighting fire with fire. Your weekdays may give your body the time to repair and replenish itself after a hard night or weekend out but what if you throw **the constant barrage of 4000 poisonous chemicals** into the mix every time you feel like **inhaling cancer causing, cell destroying smoke.** You may have enjoyed those cocktails on the night out but you paid the consequences of that enjoyment the following day. Likewise, you may enjoy standing out in the **rain like a drowned rat** or sitting in **a poisoned smoke filled shed inhaling this toxic shit** deep into your body's cells, but your body itself begs to differ. This cocktail of over **4000 poisonous chemicals**, your body understands it has to now deal with, but it doesn't understand why it has to deal with it, as it is given no respite over and over again. Even if in your false reality, you try and force yourself to believe that you are enjoying **every heart stopping cancer stick** that your body is **forced to endure,** the simple truth is that, out of the trillions of cells that make up your body, only one of them has to take on **a cancerous mutation** by dying. It is this one apple that you have caused to rot with your complete **disregard for your body** and health, which will eventually spread rotting every other cell it comes into contact with in **the form of a cancer.**

Your body may enjoy the sea weed spa, the pampering, the face packs, but it doesn't take me or anyone else to tell you that your body, **the machine which gives your life**, doesn't take kindly to being force fed a constant barrage **of poisonous chemicals**. All you get in return for this **self-harm** is **shit stinking hair, shit skin, and a shit smelling breath.** If you can agree with that, then I can guarantee you that your body is already breathing a fresh sigh of relief as it sense's a glimmer of hope. If you've just decided or had already made up your mind to allow your body**, your skin**, **your cells**, **your organs,** your very self , a chance to recuperate from the **poisonous onslaught,** then you have made a decision to stop **feeling like shit all the time**. Be prepared to see dramatic changes both internally and externally. Although time can be another enemy to a woman's skin, body or her appearance, by buying yourself some time you have given yourself the gift of **allowing your body to age at its natural pace**. Remember that all of our **biological clocks are ticking** and that our bodies produce fewer cells as time goes by. But please bear in mind that even though production may slow down and someday stop, it is wise to remember that production and destruction can often be called the opposite of each other and that the 'choice' of which word applies to 'your cells', is completely **'your** choice'. If any person feels in doubt about **skin damage** or is told by some idiot that **the wrinkles** they now have won't go away just because you **stop inhaling poisonous shitty chemicals**, then don't allow their negative comments sway your decision to **get healthy** because I have personally seen **the glow on the skin** of people who have **given up inhaling shit** even in their 80s. Your laughter lines may stay in position as the characteristics of your personality, but gone will be the **grey or yellow complexion** staring back every time you looked in the mirror with a **cancer stick, burning toxic shit** hanging from your lip. The only way to finish this chapter is to give any woman who is serious about **her health, her looks, her skin**, a simple but effective analogy to pass on to any other person they wish to help or advise. The following is my metaphorical attempt at breaking down what this poisonous shit is doing to the beautiful skin of any woman.

Collagen and Elastin or **firmness and tightness** work in a factory. This factory is called "YOUR BODY" …For the first number of years this factory was a great place to work. Firmness and tightness have been with you since day one and have worked overtime to rebuild and replenish any damage inflicted by the elements of everyday life. They work just as they should because they are designed to protect against sun, wind, rain and the daily grind of life itself. One day out of the blue, there appears to be some concern for the first time amongst your many thousands of factory workers. **Firmness and tightness** have found that for some reason, the factory they work hard in has begun to force them to work in **dangerous chemical conditions**. Not only are they being forced to work in these new **dangerous chemical conditions,** they are also expected to work overtime to repair the **damage these poisonous chemicals** cause without any form of relent. This constant barrage continues to **inflict injury** just as they have finished up repairing the **damage done** from earlier. One by one, over time, you will begin to notice that your these extremely valuable workers are growing very sick of working under such conditions and are beginning to talk of walking away. Unhappy workers produce shit products and all great manufacturers know this. For the first time ever there is talk of desertion amongst **firmness and tightness.** This will continue every minute of every day and every day of every week. Being loyal to this factory which has up until now allowed them to work in peace and without interference, they find it difficult to walk away, so some of them stay to see if repair is possible by striking a deal. But this loyalty is in vain. Eventually they begin to realise that it is time for **firmness and tightness** to hand in their notice. There is only so much work they can do and only so much they can take. **Firmness and Tightness** have worked overtime for years with complete loyalty and now they feel their hard work was in vain. Even if this factory, your body, was to offer them an incentive or truce to stick around, they would still refuse to work under such dangerous poisoned conditions. As much as it may pain your workers to leave the place they stayed for so long through equal respect and loyalty, they now feel that they couldn't possibly continue to fight against something that has turned on them. Feeling deflated, tired and unappreciated, **firmness** and **tightness** will only take so much, before they too eventually take all the onslaught it is possible to take and leave. Any **firmness and tightness** that stays behind will eventually follow them out the door for good, never to return. When this happens, the factory, the body they worked for, will quickly become dilapidated and with no one to work to maintain its appearance, will eventually begin to sag and crumble and collapse. This is the sad and inevitable truth behind **Collagen** and **Elastin**. They will stay will the person who treats them well and grow old gracefully with the body, or they will leave the body early if they are poisoned and mistreated. You only need to look at the face of a non-smoker to see this in real life.

We all know the expression "not even for a million bucks". If you are a young woman who thinks **firmness** and **tightness** are permanent fixtures and refuses to believe that the elements of time, weather and hard living and **inhaling poisonous shit** play a part in the **departure of collagen and elastin**, then keep puffing away. Watch how your **looks fade** as every new crevasse that appears on your **once supple skin** give you the **grey appearance of a person who looks almost 30 years older** than their actual age. Not for a million bucks may have more of a meaning when talking about you in all the wrong ways. The saddest part about this is that it is all totally avoidable if you were to just **STOP FUCKING SMOKING!**

THE BEST SEX YOU'VE NEVER HAD.

Time now to speak to the chaps of the world for a bit. (Ladies, please read on as you might find something to show your other half or find something that interests you.) OK, firstly, men, the boys, the fellas. We men like to be told that we are brilliant. As a man I know this! Tell a man he is brilliant and we will do anything for you because it only confirms what we already suspected or believed. Tell us men that we look very strong and like idiots; we will run out and build you a wall or fix the garden fence to try impress with our strongly manliness. Tell us we are great in bed and we will run out and build you a house. We are extremely egotistical creatures and by feeding us what we love or need to hear, you remain in control. That's the secret ladies and it's very simple. This is why women have the strength that is bigger than the muscle of any male. Tell a woman she looks fat and she will cry tears and then get on with it. Tell a man he has a small dick and he will laugh it off but secretly and sadly hold onto it forever. The woman cries to release the pain and the man doesn't, so it manifests itself in frustration and often aggression. A comment by a female either good or bad, can do one of two things to a man. It can turn a pauper to a king and a king to a pauper. Words of women reduce to rubble or keep contented in a bubble! Think about that one. We also are great most of the time at hiding our emotions. Although it's hard for some to believe, we are quite emotional creatures but our tear duct reservoir quite often seems to be in a low supply of water. When we are finally dragged to the doctor for a check-up, it is usually after being badgered to death by our better half. This concern is usually greeted with a "told you so", when the doctor says you have nothing to worry about. Now…just to shake things up a bit. Men know that we don't have to be told twice to go to the bedroom! Your partner gives you the come hither and summons you to the place of promise. You fall up the stairs in anticipation and almost take the door off the hinges. You race to the bed but somethings not right. There's a party in your head but no one invited your flaccid penis. "What the fuck?" is now the only thing racing through your mind as your frustrated partner lays there telling you it will be fine. You will now hear the lie which is that "it happens to all men". No it does not.

If; as a man of any age, you climb into the sack and before or during the main event, your jack the lad fails to answer the call of duty (.i.e.; stays as limp as wet toilet paper), do you now have to be dragged to the doctor? Or will the engine to the car be running before you can even get your underwear back up? Of course the inevitable question running through your mind is "what's happening?", or not happening in this case! You can be guaranteed one thing if you have ever experienced this problem before and that is the first question your doctor will ask you when you sit in his office…"Do you smoke?" Well, if you had previously, or are currently experiencing this problem and the answer is "yes, I do smoke" then we may have the solution to your soft approach.

The following is dedicated to all the studs out there who are aged from 15 to 55 (55 being the statistical age which show that men of the above age group are showing more and more **erectile dysfunction** than ever before). If you are **addicted to poisonous nicotine** then you should enjoy the following facts as they speak about you. Firstly, females, women, girls, the opposite sex, your other halves, the ones you can't live with or without, enjoy sex (believe it or not) just as much, (some even more) as you do. Now especially for those in need of a quick birds and bees lesson, the woman's vagina (do I hear giggles at the back) although I'm sure the reader has their own name for it, is designed for and to do many weird and wonderful things. All of us at some stage took our first gasp of air upon leaving a vagina and the trick here is not to be left gasping for air whilst you attempt to go back into one! Do you understand me? Now… for many young, old and middle aged men who have a **poisonous filthy disgusting addiction**, this sadly happens to be the case.

As well as **polluting your heart and lungs with poisons and tar**, your bloodstream is **struggling to pump blood** into what's needed to make the race horse run the race he was built to run and to win. If you are one of the few smokers who at present, can manage to get it up and keep it up, then enjoy it because it is guaranteed to be very **short lived.** There will be those of you reading this, and unfortunately for you, it is happening or has already happened. Do not fret… not yet anyway. This is very simple to grasp so listen up. Men who take care of themselves can **achieve erections**, rock hard erections, some until the day they go into a coffin (we have all heard the tale of being unable to put the lid on the coffin!). Although this may be an urban legend, being able to get and maintain a rock hard dick for a **healthy man** of any age is just a fact. It is true that the body suffers wear and tear as we get older but please bear in mind that the world's oldest marathon runner Fauja Singh ran 10km in 1 hour and 31 minutes at the age of 101 in February of 2013, and that the world's oldest man to father a child, without any medical help is Ramajit Raghav at the age ripe old of 94. These men are not medical marvels, merely examples of men's capabilities once they **look after themselves.** This is how they have been rewarded for **self-awareness** and the proper use of their bodies.

There are millions of other men worldwide who have achieved the same quality of life through **self-awareness.** When the mind is healthy the body is healthy, but this always works in reverse also. Healthy body healthy mind and healthy mind healthy body. This is one of the reasons that all aspects of health are as important as each other. There are men out there who don't inhale nicotine and still fail to get erections but you can be guaranteed there is an underlying physical, medical or mental health issue involved. There are those who may say, "I'm not really bothered either way, that's why Viagra was invented" or "there's a little blue pill I can take for that certain problem" and you are the same ones who will always use **dependency as an excuse** for the majority of problems in your **short lives**. If a man suffers from brewers droop, (the condition of **failure to get an erection** through too much consumption of alcohol) he can brush it off as an excuse as to why he didn't give that one night stand "the best sex of your life" he promised her in the heated embrace, on the taxi journey home from a club. There are those to which this may never have happened and those to which it only happened once, but what happens if this reoccurs? What happens if this happens again and again? What happens if the **one night stand king** (as he has become known as to his buddies), quickly turns into **the one second erection pauper?**

If it's a case of too much alcohol and by cutting down it resolves the problem, then good for you. But what if your casual fling has forgiven your empty promises and wants a second date? You, of course, being male are going to tell your friends in typical bravado that "she wasn't able to walk" after the sex you gave her as it was so good. The truth of the matter is that you may as well have taken **a droopy string of spaghetti off a plate** and attempted to hammer it into a wall. Your friends think you're a legend when in actual fact; the only legacy you'll leave behind is a **string of sexually frustrated and unsatisfied girlfriends** (who love to tell their friends everything!) and a strong possibility of **never conceiving a child** without expensive, evasive and extensive medical help.

You may be of any age, colour, you may be bald, short, tall, thin, obese, tanned toned rugged or ripped, but if you **fail to maintain an erection,** you cannot **provide a child naturally** and in the way nature intended. And although as I've already said, medical intervention is possible, it should not be depended upon. If you are under 60 years of age and are suffering from **erectile dysfunction** due to your inability to **say no to nicotine** then you have a **serious problem,** but also a **common one** associated with this **filthy disgusting addiction.** While some argue that the female of the species may go for **the fitter, faster stronger males,** others argue that's it's not always about the best, the fastest or the better looking but more about the character of the person or how they hold themselves. Whatever type of men women are attracted to, I challenge any woman who looks at 10 completely different men of all shapes and sizes and says **"I'm looking for a man who can't get an erection and has a low sperm count with short life expectancy**. If you are a male who is **addicted to poisonous nicotine** then you fall into this category of men. While other men of your age play for the local football team or spend time cycling, training or working out in a gym looking after and **maintaining their bodies**, you **stand outside in the cold smoking shed breathing in 4000 toxic poisonous chemicals that smells like shit** and **sticks to your clothes, teeth, gums, tongue, throat, skin, lungs, heart.** It also **clogs up every vital organ** in your **body as well as your bloodstream.** Your companions in the smoking sheds are just as bad as you are and are unaware, unintelligent with **yellow teeth** and not an ounce of real discipline between them.

To become disciplined, you must be able to push yourself further than you ever thought possible. When you conquer your **addiction to nicotine** fully, you will understand this. This is when going the extra mile actually takes place because your mental strength drives your physical endurance. The mind will give up long before the body does so if your frame of mind is strengthened, you will quickly develop stamina in all aspects of your physical life. This is because the body and mind are now working with one another instead of against each other. When nicotine is involved, the mind is begging "yes please" and the body is begging "no, not again". This is one of the reasons people suffer conflict of inner turmoil and why that extra mile is harder because you are fighting against yourself constantly. Free your mind and the rest will follow. This is what discipline is all about and smokers who often see themselves as Alpha males are often in short supply of discipline, just like the rock hard erections we discussed earlier. Now back to the subject of male/female attraction.

No matter what arguments people try to put forward in regards to what it is that attracts females to the opposite sex, id challenge any woman who has direction in her life and is conscious of her health, to genuinely say that she is attracted to **smokers**. If she is, then what is it that attracts her? The majority of **poisonous addicts** don't care about their health so it's not that his physique is going to make her go weak at the knees, Could it be that maybe she is attracted to a **smokers yellow, brown,** or **green teeth** caused by **tar** and **toxic chemicals**, or **gum disease** or the **brown stained fingers?** Or maybe you do look fit or that you have the appearance of someone that might have the stamina to "drive it home" when in actual fact you'd get **breathless whilst walking up the stairs** to the bedroom. Or maybe she's attracted to the **FACT**, remember **FACT** that a smoking addict has a **60% greater chance of erectile dysfunctional problems** in his **20s** and **30s** and has a **greatly reduced sperm count.** Maybe it's one of many of these things that you as a smoker already (or is more than likely to have), or it may be a combination of all of them, but bear this in mind. If you are one of the **hundreds of millions of idiots worldwide** who reads this and laughs, thinking none of this applies to you, then take the following test. Ask your girlfriend, boyfriend, wife, partner or significant other how they would **rate your sex life** with them and how is it compared to a previous partner who wasn't **dependant on breathing poisonous chemicals** every few minutes. If their last partner was an **addict like yourself**, then she or he keeps repeating their mistakes by shifting from one **addict** and jumping into bed with another.

Chances are if you **inhale toxic poison** then your significant other does also, but if they do happen to tell you that you are much better in the sack than **their previous non-smoking partner** (who enjoyed running the 10km every second day or training 3 days a week) then they truly do love you. This is because they are sparing your feelings by blatantly lying to your face as not to hurt your fragile emotions. To be the animal in the sack that most men believe they already are and to have the stamina that could put the smile on the Mona Lisa's face so to speak, a man must be in the **peak of his fitness** regardless of age. He doesn't have to be all Hollywood buff to achieve this; he only has to start looking after his body and taking care of himself. To start treating the body in the same way he would treat the car he invests so much money, time and effort into taking care of. You would not put petrol in a diesel car as the saying goes and the same should be said about **putting poisons into the body.** When you do finally manage to harness **the Willpower you were born with**, wait until you **see the difference in your appearance** within a very short period of time. If you don't see it in yourself, I guarantee you that your partner most certainly will.

A man who believes he is strong or powerful is only delusional if he cannot quit his addiction to nicotine. Smoking this poisonous shit is a sign of weakness, full stop. It means you are dependent on a substance to get by and you try bullshit people by telling them you enjoy inhaling addictive chemicals when the truth is that you can't handle the comedown. Limp dicks await the smoker. Maybe not today, maybe not tomorrow, but soon and for the rest of your life! This is inevitable. Blue tablets are another way of turning a blind eye. Don't rely on anything or anybody, only yourself. Strength, stamina and a strong physique await the man with Willpower and discipline. Avoid all this ridiculous self harming and be a man who is not afraid to live in the real world. **Stop fucking smoking**.

YOU'RE BREATH SMELLS LIKE SHIT.

Getting up with a yawn, a stretch and releasing your tongue from the roof of your mouth is a thing which many of us do. Morning breath, a common occurrence experienced by most people, can be treated by giving your teeth, tongue and gums a good scrub with the toothbrush or by rinsing out with a gob full of mouthwash. The odour, caused by a build-up of bacteria in your mouth as you sleep, is considered natural and goes once you've given your mouth the proper treatment. The above only applies to people who are not suffering from an **addiction to the filth** which is **nicotine**. I want you to do your own research by typing in the words faeces **(shit)** and **smokers breath** into your search engine online and to have a look at the studies into how the odours contain the same **chemicals and bacterial content**. This will give you the truthful unbiased opinion on what your breath actually smells like as a smoker. Now; for **smokers** with an **addiction to this shit**, morning breath will be the least of their problems, because the **smell of shit** which comes from their mouth is **a constant issue**. What can you expect it to smell like after **you inhale 4000 poisonous different chemicals** every time you light up? **Yes, your breath truly smells like shit** and this is a fact you needed to be made aware of if you didn't already know. You may have used mints in the past to cover or hide **the smell of shit from your breath** but there is no hiding the truth in this chapter. It is **time for you to take the shit breath challenge**.

I'm also going to let you know, how **as a slave to your poisonous substance**, your **foul smelling sewerage breath** is there to stay when combined with nicotine addiction. Here is a scenario that all of us will be familiar with. You, all excited about the big night out with the boys, girls whatever, have everything prepared. The new shoes, dress, handbag, shirt, jeans are bought, hair is done and cut, you are showered and shaved, or your make up is done with nails did. Final touches for the boys include the expensive aftershave that the ladies can't resist and for the girls, some final touch ups with the lip stick or gloss followed by the squirts of seductive perfume to drive the boys crazy. Taxi has been rung and is on its way so you just decide to have a quick smoke while you wait. You put the **cancer stick to your lips** and light up and **suck 4000 poisonous chemicals into your mouth** while you hang about. You have just counter acted or contradicted what you just spent the last couple of hours doing and that was to look and smell your best.

Looking great and feeling great as we discussed previously cannot be associated with this **horrible act.** The **4000 poisonous toxic chemicals** all of which now have to **pass through your lips, skin, mouth, teeth and gums,** before you inhale deeply into the lungs, which were designed to breathe air. Your fresh perfume or aftershave is now diluted with the smell of **stale shitty smoke** which **also clings to your new clothes, your hair, your skin and your breath.** What makes you different than the man or woman who is not **a slave to poisonous nicotine** is the following. First off, when a **non-smoker** brushes the morning breath out of their mouth, they can smile, producing a fresh white smile with a minty fresh breath whereas **the smoker of poisonous filth** can brush all they want but once they **put that poison to their lips** all day long, the **only thing they produce in their mouth is a set of yellow or brown nicotine stained teeth with a shit smelling breath.** Even if they can afford to get their teeth maintained or whitened, this is only cosmetically fake because on closer inspection, behind the false white smile, there is natural bacteria which we all have, combined with the unnatural bacteria caused by **inhaling toxic chemical shit**, thus producing a **foul shit like smelling odour.** I would like to challenge **any slave to nicotine** to take the following test and ask someone to **smell their breath** and to give a truthful answer by allowing them to **smell their foul smelling sewerage breath** and to see **what kind of smell they get.** I can guarantee you when they get it, they will agree that **it's the closest thing you will get to the smell of human shit.** Unless the person you ask enjoys **this smell of shit on your breath** you won't get an honest answer, and by that I mean someone afraid to be honest as not to offend you, so ask someone who will be straight out with you.

If you are surrounded by politeness, the allow me to tell you like it is… **YOUR BREATH SMELLS LIKE SHIT!** From the roof of your mouth to your tip of your tongue…**shit.** From the **brown yellow black and green stains on your teeth**, to the bright red poisonous blood when you brush your gums…**shit.** The **brown/green phlegm in your throat** that is coughed up from your lungs doesn't contain a subtle taste of strawberry either because unfortunately, that's shit you're tasting. If you refute this, just try to imagine the first thing you hear from a person after you've ate a meal or snack containing garlic. They tell you to back off because your breath reeks! If a garlic gourmet is enough to make someone turn their head whilst speaking to you close up, then try factor in the **poisoned shitty ingredients** in your **horrible 20 box.** Do you have some sort of romantic view of how these **cancer sticks** are produced? Do you think that these chemicals which you put near or in your mouth, lungs and body are mixed in a factory by hand? No they most certainly are not and anyone who handles **these poisons** are wearing advanced safety breathing apparatuses and clothing in order to even be allowed stand in the same room in which these chemicals are stored. And yet you put them in your mouth.

You swish that **stale shitty smoke** into your own breathing apparatus as if you were sampling a fine wine and then exhale it into someone's face as if you were spitting wine into a taste bucket. The connoisseur of **this filth** is only sampling different types of cancer and death. I can imagine someone taking a drag and saying "mmm… **taste of Ammonia** with a subtle hint of **Arsenic** or perhaps a slight tickle of **Formaldehyde**". As funny as this may sound, there is fuck all funny about this **filthy** shit. **Mouth cancer, tongue cancer, throat cancer, lung cancer** is not funny nor is any type of cancer for that matter. Ask any individual or their family how funny it is to watch a loved one who wastes away needlessly because of addiction to **this filthy shit.**

If I was to ask you to allow someone to take a paint brush, dip it into **4000 poisonous chemicals** and dab it all around your teeth, gums, tongue and throat, how many of you would let them do it? None of you would because it would seem ridiculous to do such a thing and yet you do it regularly with smoke because you foolishly think it's somehow acceptable. There are couples out there who don't realise this because they both **inhale this shit** and don't seem to mind each other's breath, but ask them to step outside their smoke filled circle to take the **shit breath challenge**. If they are told that their breath smells like warm apple pie then they are talking to a liar. Go to your doctor and he will tell you that you have what's medically known as **'faecal breath'**. He is basically very politely telling you that **your breath smells like shit** and that **your addiction to inhaling poisonous shit** is the root cause of it. The cure is to **stop fucking smoking** but first stop feeling sorry for yourself. And before you say "I don't feel sorry for myself", let me cut across you by saying, yes you do, because all smokers do. Anyone who can't quit fails because they feel sorry for themselves. It is a common trait with every **'exhaler of the stink breath'** to feel hard done by.

"WOE IS ME"

"Woe is me" or "Woe unto me" as Shakespeare said in Hamlet, was also quoted in the bible. In other words people have been **feeling sorry for themselves** for a long time. It is not a new thing this **whining** and **whinging** about the self. In order to really feel sorry for any human being these days, all someone has to do is to turn on the television, open a newspaper, browse the internet or even to speak to somebody on the street. These are the places where some of the real problems of the world are taking place. War is everywhere and peace seems like a word from a romantic novel. At a time when our planet seems to see more and more doom and gloom, it is very easy for anyone to get caught up in the hype of misery and start feeling sorry for themselves. But what have you genuinely got to feel sorry for regarding your own life? What I want you to do here is to grab a pen and turn to the blank page left for notes at the back of this book. Grab a scrap of paper and a pen if it's an eBook. Write down 5 of the most important things in your life and 5 things you would like to change. If you are having difficulty in coming up with 5 things for each, I will give you an example using what most people would change in their lives or 5 things that may be important to them…

5 THINGS IMPORTANT IN MY LIFE.

- FAMILY.
- HEALTH.
- RELATIONSHIPS.
- LOVE.
- FINANCE/MONEY/WORK.

5 THINGS I WOULD LIKE TO CHANGE ABOUT MY LIFE.

- FAMILY!
- HEALTH!
- RELATIONSHIPS!
- LOVE!
- FINANCE/MONEY/WORK!

You see what I've written applies to almost all of us. When it's broken down, most of us want to change what we already have for the better. We want to improve all the time. That is because as human beings we are always changing, forever evolving. Quite often we humans are never happy. Human beings or being human, what is the difference? The difference is that anyone can be a human being but being a human takes a person who is at a stage of full awareness and understands what it is to be grateful (to have true gratitude). Being human is having an understanding that you are alive and that this is a remarkable gift. It is this person who is at a more evolved stage and realises that human beings were designed to breathe air and **not poisonous addictive chemicals**. That is what sets them apart from those who continue **to poison** their bodies and the bodies of the others around them with unevolved ignorance. These people are more than happy to dwell in amongst other **nicotine addicts** who are just as ignorant, unevolved or as unaware as themselves. Those who understand what their lungs were designed for and live a life without toxic poisonous smoke in their bloodstreams have a better grasp of the 5 things that a person counts as important and the 5 things that they would change. Because of this awareness, those being human will have a greater chance of living a lot longer, thus seeing their grandchildren, maybe even great grandchildren. They will have their health if they decide not to pollute their bodies with **this filthy shit.** Their relationships will not involve **poisoning one another with nicotine**, giving them longevity of life with their significant other. Their love will be for things natural such as the air we breathe, and not confused with an **unnatural addiction to poisons**. Their financial or money situation will always be better off than those who suffer the weakness of **addiction to 4000 poisonous chemicals**. Lighting up and enlightenment are two different things and should never be confused. Enlightenment in this sense only takes place when knowing that lighting up is wrong. Im not saying that enlightenment guarantees you will live forever, but it will give you a chance of living a lot longer.

When a person gets to this stage of knowing, it is then that they become more aware of their mortality, and quite often more aware of the damage they inflict on themselves and those around them. It is then and only then, have they become more evolved. When, what is written here, not only the last few pages, but all of the pages from cover to cover of this book, make perfect sense to you and you decide to put thoughts into action, to declare **" enough of this shit"** and act on it instead of just talking or thinking about it. Then you are taking your awareness up a notch and now you are starting to see sense. If on the other hand you've read what's written so far and like a moody teenager sulk to yourself for feeling as though you've been told to go clean your room, then the truth of the matter is that the truth hurts and you instinctively know this. Remember how we said you cannot lie to yourself; that's what you've been doing up until this point, attempting to lie to yourself. The addicted side of you is like your bad conscience sitting on your shoulder begging you not to read this book, because your bad conscience knows that you no longer being addicted means that it is out of work. The same little demon who sits on your shoulder and whispers its shit advice on addiction into your ear is the same little shit bag who is responsible for the breathlessness you feel when you try running any further than a few paces and is also responsible for making you stand out in the cold and rain **whilst inhaling poisonous chemicals with a chest infection.** If you are one of the many inhalers of the poison reading this who at times found that they feel sorry for themselves, then snap the fuck out of it. What do you expect? You **knowingly inhale poisonous chemicals** in the thousands even though you are aware of this and you only have to look in the mirror or look around you to see the misery that your filthy disgusting addiction has caused.

Again, all of us, no matter our background or geographical our nationality is either aware at this moment in time or has known someone who has **died prematurely from inhaling chemical poisons,** (be it self-inflicted or by being force fed chemicals by **inhaling the second hand poisonous shit of others**). To be aware of the damage it is doing and to keep **pumping poisonous chemicals into the body** is not being aware in any way whatsoever. I once met a friend out walking and asked him "how are you keeping these days?" as is customary when meeting on the street. He answered whilst taking a drag of a **cancer stick**, "I'd be doing a lot better if they'd never invented these damned things" gesturing at the **cancer stick** with his eyes. I nodded in agreement, but now that I look back and think about our meeting and the statement he made, I think to myself "What a ridiculous thing to say". Did the inventor of these **horrible cancer sticks** also invent a machine that forces people against their will to place a **cancerous piece of shit** between their lips and set fire to it to ignite its **poisonous chemicals?** If he did invent such a contraption, was it also designed to force these same self-pitying victims to breathe in deeply and inhale **the same poisons continuously?**

And if you happen to be a person who is addicted to **inhaling a poisonous chemical like nicotine**, were you born addicted to it? Was it inevitable that you were to become addicted to a substance of some kind? If the inventor of the packaged **poisoned product** you purchase every day like a slave hadn't invented them in the first place or if tobacco never existed, what would you have become addicted to instead? Perhaps heroin, cocaine, or alcohol? Were you born with an addictive personality? If no one had ever mentioned smoking in the first place or a **cancer stick** was completely alien to you, do you think you would perhaps go looking for superglue or a deodorant can or some other type of solvent to fill your lungs up with chemicals and poisons to help you cope with stress or worry or because it makes you feel good? What reason can be concocted or feeble excuse can you give as to a good reason for causing such damage to your body?

It is time for anyone who **inhales the poisonous chemicals** that are **killing every cell in their body** and creating numerous **deadly dangerous health issues** to the very body which keeps them alive, to have a genuine, good hard look at the serious damage they are doing to themselves and to take some responsibility for the mistakes and actions which have had a very negative impact on their health, their bodies, their lives, the lives of those around them and their pocket. It's time to stop being a whinge bag and pissing and moaning about the difficulties in life that you face and how you need your **poison to get you through the day** or through a stressful event that requires **poisonous chemicals** directly into your bloodstream and lungs, to get poor little you through. If you continue to play the part of the victim then a victim is what you will soon become. There are those who may say "oh , but I've seen sports stars who were as fit as a fiddle dropping dead in the middle of as game" or the defeatist ridiculous statement used by **idiots of addiction** which is "when it's your time, it's your time". Again, I will say this; over **100 million smokers have died prematurely in the 21st century** so you can take that number and put it against the probably 100 sports star who have died in the same period of time (and possibly did so because of an undetected heart condition or sudden adult death syndrome) and not because they were **sucking 4000 poisons into their lungs** before the big game. Going back to the famous "when it's your time" comment for a moment. Although I am quite aware of the fact that an undetected heart condition or a sudden adult death syndrome can claim the lives of many unsuspecting people globally who are in no way connected to sports, it is still a fucking idiot who tries to compare sudden death as to a good reason to **suck chemicals into your lungs** as if its enjoyable enough, that it justifies doing it just in case you drop dead.

It is an even bigger fool who chooses to live their life by this code or mantra of "when it's your time, it's your time". Such ridiculous statements are outdated and were first used by people who didn't understand that the human body is the very essence of nature and what nature or life stands for. This should never be mistaken for bravado. By taking what's natural and combining it **with unnatural poisons which are inhaled into our lungs** confuses the difference between a natural way to die and an unnatural way to die. We are all on the clock, that is to say borrowed time as we've already discussed. Whether or not you choose to fill that time wisely is up to you. When you take an average of 15 years **off your life** because you purposely inhale poisons, then your desire to live will be cut short with every single toxic cancer stick you put in your mouth. To say "when it's your time, it's your time" is for the movies and when you say this in real life, it is such a defeatist attitude for any person to have and you must seriously take a look at how you view your life, your role in this life, your health and the signs your body has been screaming at you, that go unheard along with the smoke signals that go unheeded. If you choose to continue to blame your parents for poisoning you to begin with as a child, or those around you who inhaled poison in your company or even peer pressure from the teenage group you kicked about with, then stop playing the victim by **continuing your filthy disgusting addiction,** even if you feel you were not responsible for getting you hooked in the first place. I do agree with you if believe you may not have had the best of starts in life if your parents smoked while you were in the womb, or you grew up in a house full of those who forced you to inhale their **1st, 2nd, and 3rd hand smoke and poisonous pollution**, but just because your grandfather used to slap your grandmother about, doesn't mean that you have to repeat the sins of the father, or grandfather or whatever. The point being, in this case the chain can be broken and it doesn't have to be monkey see monkey do. It may not have been the ideal gift or start in life for a child to have **poison in their bloodstream**, but one of the greatest things about becoming an adult and discovering ourselves, is that we make our own decisions as we get older in life and as we grow. Some of these choices are trial and error with some decisions working in our favour and some going against our better judgement, but it is the adult who learns from the mistakes that they've made and from the mistakes of others who will receive all of the good things life has to offer.

You will, at some stage of your life, be given the option to say no, to walk away and break the **vicious circle of poison** which has engulfed you up until this point. Is today the day you make that decision? The key to surviving many of the things this life has to throw in our direction, is to take responsibility for your part in any given situation, whether or not you believe what happens is your responsibility or not. To own ones mistakes is to master ones mistakes and this allows you to move forward with the invaluable knowledge which allows you not to repeat the same errors. When you do find that you are feeling sorry for yourself for any particular reason, remember this old expression that we are all familiar with; No matter where we are in the world or who in the world you may be, there is always someone who has suffered so much more than what you are suffering right now. Every person meets trials in life and if you think that "nobody knows the trouble I see", then you are very much mistaken. The majority of those **who inhale poisonous shit** must remember that they live in a world where they can afford to **poison themselves** and that they have the legs and arms or the transport to drive them to a location to **purchase more poison** once their **shitty chemicals** run out. They also have the air in their lungs with which to **breathe in and out this horrible shit**. There are people on this planet who are born without the ability to breathe in and out properly without a machine, people born without limbs or without food to feed new-borns. Some born on this planet will die within 24 hours of arriving here because of poor medical supplies or living standards or thirst or war or of malnutrition. Fair enough you could say, "Well I'm not Bono or Bob Geldof or a politician who has any input into this, I can't change this world even if I wanted to". And nor am in asking you to. What I am saying is to take your own life up until this point and remember this; you are alive. While others have gone before you under whatever circumstances, you are still breathing. This in itself is something to be extremely grateful for. To truly have gratitude for being alive is unfortunately only realised by some when they have come face to face with tragedy or an event that could have had tragic consequences. If you've had this type of experience where you took a deep breath and counted your blessings, then you understand exactly what I'm saying. Usually after such a fright or health scare a person realises how foolish they have been and in respect to your health and will now have a new view of the world around them by looking at the precious fragility of life and the world around them.

If, on the other hand, you have never been faced with any great trials in life and you continue to force either yourself or those around you with **your filthy disgusting addiction**, then it's time to wake up, look at your reflection and start **using your lungs to breathe in the fresh air** you have long being denying them. It is sad to still see those who wait for the bad news or an official warning from their doctor before they make **decision to quit smoking shit**. It is even sadder to see those who get these warnings and ignore them. This is the sad realisation that all the **pain, misery, suffering,** and all the **self-pity,** excuses made are the sad signs of **an addict** who uses **pathetic excuse** after pathetic excuse to **inhale poisonous chemicals** into their bodies and not have the knowledge through chosen ignorance, to question the damage that they are actually doing by **admitting to being an addict,** but not really understanding or caring what **an addict** actually is. It is a person who is quite blatantly showing disregard for the many things they have in life and who in their right mind is willing to trade **14 to 16 years of their life for poisonous chemicals.** This is time that could be spent with loved ones and all lost for the sake of **inhaling the shitty chemicals** in a dried up piece of toxic paper which is guaranteed to offer them fuck all but **misery, pain suffering and an early grave**. Even to read this and agree and then light up is madness. This doesn't make sense. Get a grip. Stop feeling sorry for yourself and **STOP FUCKING SMOKING.**

SMOKE SIGNALS.

Warning signs are everywhere… We all know what they are and we see them almost anywhere where we go. They often represent danger and let us know that injury or **death is imminent** if we proceed any further, or go against the **warning sign** which has been left quite apparent for all to see. Be they small, such as "mind your step", "do not touch" or large such as "danger high voltage", STOP or GO, we as humans in 9 times out of 10 circumstances, will obey what these signs stand for. Our instinct **to survive,** allows us on a conscious level to take heed and to spot these signs even if it's out of the corner of our eye. As with many things in our lives, unfortunately there are those who risk life and limb simply because they could not see these signs. And then we have those with the rebellious "fuck danger" outlook who like to take "the salmon who swims the wrong way up the stream" attitude. They don't seem to realise just how easier their lives would be if they didn't fight against the current to just go with the flow. These same "die hards" come in all age groups and not just in the rebellious teen stage of life. They like to use expressions similar to those in our previous chapters such as the ridiculous "live fast and die young", or "I'm here for a good time and not a long time" or the idiotic "whatever doesn't kill me only makes me stronger". These statements might look good on a t-shirt, a poster or tattooed on a rappers back, but believe me, when it comes to the crunch and the body starts to send you the **smoke signals**, you will see these statements for what they actually are. They are the false words of bravado from a person who fears death more than they let on and usually spoken by those who have **the most to live for** and who really want to know how to **embrace life**.

Remember, that we all were put on this planet **to live,** regardless of whether some only survive for a number of minutes, or hold on until they were 116 years of age like Jiroemon Kimura, the world's oldest man. Point being to embrace death, without putting any thought into your mortality, as someone who thinks "to hell with the consequences", may get the harsh landing back on planet earth, or the wakeup call they now wish they had never woken up to. Embracing ones death can be a wonderful freedom if preparation and acceptance is carefully thought about. If you are one of the billions on this planet who likes to live the **precious life** they have been given, by living it with the "look how shit hot I look" approach by walking around **with a cancer stick hanging out from their lips** wearing a "fuck life" t-shirt, you might try this old expression instead…"be careful what you wish for". The world has too many idiots who take life for granted and is in short supply of those who work overtime to reverse **damage caused to our bodies through stupidity**. It is the doctors of the world who usually have the terrible task of breaking the news no person ever wants to hear. As devastating for any medical professional as it must be to read the results of a patients test results (and to see a positive result for **a terminally ill patient),** it must pale in significance to **the patient** who receives the devastating news. I wonder if any doctor has sat a patient down and said **"I'm afraid the news isn't good",** and has ever been greeted by the patient hearing this with "oh that's fine, I was only here for a good time anyway and not a long time", or maybe "well my plan was to live fast and to die young so this works well for me" or perhaps they might say, I thought because **the poisonous chemicals** didn't actually kill me , that they were only making me stronger".

Although sarcasm can be classed as the lowest form of wit, **a filthy disgusting addiction** can be classed as one of the **lowest forms of body abuse**. And that's calling it exactly what it is, **a toxic poisonous disgusting abuse**, inflicted on you and by you, and a dangerous invasion on **your major organs** that are already working overtime to keep you **breathing and alive**. If you ever happen to be the unfortunate individual who's given the bad news, (like anyone whose been misfortunate enough to understands how it feels),you will most certainly react with complete shock and I would challenge anyone, no matter how tough they think they are or how hard they've lived to say "oh well, I expected that" or to put their hand up in the doctors face and say "high five doc". The first thing most of us will do whilst trying to remain in a state of composure after being hit with such a sledgehammer of the **worst possible news** is to ask the five W's. Who? When? What? Where? And Why? **Who will take care of my family? When am I going to die? What can be done** to save me or to **give me more time? Where do we go from here? Why is this happening to me?** The saddest part of all of the questions you are reading is that the person who's asking them is sitting there because they have gotten the results back on an illness, (directly associated with **inhaling 4000 poisonous chemicals,** every time they partook in their **filthy disgusting addiction**), is that all of it could have been avoided if you had not have waited for **smoke signals,** which the body has been giving ever since the **spluttering and coughing** of the first ever **drag of poisonous nicotine** right up to the first piece of **black phlegm** or **piece of lung**, which led to this **horrible prognosis of uncertainty** of ones future.

For anyone reading this, thinking it is a horrible way of me saying "I told you so", then you are wrong, as your life and **inevitable death** is fuck all to do with me and vice versa. To be quite honest, the chances are, that I am never going to come face to face with the millions of those of you with **a filthy disgusting addiction,** that will at some stage of their lives be given the exact line **"I'm afraid its bad news",** from their doctor and nor could I give a fuck whether or not they care to take advice from a book which clearly demonstrates **the stupidity** and **idiocrasy** of **smoking poisonous** and **heart stopping addictive shit**. I am not the babysitter for these people and if they wish to continue playing games with their health then who am I to interfere? The people I want to reach are the people who are reading this book as a last resort and the people who are just **sick and tired of feeling sick and tired** all the time **because of an addiction to inhaling this dangerous poison**. The ones who are taking heed and not the ones saying "fuck this guy" because little written words make them uncomfortable. There are people as we speak are now crushing their box of poison because they understand this poisoning of the body has to stop this instant. These are the ones who, just like myself, have tried all the patches, gums, books, hypnotherapy, counselling and e cigarettes, the cold turkey and have up until this point failed.

These are the **people who give a fuck.** They have had their moments of darkness and now wish to step back into the light. Someone once wrote, "There is no way of saving a person who does not wish to be saved" but I'd prefer to look at it this way **"why give a fuck about people who don't give a fuck about themselves?"** On a human level of course I have the utmost of respect for any person who is diagnosed with any form of sickness or who has to go through any kind of **suffering.** I am also aware that there are many people even now as I write this who either, have recently died or recently been given the **heart breaking news** that they must **prepare for the worst.** These same people, many of whom have been **given their prognosis** because they've **inhaled poisonous chemicals into their organs and bodies**, are our father's mother's sister's brother's sons and daughters. Most of them will, after a time come to accept the cards they've been dealt and will decide either to accept the **treacherous cancer** which has **engulfed their body** or stand up and fight to the very end , whatever treatment, be it chemotherapy, radiotherapy, both or any other alternative treatments that may give them a **fighting chance**. A lot of families would like to say that after **being diagnosed** with a **terminal illness** caused by **inhaling poisonous nicotine** that their loved one fought bravely until the end and **died with dignity.** I spoke to a doctor in the US one day, who told me that after diagnosing a 29 year old college lecturer **with terminal throat cancer**, he was **inconsolable with grief** and cried from the moment he broke the news, right up until the moment of **his death only seven weeks later.** I can't see why people fight with every ounce of strength in their body to stay alive **if diagnosed with a smoking related cancer,** when the battle to **conquer addiction** can be made with a **very simple decision to live.** People may cope with **grief or loss** in many different ways and what I'm trying to say or to make clear to you is this; what if **all of this grief and suffering** was in vain and was

avoidable. I'm hoping the penny drops with every one of you and you are now saying "do you know what, he's right, **fuck this poisonous shit**" and takes instant action. Think about it? Why take any risks at all. Why not cut out the risks altogether. Doesn't it make sense? **Cut poisons out of the equation…** = healthiness, healthy mind, healthy body, more energy and less chance of a **slow painful death,** simple. Then, there are those who will say "I wish it was that simple" and to you I will say that **your decision to quit**, to stop inhaling **4000 poisonous chemicals** into **your bloodstream, heart** and **lungs** should involve whatever the hell you've got to do to stick with it, once **your decision to live** has been made. Of course, everyone is different and everyone's approach in dealing with the physical or mental anguish will vary from person to person. For some, a graphic image is enough whilst with others; a spell alone on a desert island with **no cancer sticks,** food and solitude is the only way they could deal with the very real feeling but false urges (Remember, false being the mind tricking the body, which is **addiction**).

This believe it or not were the steps that one man felt he needed to take in the much publicised case of one man's battle **against nicotine addiction.** In the UK, Geoff Spice at 56 years young was a retired senior banker who felt that he had tried everything available to help himself quit his addiction. Mr Spice smoked **30 cancer sticks a day (that's 4000 poisonous chemicals) into his body daily for over 43 years.** He decided that his cravings were so overwhelming that he needed to stay on a deserted island for one month with only sheep to keep him company. He had previously tried nicotine patches and gum, self-help books and going cold turkey in his effort to **kick the addiction** but nothing seemed to work. As I said earlier, whatever works for you, but let me give you my honest opinion on Mr Spice. Working for Rothschild bank for 30 years may have taught Mr Spice the value of the pound, but absolutely nothing about the **value of his health and his life**. To punish his body **for 43 years with poison after poison** is a perfect example of how someone who although extremely successful and wealthy by societies standards, was actually **piss poor** when it came to understanding how his health and family were coming second place to **a filthy disgusting addiction**. 'Time is money', is a phrase that Mr Spice no doubt would be quite familiar with, and money (although a nice survival tool) realistically means fuck all at the end of the day. People gasping their last breaths understand that the value of time over money is priceless. If Mr Spice had been using his mathematical skills to calculate how many cancer sticks he had inhaled (**30 per day** by **365 days by 43 years** equals £470,850) vs how many years he's knocked off his life, then he may have used this shock as a deterrent. Regarding Geoff Spices' case, he felt he done what he had to do in order to quit smoking shit. In doing so he probably doesn't realise that he has left a legacy by showing smokers the lengths he personally felt he had to go to beat this horrible deadly addiction, as its grasp on him was so strong. Not everyone will go to this extreme and not everyone should have to. Had he listened or read some common sense, he may not have had to spend a precious month alone on an island, spending even more time away with his family.

Do not, whilst reading the story of Geoff Spice allow yourself to doubt **your own ability** for even one moment. Geoff Spice had been listening to the **smoke signals** his body had been sending him for years. His story should be told as a warning that this is the effect **that inhaling addictive poison** into your body can drive you to. Prevention is better than cure and all that jazz. Don't allow yourself get to that stage in the first place. Don't feel the need to spend time away from your family to **withdraw from poison**. Do it because you want to spend time with your family and to be there for them when they need you. If you haven't done so already, then start now to listen to the signs your body is giving you. Watch out for the signals every time you look in the mirror or when you see another person who is **inhaling this poisonous shit.** Take in the sights of their skin, the raspy sounds they make and the smells as you watch another **nicotine addict inhale their fix.** Watch look and listen to the **smoke signals** that their bodies are giving to them. If you are confused about what to look out for, then watch for any one of the following; **coughing constantly,** (smokers cough), **wheezing** (at any kind of normal physical activity, i.e. stairs or up a hill), **spluttering, spitting phlegm** (a filthy disgusting trait) **bleeding gums, bad breath, aging skin, yellow, green or brown teeth, gum disease or brown or yellow stained fingers.** These are just a few of the **smoke signals** or visual physical signs that the body sends out to let someone know that it is under pressure and is rapidly growing tired and is beginning to fight even harder to survive against **this poisonous onslaught** and is sending you signals from your interior which can now be seen on your exterior physical appearance.

When at 30 years of age you have the skin or appearance of a 50 year old or you **are 50 years of age and have the skin of a 70 year old**, then can you begin to imagine what the inside of your body looks like after taking a direct hit of **4000 poisonous chemicals** constantly day in and day out for the last 5, 10, 20, 30, 40, 50 years. It's time to **listen to the body for once.** It's time to give back what you have taken away. You could be one of the **many addicts** out there who is foolish enough to go on about their daily life, either unaware or blind to the fact that **your mortal existence may soon be coming to a premature end.** Don't allow yourself be fooled by the nonsense you hear in the workplace or on the street about someone's uncle or grandmother who smoked right up until they were 95 years of age. If they lived to that age whilst **inhaling this dirty shitty poison,** then they were some of the very few and would have been around for their families for another **15 or 20 years** if they **had quit,** or never taken up **this filthy disgusting addiction** in the first place. Take that one person's story and put it up against the statistics of the thousands in your home town who **have died from cancer, heart attacks or strokes in their 40s 50s 60s and 70s** and you'll soon begin to see it wasn't **the poisonous chemicals in cancer sticks** that was keeping that 95 year old alive. People for whatever reason cling on to the one who survives and forgets about the thousands who die. The one is often seen as a beacon of hope for smokers in this fucked up view on early demise through addiction.

This is the foolish notion some idiots take when they look at **this filthy and dangerous addiction.** And this is what this is; a fool's game; **a dangerous game** played only by fools. If someone would like to point out that their elderly parent or grandparents are too old to quit and to let them enjoy it while it lasts, then go and do some research. From the day you quit, you are beginning to **add extra time onto your biological clock.** If you say "but the cigarettes are the only bit of comfort they have left at this stage of their life" then you are without realising it, stating that your parent or grandparent is **so addicted to poisonous nicotine** that without the ability **to inhale it into their bloodstreams**, they will be climbing the walls **like a heroin addict deprived of their fix.** This is the **cold hard truth** of the matter and if this is what our modern society sees as normality when saying that an **elderly person can be addicted to a substance that is killing them** and it is accepted!

No matter who you are or where you live, if you are beginning to receive **smoke signals** from the body, or if you feel on top of the world even though you **inhale this addictive shit,** I want you to reflect on what you are actually doing to every part of your body. You are forcing it to do everything **it was not designed to do.** You are taking the most **natural** and **poisoning it** with the most **unnatural.** If you've made your mind up again, I am telling you **to stick with it.** The results you will begin to see and feel within weeks will astound you. Don't wait until you are given the news that no one wants to hear, which will change the destiny that you believed involved being with your family and loved ones for as long as you deserve. **Take heed, take notice and listen to your body.** You may not hear or see **the smoke signals** all of the time but they are always there. When you get them, **beware!** These signals are here to tell you of what is to come. Smoke signals are the body's cry for help and the heart and lungs begging for mercy. A cough, a splutter in a car or the battery beginning to give trouble are enough signals to alert you that your vehicle may require fixing or an adjustment of some sort. This car may struggle to go up hills or crawl along a motor way as it struggles under pressure, but it will eventually (as all things under pressure do) come to an abrupt end. This is usually expected but at the same time unexpected when it actually takes place. A backfiring engine with a loud puff of black smoke is enough to make people jump and look at you shaking their head. "That car is fucked" is an expression used when this happens. You get what im saying…**stop fucking smoking**

PUTTING YOUR MONEY WHERE YOUR MOUTH IS.

Time to engage in some simple maths. This is a great way to grasp very easily, **the damage your filthy disgusting addiction** has done to **your pocket** as well as **your health.** I'm sure most of you have a rough idea or estimate of how much you spend per day, week month, year, etc., but let's have a more in depth look at what kind of cash you have **spent pumping poison into your veins heart and lungs**, from the moment your **dirty little habit** became an **addiction.** To help, just grab yourself a pen, a calculator and there's a blank notes page at the back of the book to write out your calculations, if you feel you need it (grab a notepad if it's an e book). Now just in case you pull away making excuses at this point claiming you are shit at maths or that you couldn't add 2 and 2 together, please bear in mind that the book you are reading was written by a man who failed foundation maths at school, so no excuses! This is not rocket science by any means. I have made it so any one of you can grasp it very easily, whether like me, you are mathematically challenged or not. I am going to use my own **poison** laced history as an example and I want you to write down the following information, instead only using your own details, name, age, etc.

I started smoking in 1990,

I smoked 20 a day,

I stopped smoking in **2003,**

This means I smoked for **13 years,**

If **1 year** has **365 days** and I smoked **20 on average a day**,

This means that I have smoked **94,900 cancer sticks,**

Each box on average cost the equivalent of **8 dollars**…..

So, to recap and do a little math, this means that a box of cancer sticks at **8 dollars a day** for **365 days** equals **2,920 dollars per year** for **13 years** is equal to **37,960 dollars.**

It also means that I have smoked an average of **4,745** boxes of a **20 pack** of **cancer sticks.** Now as I write this and read it back to myself whilst doing the calculations, I feel stupid. I feel like a fucking idiot, and here's why…I have spent almost **40,000 dollars on poisoning my body and killing myself slowly**. I almost worked myself **to death** to try getting the **deposit money** together to take out a **35 year mortgage** on my home. I worked for as many hours as the day would allow for many years in hail, rain and snow to furnish that house, to keep up mortgage payments and to pay the mounting bills that kept climbing and climbing, all whilst a **poisonous addictive substance like nicotine** took first place to help me cope with the stresses of life. The maths you have just read is my mortgage paid for 4 years. It is my children's college fund. It is a person's **life savings**, rainy day money, holiday money, retirement money, investment money and it has quite **literally gone up in smoke**. I don't dwell on the past so I'll leave it there in regards to the 'what ifs' in my life. Since I quit **smoking shit** I have a lot to be grateful for. I'm not tied into a **poisonous subscription** any longer and since 2003, I have never looked back. Now, back to yourselves. Let's see if we can give you the reality check you so badly need. I'm sure some of you are eager to find out their own results while others are afraid to even total it all up but it is important for you to do so. Every one of you obviously will have different amounts, but even if you consider your **addiction** to be new or a year old, bear in mind if you smoke 20 a day, you are still down **3000 dollars** already in a year. If you are smoking 60 years or more, don't despair. The fact you are reading this means you want to live and this is a great step forward so don't dwell on what's already done. Write your own calculation down now if you haven't already done so. If you are still smoking today, then write this down too.

Follow like so.....

What year did I start?

What year did I stop?

How many do I smoke a day?

How many days in a year,

I have smoked for   Years,

Now, just to give you an example of the mature smoker in regards to the calculation above. If the person filling this out has been **inhaling poisonous shit for say 45 years** and we apply this to our maths, this is what we unfortunately come up with.....

So, 20 a day for 365 days = 7300 inhaled per year multiplied by 45 years is 328,500 cancer sticks or 16,425 20 packs of cancer sticks at 8 dollars a box, meaning they have spent 131,400 dollars on 16,425 boxes of addic-

tive poisonous shit!

So, how do you like them rotten apples? It's a fair old kick in the guts, RIGHT? Now as I've said, everyone's results will be different, but let's try this on for size. Let's just say your partner, husband/wife or another family member who lives with you in the same household, has also spent that amount of money and time **inhaling this shitty poison with you.** That means that the maths for both of you is as simple as taking your result and multiplying it. Using the example above I just gave, take the **smoker of 45 years** who **has spent 131,400 dollars** and double it. That's **262,800** dollars or a new 4 bedroom house where I come from. If both you and your partner partake in **this poisonous addiction**, you are taking your hard earned cash and giving it to a billion dollar Tobacco Company who **doesn't give a fuck about either of you.**

When a family gets together to discuss financial difficulties, they should never have to factor in **needless addiction to a poisonous chemical like nicotine.** Some of us will work very hard for every penny we earn so why should we spend it on poisonous **chemicals** which are running us into an early grave. If you are already struggling to pay your bills whilst at the same time paying some wanker you're **hard earned money to inhale a pesticide designed to kill**, then you are going to continue to struggle every day with your wealth and health. **Fuck the tobacco companies;** say that to yourself as loud and as proud as you wish. Remember that you have given more than enough of your time and money, and all you have gotten in return is **poor health** and **empty pockets.** I ask you this. Have you ever taken really ill with **a smoking related illness** or **cancer?** Have you ever received a get well soon card or a letter from a director or from a representative from the tobacco company you **purchased your poison from?** What? Not even a letter asking how you are or a donation to help pay for **your treatment or medical bills?** Or even a contribution towards family support when you are flat on your back **struggling to breathe,** or worse, **stuck in a permanent wooden box?** I feel your answer is like many of the billion people worldwide who **purchase poison** (from **these parasitic companies**) is going to be no. And let me tell you why again. It's like a drug dealer worried about the injury caused to a vein when **an addict** drives a syringe full of heroin into their arm. The drug dealer **doesn't give a fuck** and as long as the **addict is stupid** enough to pay for the drugs, the dealer **will feed it to them.** They don't care who buys it off them and who uses it. When is the last time anyone reading this can remember a tobacco company paying for the treatment of a woman's **lung cancer** or the funeral of a man who has gone into the ground because of **nicotine addiction?** You don't remember because it doesn't happen and because the **sickness** or **death of a smoker** doesn't matter to them. And just like the drug **addict** whose **death** is caused by their **addiction**, the **nico-**

tine addict who **dies** is quickly replaced by **the next up and coming addict.** The loyal customers of these **dealers in death** are in most cases youths, who get themselves involved in **an addiction some of them will die with**. While we are on the subject of **death, life, addiction** and maths, let's now take a look at another little maths equation to get your mind expanded with a little common sense to try getting you more level headed, in your attitude to the **filthy poison** you have decided to no longer partake in. This is another little maths I devised to calculate our longevity on this planet, using the World Health Organisation's statistics on the mortality rates of men and women in Europe and the United States as of 2016. Because our medicines and sciences are improving by the day, we now have a higher mortality rate than ever before with males living an **average of 80 years** and females at a whopping **88 years** young in the western world (depending on country of residence). Again, I will use my own details as a guideline or example to follow.

I was born in 1978,

The year today is 2016,

If I live until I am 80,

Statistically, I will die in 2058,

If I was still smoking, minus 15 years, which means,

My age of death if I continued to smoke is 65, meaning,

My premature death from inhaling poisonous shit would occur in 2043,

Now…That really is a kick in the teeth. The only good thing I could wish for in this case would be to get a quick belt in the chest (or **heart attack** to the layman) and hopefully be **dead** before I hit the ground. Even to write this statement pains me even if I say it with dark humour. The truth of the matter is that I very much love my life since **I stopped inhaling poisonous shit.** I'm not trying to get you to imagine a shampoo commercial where I'm running up a beach smiling and happy. I'm not trying to sell you anything but the truth and the truth is that I'm very grateful that I was able to conquer my **addiction to poisonous nicotine.** I feel good in myself. I **feel positive, healthy and strong**. I want you to feel like this and I know also that **you are strong** and **very capable** of **giving this filthy addiction up for good.**

Since my children have been born, I value my health so much more. I want to be around for them as much as possible and to be a part of their future. I want to see them grow up to become adults. I want to see them go to school, college, and follow their careers, watch them find love, get married and have their own families. I want to walk my daughters down the aisle and if I really manage to push the boat out a bit, hopefully dance with my granddaughter on her wedding day! I could not imagine having to leave them suddenly, although if I was still **addicted to nicotine and poisonous chemicals,** I might not get the chance to stick around. I don't want to spend months or weeks **arranging a funeral unnecessarily.** I don't want my **family to see me suffer** when I don't have to. I want to be of sound mind for as long as I can when my time comes and not knocked out **with pain handling medication** to treat a **self-inflicted cancer** which has me **wasting away.**

These are some, but not all, of the reasons I decided to **stop fucking smoking.** They should be some of the reasons that you decide also and for good this time. It doesn't matter if you are 80 years of age and feel as though this doesn't apply to you because it does. It applies to any person reading this now who is at their wits end with addiction to **this poisonous horrible shit.** There is never a bad time to want to quit. The **benefits of quitting** will hit you in a matter of weeks regardless of age or how long you have been **addicted.** Everything you read in this chapter should make you realise that what you are doing to your body is downright crazy. The maths figures you have calculated are accurate give or take a few years and a couple of dollars here and there. Whilst I understand no one really has a crystal ball to determine their future, it is somewhat frightening to see that this guideline based on **the mortality statistics** means quite literally that **you are paying big money to kill yourself.** You may finally pay your mortgage after 35 years only to have to re mortgage or sell off your home or property to pay for **your medical bills.** Whilst we talk about statistics always bear in mind that **1 in 2 people who are addicted to this horrible chemical will die from a smoking related cancer.** This is fucked up. Again, as I write this, I am struggling to believe how obviously ridiculous it all seems yet how realistic this issue really is. Do me a favour and do yourself and your family an even bigger one, **bin the cancer sticks** if you haven't already done so and **stick two fingers up to the tobacco companies** and **say fuck you, I'm done.** Don't give these **horrible fuckers** another penny. Go out now and get yourself one of those money boxes you have to open with a can opener. Take a piece of paper and ask your child where they would like to go on holiday in 12 months. If they say Disneyland, then write that down on the piece of paper and tape it to the box with your child's name also written above the destination. Now, for the next couple of days weeks and months, every time you would have bought a **20 pack of poisonous chemical shit**, stick the money in your child's holiday fund instead. Your child's happiness should always take precedent over **your addiction** to anything. A real parent knows this. Time will fly as time always does and after 12 months, you could be flying to Disneyland with **your 3,640 dollars** that you originally would have slaved for only to give it to **a billion dollar tobacco industry** who **doesn't know or care that their products are poisoning and killing you.** I know what choice I would make every time.

None of what you've read is possible unless you **wake the fuck up to what you are allowing nicotine to do to you.** Nothing you read in this book is for shock value. It is what it is and that's what it is. If it gives you clarity, then good. This is your life and it is short so if you don't want to do it for yourself, just think of your family. **Your health** may be a thing you take for granted but **your family cannot afford to be without it**. When you do manage to raise the funds for a family holiday, your family will have memories to remember forever and will thank you, whereas **the tobacco companies** who get you **hooked on their poison** will never send you a thank you or send you a get well soon card. Even if you don't have kids or a family, it doesn't matter. We all have goals and little projects, holidays, etc. and wouldn't it be nice to have **a 3,640 dollar bonus at the end of the year.** Wouldn't it be nicer to have that money in your hand to play around with instead of **trying to shift 3,640 dollars' worth of poisonous phlegm out of your lungs?** Of course there are those reading this who may think that because they have no money worries, they are somehow excused from **stupidity**. "I'm a billionaire so this doesn't apply to me" syndrome. Listen! The best money that doctors could buy will see an empty pit when it comes to a smoking related **terminal cancer.** In other words, you cannot buy time, remember this. Our next couple of chapters will look at some of these powerful **nicotine addicted fools**. Finally, for those who continue to struggle financially, take the results of your little maths calculation and stick it on a place like the fridge or the steering wheel of your car. Look at it when you drive to work to slave for a wage or when looking into an empty fridge you find hard to keep stocked. Remind yourself of what you are spending your money on and **what really takes priority in your life**. Do what's right for your family, do what's right for your body, and do what's right for yourself. And let's say it once more…..**fuck the tobacco companies, fuck em, fuck em, fuck em!** And most importantly, **STOP FUCKING SMOKING…**

SIMON COWELL (1959-2025) REST IN PEACE.

Whilst sitting watching the world famous X factor one Saturday evening, I noticed how one very powerful and influential individual had absolutely no power of control or influence over his own addiction. The running joke on the show seemed to be about stress and ciggie breaks amongst some of the judges and in this case, Mr Simon Cowell. One of television, music and Media's most famous sons, loved by some and hated by others is also famous for his very own love/hate relationship with his **poisonous addiction** to **nicotine.** Because of this, I have entitled this chapter with a medical or scientific prediction (or I suppose, learned guess) using the (WHO)'s statistics on the **life expectancy** of one of television's most powerful men, based on his ability **to say no** to the one thing in his life of which he has no control. This chapter will give you an insight into how one man can be seen to be totally in control of every aspect of his life and conquered everything he attempted to challenge, except for **addiction.**

Whoever invented the game 'Simon says' must have had this man in mind because that is how Simon Cowell seems to live his life. What gives him the respect and power that he commands is not only his knowledge of his industry, but also his understanding of being up in life as well as down. His life story will tell you he doesn't take much for granted. If anyone has heard or read this man's story, you will know that he has taken harsh blows several times in the trials of life. Simon has bounced back every time, with the positive self-belief that few are born with to remain positive and confident enough to dust himself off and carry on. Men and women who push through what others see as impossible can be found in every corner of the globe and Cowell has had it, lost it, had it, lost, and had it again. It shows that he's one of the resilient few on this planet who when it's needed, can display an amazing talent of survivors instinct in regards to hardships of life and the business world. Simon was born with bouncebackability! as a co-worker once told me.

Unfortunately for Simon, his ability to survive and to adapt to what life throws at him is overshadowed even overpowered by his **lack of self-control**. Because of these factors, the x factor he is missing out on regarding himself is **self-awareness.** Like billions of other similar **nicotine addicts,** he could talk about it all day long, even write a book on it, but cannot actually grasp what it means to actually live it and to be **self-aware.** When it comes to **self-awareness**, the money man Simon Cowell, one of the entertainments industries most powerful and wealthy individuals, is actually piss poor. He is broke and the balance in his **self-awareness** account is at zero. You see, it is not possible to have **complete self-awareness** and **inhale poisonous shit** into the body which works overtime to protect you. Thinking and knowing are two completely different things when your life is on the line. In order for Simon to add currency in the form of **precious time** into his account, he must finally conquer his demons and have the balls to finally say no to his **poisonous addiction** once and for all. His reputation has been built on his often outspoken or controversial ability to say no to anyone or anything that doesn't fit into his game plan. It is ironic that his refusal to **say no to inhaling poisonous chemicals** may put an end to everything he has amassed, including this game plan and his life.

If Simon was to be **diagnosed** with any of the **life changing** or **life ending diseases** associated with the **inhalation of these disgusting poisonous chemicals**, he would do well to remember that it has been responsible for **the demise** and for the **short lived lives** of some of the showbiz world's best known and powerful people including Walt Disney (65), Humphrey Bogart (57) Clarke Gable (59) and the great Ian Fleming (56). All men in or around Cowells age group, all men with money and all men with an **addiction**. Money may pay for the best treatment but with many of the **illnesses** and **diseases** associated with **inhaling this toxic shit,** sometimes the best treatments around are just not enough. **Cancer doesn't give a fuck** whose name is written on test results from the doctor, or whose name is written on the cheque for the treatment. It can't tell the difference in a person's skin colour, age, and will ravage the body of an infant or of an elderly pensioner. It is the **scourge** and one of the **largest ills** of all humanity and if Simon, just like every other **inhaler of this carcinogenic poison,** chooses to believe that he is free from the **50/50** or the **1** in every **2 club**, then he is deluded and very much mistaken. Whilst writing this, it has come to the world's attention that Simon Cowell, has fathered a child with an American socialite. I'm not one for newspaper tabloids or media for that matter as speculation seems to be the key ingredient often taken as truth, but according to reliable news outlets and associated press, Simon most definitely is going to become a first time father very soon.

If there was ever a better reason for Simon to get his priorities in check, then this is it. Unfortunately, **nicotine and its control over Simon** will either relate to this news as stress allowing him to deal with it by **inhaling 4000 poisonous chemicals** or as a reason to celebrate by **inhaling 4000 poisonous chemicals.** Either way, what he is doing is wrong. If he decides to **poison his body** in any way and for any reason, **he is wrong**, regardless of what happens in his life. It is time for Simon to listen to his own voice for a change and not the contestants on his shows or the voices of the brown nosing yes men and women he surrounds himself with. These voices of yes Simon, no Simon, whenever he wants to hear it are guilty of enabling him and are as **dangerous to his health** as the voice of the **addictive nicotine,** and each of its **poisonous co-defendants** who whisper sweet cravings into his ear at any given moment. Simon Cowell, with the power and wealth he has built from nothing could if he desired, celebrate or announce to the world in any way he wished, that he was expecting his first born child and in a way that very few men could. While most men feel as though they could shout it from the rooftops to let everyone know of their joy, Simon could be carried to the top of the world's highest mountain by Sherpas to make his announcement that he has achieved something that every man wishes to achieve, or hopes to become at some stage of their lives.

If someone reading this were to say that "Simons baby won't want for anything" that they will have private schooling, nanny's, wealth beyond and blahhdy blah, whatever. Just remember how we already have discussed that on the grand scale of things, money is quite nice to have, but in reality it means fuck all. Money can buy you a clock made from solid gold and can be encrusted with the world's most expensive diamonds and even though the hands of this clock may be manipulated by those with wealth, the time itself cannot be controlled by any man or any amount of money. It is the person who understands this that knows that the most valuable asset we all hold a percentage of, is time.

If Simon Cowell was '**truly aware**' of this fact, he would make a conscious decision the very moment he felt this '**true awareness**' and say **"enough, that's it, I'm done"**. He would then finally walk away from the **filthy disgusting addiction** he has long had this **master/slave** relationship with. Sadly Simon has never had this awareness. He has merely smelt the fresh air of awareness but not of true awareness. With true awareness there is no going back. Awareness is a nice temporary fix regarding the 'want to quit'. One could be forgiven for thinking such a giant has it all but alas he is lacking in morals of the self. Those who seem to have it all, for little things soon tend to fall! As streetwise, business minded and intelligent as this man may appear, **he is still stupid** enough to give these **poisonous toxic cancer causing pieces of shit** another chance after another chance after another chance. The same man who doesn't flinch whilst reducing a teenage girl to tears or shattering the hopes of the next big one direction at an x factor audition, by repeatedly using the word no, will struggle to use this same little word when it comes to **polluting every major organ and arteries in his bloodstream with poisonous tar**. If Simon does get his hands on a copy of this book then I will take the opportunity here and now to tell him in black and white what those around him won't for fear of his wrath and that is **"Simon, stop being such a dick"**. Sipping expensive water and vitamin injections do absolutely fuck all to help a **body that has thousands of poisonous chemicals running around its bloodstream, heart and lungs**. You have conquered all there is to conquer except **your health**. If you are to become a father, then don't allow that child to grow up without a dad just because **you are too weak and addicted to a poisonous addictive substance like nicotine**. Give your child at least another 15 years of your life if you make your decision today. And when it is your time, don't leave this planet as a **celebrity statistic of demise** by **nicotine addiction**. Responsibility starts today. **Leave the legacy** of someone who conquered the odds in life to succeed and who got to the top. Do not leave the legacy of a reclusive **lung diseased** middle aged man who fought bravely to the end, against a disease which never had to be fought in the first place.

The main thing about all this avoidance of illness and **premature death** is that, like in the case of **every addict of this poisonous shit**, it is completely up to the person themselves whether or not they just talk about it or act on it and Mr Simon Cowell is no exception. Until Simon realises this, he will always be a **humble subject** like all the **other addicts** who bow down to **nicotine and filthy poison addictive tobacco**. He may indeed be the king of all he surveys in the entertainment industry but as far as his life's force, energy and health are concerned, he is on very thin ice as they say and **like every other addict of this poisonous shit**, is **living on borrowed time**. The only certainty is his **1 in 2 chance**, like every other **addict**, so he is either **going to die prematurely** from a **smoking related death**, such as its **many cancers**, or he will not. It is only when Simon becomes **truly aware of his mortality** and when he, (like myself and the lucky few), makes a conscious decision that enough is enough, will he realise that time becomes not only important, but everything. True awareness of the self brings an understanding of the essence of the precious commodity of time.

Simon who once famously said that he would prefer to **drop dead** instead of giving up working, will find that ironically, that is how he will probably **meet his demise** either sipping a cocktail while being fanned by his adoring ex Sinnita in the hills of Spain whilst **taking a drag from a poisonous toxic cancer stick** or shouting orders from a boardroom while taking his last pull of **chemical toxic smoke** on this planet. Either way, it doesn't matter about hypothetical situations in which Simon Cowell might pop his clogs. What matters is that it is inevitable. Simon Cowell is a person very much admired by many, including myself. The reason for my admiration is because of his work ethic and his ability to insist upon and settle for nothing less than the very best. I think it's a shame to see a man with such a vision in regards to how he sees potential in those unassuming individuals and changes their life status overnight refusing to or failing to give proper consideration to his own future. With the **damage he is forcing his body to endure** on a daily basis, his own life could be changed overnight for all the wrong reasons and like many **addicts of nicotine**, he no doubt lives the "it'll never happen to me" mantra or the infamous "we'll cross that bridge when we come to it". I do understand his comment about **dropping dead** was not to be taken as **a death wish,** but about his passion for the empire he has built up and how much it means to him, but if he was to quit **inhaling this poisonous shit,** then he could gradually just slow down as **nature intended** and ease himself towards the inevitable we all face, instead of **clutching his chest** and **falling face down**. I have no doubt Simon Cowell likes to take care of himself with exercise but combining the fresh oxygen you give the cells of your body with **4000 poisonous chemicals** is the **contradiction** of pissing against the wind and we all know what happens when we do this.

Personally, if I use my own experience in **overcoming this poisonous addiction,** I am sure that Simons real awakening will be the birth of his new born child. I have seen it change the lifestyles of men and women before and I have hope it will do the same for Mr Cowell. For some people it gives them **a new lease of life** or something to really live for which holds an amazing **responsibility**. I'm not saying that those who are without children don't have anything to live for, it's just that some people are either married to their work or their social life and all that seems to go in a different direction when a life is created and a new born baby comes into the picture. **Responsibilities** and **priorities** are now the key words. **Your responsibilities** are to make sure that this little person has you around for as long as is possible so they can learn and grow up with the very person who created them. **Priorities** now circle around the new addition to your life and the life you've up until this moment led. Call it selfish if you will, but priority now sits in the back row so the new baby can take centre stage. I don't think Simon Cowell is really in for a shock to the system because he doesn't seem the easily shocked type of individual, based on what I've seen of him and I do think he'll adapt to fatherhood very quickly. Only time (**remember how limited it is**), will tell whether he takes his **responsibilities** as a parent seriously and whether he prioritises his health over a **poisonous** and **ridiculous addiction** to dried up leaves and paper. All Simon needs to remember in his quest to **beat his addiction** is this. When the **addictive chemicals** have left the body, there is **no physical dependency**. This happens over a number of hours and after that, it truly is, all in the mind. If Simon can conquer this in the exact same way that he has conquered every other aspect of his life, then he has **a long future to look forward to**. The main thing to remember is not to bow down to cravings through self-pity and weakness. If he is putting his own cravings or urges toward a make belief stress reducer or **false pleasure** before everything else in his life including life's real pleasures, such as **fresh air** and **family** then he's no mogul, just a mug. Anyone who can put their body through **hours or days of withdrawal without poisoning it,** only to pollute it all over again just because they felt like it or got a bit of bad or stressful news is a **fucking idiot** and if Simon Cowell takes this route and fails then he is no exception. All Simon needs to remember is the following. He is soon going to have an heir or heiress to the throne. Give you're unborn what they deserve and that is as much time with you as is possible. **Don't deprive** the child of memories, many of which they will carry until the day they will have their own children. **Don't be weak, be strong**. Say "fuck off" to anyone who tries to knock you off the path, when you do find the enlightenment and **freedom from inhaling this poisonous shit.**

Get your shit together and make sure you do it before this child arrives. Don't use the news of becoming a father as **an excuse or a reason to inhale poisonous chemicals** regardless of the situation, no matter whether the news of any occasion or event is stressful or indeed like this one, joyous. Don't make empty promises, especially to yourself as it is yourself you are hurting in the physical sense in the long run. And finally, instead of playing games with your life regarding every **cancer stick** you put to your lips, the only game Simon Cowell should be playing is Simon says NO, or **Simon says ENOUGH** or a polite **"no thanks"** or Simon says **"get that poisonous shit out of my face",** anytime that **nicotine** is either offered to, or is around the music mogul himself. If Simon is stupid enough to think he is above **cancer** then it would do well for him to remember that the scourge of **cancer** looks down on everyone.

-PATRICK SWAYZE AS I REMEMBER HIM AND LATER ON AS HE BATTLES PANCREATIC CANCER- HOLLYWOOD AND THE BLAME GAME.

For those of you too young to remember; smoking and Hollywood movies, televisions, the entertainment industry in general, used to go hand in hand with **filthy nicotine addiction** but was never marketed or advertised in a negative way. **Cancer sticks** were used on billboards, the big screen, television shows, magazines, books and newspapers as something that you had to have or that you couldn't be seen without. Iconic stars such as James Dean, Marilyn Monroe and Audrey Hepburn wouldn't be seen without **a cancer stick** between their fingers or lips and they featured in some of their most iconic images in the 1950s. Now in 2016, there are still celebs that won't be pictured without cancer hanging out of their mouth. Thankfully, as the years have progressed, the advertising standards of the business have taken younger impressionable people into consideration when it comes to its distribution of movies and programmes regarding the glamourizing of **inhaling this poisonous shit**. Now whilst I can see why millions of young girls worldwide would begin to **start smoking**

nicotine if they see one of their biggest idols with a **breathing in smoke**, this still doesn't lead me to believe that a person can say that just because Rihanna or whoever started smoking, I also became **addicted to nicotine**, and here's why. Unless Rihanna or Justin Bieber or Harry Styles or whichever celebrity you worship, knocked on your door with a couple of months supply of **cancer sticks** and forced you by hand or gunpoint, making you **inhale deeply into your lungs,** (until you found yourself a hopeless **nicotine addict** who couldn't get through 5 minutes without lighting up), then you are playing Hollywood and the blame game. It goes back to the any excuse chapter except celebrity influence is used as a reason for self-harming.

Try to look it this way. If a person is 10, 12, 14, or 22 years of age just for example, and they try out **this filthy substance** for whatever reason, be it peer pressure, curiosity, or because they saw so and so doing it. This still means the **act of inhalation** (which is a physical act carried out by the person's organs/body), involves **voluntarily breathing in and out.** No individual, no matter what age, is going to become **addicted to nicotine** the first, second, or even third time around, even if the **cancer stick** is quite literally rammed down a person's throat. Becoming **addicted to this poisonous shit** happens very easily, but it is a gradual process that usually sneaks up on the person who usually thinks they can quit whenever they feel like it, until they actually attempt to do so. Smokers as young and as impressionable as many of them are, make choices and unfortunately, like **the sticky poisonous tar they inhale**, it sticks with them **as an addiction** but only if they persist in turning a filthy habit into a filthy disgusting addiction. Peer pressure can be blamed far too often in circumstances, but the buck stops firmly in my opinion, with the person who started something (that they once saw as harmless fun) themselves, and continues to do so until it **becomes a dangerous threat**. If a parent reading this says "my son or my daughter only started because of the crowd they were involved with", then **tough shit,** that's down to your bad parenting skills by allowing them to run with the wolves in the first place. I personally, was a child who followed this path and it falls back once again on bad parenting, simple as that. My job today as a parent is to now teach my children to be street wise and respectful to others but more importantly, to respect themselves. If one of my children comes back **smelling of smoke** or becomes **addicted** to a harder drug such as heroin, then I have done a shit job as a parent and this is my stance on the subject.

No parent has complete control over their children when they reach certain age and if a 12 year old girl who is caught with a packet of **cancer sticks** under her pillow with a lighter tells her parents that she "only smoked because Miley Cyrus does it" then she should be told by her parents that Miley is a fucking idiot for doing so, instead of the "if Miley jumped off a bridge" speech. George Best (for some of our younger readers) the Irish footballer, was one of the greatest players that ever lived and unfortunately also one of the greatest alcoholics by his own admission. After many attempts to give up alcohol and to regain the control of the life he had **lost to addiction**, he finally **succumbed** as a result of complications from a liver transplant while still a relatively young man at 59 years young. His short life was lived in the public eye and he was brave in admitting his weaknesses were killing him. George was never force fed alcohol and in the same way, a person can wish all they want that they had never met someone who affected them negatively by introducing them to a substance, be it drugs alcohol or **nicotine.** The buck as I've already said before, has to stop with the person whose who has the option at any given stage **to quit**. This isn't possible (as became clear in Georges case) if the person doesn't give it everything they've got. Although I agree as I've said, with the fact that some kids only start by the whole monkey see monkey do scenario, I also believe that any young person who is made fully aware of their **responsibility to themselves,** will think and instinctively know not to even contemplate lighting up under any circumstances, be it peer pressure or because their favourite celebrity doesn't show respect for themselves by **inhaling poisonous shit.**

This shouldn't be because they think the consequences of their actions will be punishable with being grounded or because they are told to "wait till your father gets home". It should be that they understand **the damage that this shit does to the body** and to understand fully that **the consequences.** They should be aware of the effects of such poisons will follow them into adulthood. The youngster should frown upon it and have the sense to know every **negative aspect** of using this **poisonous product** and we should school our children on the use of **this substance** in the same way we teach them never to talk to strangers, or to take the offer of lift or a ride with someone they don't know. When they are at this stage, where it becomes second nature for a child to refuse any type of offer of a **cancer stick,** or that their knowledge of its danger is so finely tuned that they wouldn't conceive of even expressing interest in experimenting with **this poison**, it should be then that they may look at a celebrity crush or someone they idolise, and recognise that the ones who are **addicted to this poisonous shit** are in fact not really worth worshipping at all. Worshipping is for gods and celebrities who quite often have a god like complex sometime quickly learn that immortality doesn't apply to them. This is where addiction and celebrity fall out as addiction doesn't give a fuck about a name. This is unfortunately why some big names become remembered for the final battle in life instead of the fight to become famous.

What happens when the celebrities meet their demise from a **smoking** related incident be it a **cancer or emphysema** or anyone of **the numerous illness or deaths** this **disgusting addiction can cause?** One of many people's favourite films and definitely one that some of the older readers will remember or have seen at some stage growing up is Dirty Dancing or Ghost (highly recommended if you have never seen them both!). Both of these classics starred the late Patrick Swayze who has since died of a pancreatic cancer, which he put down to his sometimes… 40 a day **disgusting addiction.** The actor I personally remember best for his role in the movie Road House died a shadow of the former heart throb of the 80s and 90s, which saw him worshipped by men and women worldwide. After watching Road House for the 20th time I had decided I wanted to be a bouncer in a troubled redneck county that needed regulating!

Swayze's physique was famous worldwide so to see pancreatic cancer cause him to deteriorate was hard to bear. His body was ravaged by the **cancer** that had **spread throughout** and by the high doses of chemotherapy the poor man endured to try and stay alive and have some sort of a fighting chance. Although I would like to say that I had known the man, I unfortunately did not, but I was a huge fan and admired him greatly as both an actor and for his charitable work in his private life. I loved the fact that he remained married to the same woman for 30 years and that they remained together until he passed from this life with his wife at his side. I only write in regards to his **illness,** life and **death** from what I've seen and heard in the media but it seems from these reports that he faced his final days with great courage. Hollywood knew Patrick Swayze and all of Hollywood's up and coming stars would have followed his final months on air or in the tabloids. How any of these people witnessed the **suffering of another human** being as he was **ravaged by cancer** and still lit up while looking at his picture or after seeing how **frail** and **ill** he was, I find shockingly stupid. The images showed the man who spent decades as one of the most sought after actors, looking **gaunt, pale, skeletal,** and **weak,** struggling to get in and out of a wheelchair.

It shows that many of these famous people (some, whose pictures adorn the bedroom of kid's walls) haven't got a brain cell in their heads. These same celebrities are the ones who look but don't see. Here's a look at celebrities who are blind choosing blindness over their future. These are some of the ostriches today with their head in the sand. From Angelina Jolie and Justin Beiber to Robert Pattinson, from Ellen DeGeneres to Mila Kunis and brad Pitt to Cheryl Tweedy. To be honest it is easier for you to just research celebs who smoke online. There are those who inhale this poisonous shit that have a clean cut image but anyone who inhales an addictive substance is an addict. Every one of these household names is **living on borrowed time**. If they are foolish enough to believe that youth is on their side then they are more foolish than they realise.

The skin they possess and depend on, not only for their looks, but life itself is quickly being aged with every **poisonous cancer stick they inhale.**

Statistically, because **1 in 2** of the above will **die prematurely** through a **smoking related illness** and as we know, that's a scientific and medical fact. I'm not a yes man to any of the above but if they were to ask me "could I be one of the **1 out of the 2** who **dies**" it would have to be the most honest answer I could give them, YES most certainly. If any of the celebrities named, **thinks that death, cancer or a long painful illness** or any **smoking related ailment** doesn't apply to them because they see themselves as the elite, then I would like to give them the names of other well-known individuals who foolishly believed the same **never happen to me bullshit.** The Beatle George Harrison, Betty Grable, Nat king Cole, Walt Disney, Yul Brenner, Steve McQueen, John Gotti, Humphrey Bogart, Errol Flynn and Clarke Gable, **all succumbed** to an **early demise** in some form or another from the use of this **deadly dangerous addictive shit.** Now, the only difference in the lists of the people who are still alive and those who are beneath the clay is this. The names of the people who are dead, grew up in the last 40, 50, 60 decades where they can plead absolute ignorance to not knowing what they were doing was actually **harmful to their health.** Remember that as far back as only 10 years ago, smoking was advertised at sporting events even though it was acknowledged to be **unhealthy and dangerous.** 20 years ago, newsreaders could read the news, interview a guest or present a show with **a cancer stick** in their mouth without reaction from anyone because it was accepted as normal or as a natural right to do so.

Social normality at its worst. There has also been a number of sporting events over the years that have endorsed brands such as John Player, Rothmans and tobaccos such as Marlboro. Now I'd like to talk to you a little about the real Marlboro men and their poisonous place in Hollywood history. Many moons ago, actors in America who were blessed with a good physique and an all American male model look, would portray this character in ad campaigns that could be seen on billboards, magazines, and televisions across the world. The Marlboro man, always dressed in a cowboy's attire quickly grew as a representation of a real rugged or a man's man type hero. Those who were given the job of the Marlboro men became known throughout the decades by this title, or as the Marlboro cowboys. The pictures of them leaning back on a wooden post or sitting on horseback whilst wrangling a bull became synonymous with this particular product, in the same way that cowboy movies in the states always promoted the cowboy as the good guy who always won the day and always got the girl. These images were designed not only to entice men but women who saw these bare chested smoking cowboys as sex symbols who made **inhaling a cancer stick** look shit hot.

Bearing in mind, those who work in marketing and PR had the good sense not to use toothless, balding, overweight men in a wife beaters vest who gasped for breath as they took a pull from a **cancer stick** deep into **their lungs** whereas ironically, these are the effects of long term use of this **poisonous chemical shit.** Now, here's an interesting fact for you to consider whether you happen to be a rising star on the factory floor or the latest star on Hollywood Boulevard. I want you to check out who the Marlboro men were and to pay attention to one particular part of their story. Three of the men who were involved in the role of this character or starred as the Marlboro men in adverts or in their ad campaigns **died of lung cancer.** Dick Hammer, Wayne McLaren and David McLean **all met their demise** because of the product they endorsed. Wayne McLaren **campaigned against smoking poisonous chemicals** right up until his death in 1992. Over 20 years later, how many people have listened to reason? Have a think about this and try and see if there's any rationale in it whatsoever. The product **they inhaled** and advertised for a living, ended up **killing them** in the permanent, lights out sense… as in dead, gone, no more! Isn't this not a clear message that even the most idiotic of people could understand?

If I was to say for example, that a certain brand or make of car had a fault that killed 3 people in 3 separate collisions over 2 days? Those cars would be recalled by the manufacturers and people would refuse to drive them, or hand back the keys to the garage where they purchased the vehicle demanding either a refund, a replacement or that the fault was quickly fixed. They wouldn't endanger themselves or their families by continuing to take a risk or a chance when in actual fact the risk or chance of them injuring or killing themselves could be 1 in 10,000 or more. It's the same when an electrical appliance is recalled because of a fault; people will avoid it like the plague, boycott it or bad mouth it so that everyone knows about the particular product which has caused offence to the consumer and to stay away from it.

Again… 3 men who endorsed and advertised this Marlboro product **died** from the **same lung cancer** that attacked and **destroyed their lungs.** You cannot pay for that kind of advertising and yet so many people still refuse to listen or choose to turn a blind eye to an obvious **deadly addiction.** How can this not be a wakeup call to people? There are also fads in Hollywood where weight loss and smoking this poisonous shit is considered or even endorsed to aid weight loss. They are told that this poisonous shit supresses hunger!! Then eat apples, porridge and drink water or chew gum, same thing! These idiots who are foolish enough to believe that **inhaling 4000 different chemicals with every cancer** stick they light up has any bearing on a woman's weight, as if in order to stay looking like a stick thin emaciated corpse, that a woman has to poison her body…… let me just say that some of the world's most beautiful women

don't depend on poisonous chemicals to stave off the unwanted pounds, but keep themselves looking great and feeling fit with a combination of healthy eating and exercise. It's like this; don't think that just because **you have decided to stop poisoning your system** with **chemicals** means that you have to start putting in a different type of **poison** to replace the longing of **addiction**, such as greasy take away foods and dinners. Exchange bars of chocolate, crisps and biscuits for fresh fruit, a low fat yogurt or a bowl of healthy cereal and you are onto a winner. You don't need to pay too much attention to any expensive dietician or food guru. Your body knows what it needs and it doesn't have to be told in order to know the difference between what's shit and what's shit hot. Although **inhaling poisonous chemicals** will suppress hunger for some and not for others, you still have to remember that **nicotine; heart attacks** and **cancer don't give a fuck** about your new diets and plans at fitness. People of all shapes and sizes **have fallen and died due to a smoking related illness,** and the diseases that are associated with this **poisonous shit**, again, don't discriminate.

If I was to ask the same persons to take a potion that would put them asleep if they had insomnia but would also give them a **1 in 2** chance of getting cancer, how many would accept it? I would be told to "fuck off" even it was only one tablet over one night. But the same persons play Russian roulette **20** or **30** times a day every day for years on end with their fingers crossed that they won't get the dreaded news no one wants to ever hear or choose to **live in ignorance** hoping not **to die** in it also.

Every single cancer stick you smoke is giving you just that, a **1 in 2** chance of **dying young.** Every breath **full of poisonous chemical shit** is the one that **can mutate** a damaged or **weakened cell** in your body and be the straw that breaks the camel's back, the final straw, so to speak. Bearing in mind that there are those who will say "sure, if I lived the life of a Hollywood star, I'd be able to afford a personal trainer" and to that I would say, **stop being weak and talking shit.** There can be **no feeble excuses** for not getting fit. Even prisoners doing short, long and life sentences in 24 hour lock up are still like professional athletes when interviewed in documentaries on television and some of these individuals use their time and body weight to get fit. Anyone who argues " yeah but they have time when I have collect the kids and work an blah blah blah, is again **making feeble excuses.** If you have time to stand for 10 minutes outside in a **smoking shed inhaling poisonous toxic chemicals**, you can do a hell of a lot of push ups, sit ups or cardio like skipping in 10 minutes ,and how many times a day? Think about it and **stop talking shit.** If people like the idea of Hollywood, the look, the body, the teeth, the healthy skin. It's all there right in front of the mirror. Sure enough we all need a little adjusting or to tweak a bit of weight here and build a bit of muscle there, but you are the master of this ship. By **casting out a poisonous addictive chemical** that's holding you back, you are taking control of this ship and steering it away in the direction of your choosing. One where you can restore the old you and away from the **addiction** and the **poison** which has almost succeeded in stopping you **dead in your tracks**. Believe me when I say this; when you start using your brain without it being tormented by an **addictive craving** for **poisonous nicotine** and you accept responsibility for the actions of **self-harm,** you will not have to travel to Hollywood to look a million dollars.

For the thousands you spend on **poisonous cancer sticks** per year, you could in fact purchase a platinum membership card to the most exclusive gym or fitness centre in your area and all with a one on one fitness instructor at your beck and call. You also spend hundreds of bucks per year on beauty treatments and make up to look like your favourite celebs, (some even spending thousands they have to borrow), on medical or cosmetic procedures that could in fact have been avoided, by just taking care of your body in the first place and breathing in the air like you were designed to. Hollywood is often described as fake, but in real life where many of you have to reside, more and more people are beginning to realise that the reality of **inhaling a poisonous addictive substance** means living in a fantasy land of pretence, if you continue to do so without expecting lethal consequences. They say you should never meet your hero's and this is true, especially if you are encouraged to kill yourself with addiction to nicotine, just because they do and because they couldn't give a fuck about their own health. Be your own hero. Look up to yourself and look after yourself. Worship your body instead of destroying it. Be famous for fitness not because you were a smoking related cancer statistic.

Before I finish this chapter, I'd like to talk about influence and the Hollywood machine. In the last chapter I spoke about my admiration for Simon Cowell and his tenacity in adversity. I spoke about Patrick Swayze in this chapter and how I admired his loyalty to his wife and the strength he displayed during the course of his illness. Now I would like to speak on a lady I mentioned earlier who has suffered her own losses and beaten her own demons in life to become revered as an icon and beacon for many women to follow today. The beautiful Mrs Angelina Jolie Pitt. The daughter of a Hollywood actor may be seen as privileged by most people and there is no doubt that hunger for food was ever an issue in her younger years. Unfortunately, a tortured soul doesn't always require food in order to be fed and a young Miss Jolie had to taste much bitterness before she finally found the peace of mind she so badly sought. This peace came in the form of her large brood of children. Her love for her many children cannot be debated and she revels in motherhood. This lady has often spoken of the devastation felt by the loss of her own mother and the deep impact it has taken on her. She recently underwent a double mastectomy after discovering that she carried the same cancerous gene that caused her beloved mothers **untimely death.** This very personal decision was made after much deliberation and paved the way for many women worldwide who took the same brave step in order to cut their own cancer risk. The days and weeks spent weighing up the pros and cons of such a painstaking decision must **all revolve around future health, family** and **life or death.** In Angelina's case, there was **so much to lose.** This lady can often be seen at UN council meetings and as a goodwill ambassador; she is frequently seen in third world countries fulfilling her role to bring hope to children and women who continue to suffer through war and famine. I admire this woman, I really do. Although, when it comes to the contradiction of her actions, regarding **the poisoning of her blood and body by inhaling deadly chemicals**, it is hard for my respect not to diminish greatly. If Brad Pitt smokes and Angelina smokes then **one of the two or both is going to die from a smoking related illness** or death. It's that simple. Again, the real statistics. If the world watches their every move, then let them advertise the damage **this poisonous shit** does by **stubbing it out permanently.** There is only tragedy and contradiction associated with this scourge and if Angelina is willing to go through such evasive personal surgery to counteract a genetic flaw in her body, then **a one in two risk of cancer through a carcinogenic product** shouldn't even be up for discussion. They can read this and say "do you know what, he's right" or they can say "fuck him, talking that shit about me" and light up **a cancer stick**. Hopefully, because of their influence on much of the world, they may see sense and **stop fucking smoking**. This cannot even be argued and to attempt to, is to bury your head in the sand.

To finish, I would like to mention some words by the man we started talking about, the late Mr Patrick Swayze. In my research on this man and his **addiction and illness,** I came across an article where the doctor treating him said that because his pancreatic cancer was at stage 4, it didn't really matter if a patient continues to smoke as the longest prognosis is usually about 5 months if the individual was quite physically strong and resilient. This is exactly what Patrick Swayze was. He grew up in his mother's dance school, was a rancher and an actor who carried out his own stunts. Patrick Swayze truly was made of the tough stuff. He also continued to **inhale the shit** that he spoke about in the months before **his death** when asked if there was a connection between his pancreatic cancer and **his addiction.**

Speaking to Barbara Walters on ABC in 2009 he said "I've seriously cut down," "I was one of those dumb ones that started back in the Marlborough Man days whose — you know, it was cool. I'm a cowboy. But I'll tell you one thing. I will talk so hard core against, against smoking for kids. That's one reason I've never smoked in front of children.

"When asked if he thought his smoking caused his cancer, Patrick said it may have had an effect.

"Ooh, I don't know... I will go so far as to say probably smoking had something to do with my pancreatic cancer," he said.

Patrick said one reason he continues to smoke is to lesson his daily battles.

"I've got... priorities," he said. "It's just I've been dealing with one thing as it comes at a time, you know... in the... order that it's trying to kill me. Will stopping smoking now stop anything, change anything? No. But, when it looks like I may live longer than five minutes, I'll drop cigarettes like a hot potato."

Patrick Swayze was a legend not only to me, but to many of my age. It's a pity that a death can be possibly somehow attributed to **a filthy worthless addiction to this shit.** Time waits for no man and most certainly not for those who beckon death forward and often years and years before its due date. **Don't throw it all away because of a weakness for an addictive poison**. Live long and live strong. **Stop fucking smoking** and don't throw it all away for a **filthy smelly addiction.** It can take years to build a life and everything that revolves around life. It only takes a second for an unnecessary diagnosis to tear it all down. Be truly aware that I'm talking about you and to you directly.

MY KINGDOM FOR A HEARSE!

Every person alive would like a place that they can call home. A place where either alone or with their family, they can close the doors and forget the world outside. To be the King or Queen of their own castle, your very own private kingdom. For some this is something that has already been achieved while for others, the next 30 or 35 years of paying monthly instalment to the banks is the only way they'll truly get their hands on a permanent front door key. Now, like me, if you have already done the smoking calculator in the previous chapter, you should be aware of how much money you've already wasted over the last number of years on paying a multi-billion dollar company to **slowly kill you in a painful way.** This as we now know means leading either you or your partner to **an early grave**. People spend money on their children, people spend money on food, and people spend money on holidays. All of which allow us to grow as families with happy memories to carry throughout life and to eat thrive and survive. You cannot be in your right mind to spend the hard earned money you make on this **cancerous shit.** You waste everything that you **kill yourself** for and in the worst possible way. All that you have to show after every box you purchase is yellow teeth, rotten shitty breath, poisonous mucus filled lungs, brown fingers, wrinkled horrible skin, long **term illness, sickness misery, pain** and then a **premature death**. Every word I've just written **involves waste** and **the smoker owns** and is entitled to every one of them. He or she after all, is the one **literally coughing up their hard earned wages** in order to pursue their **filthy addiction.** When the person who **works hard all their life** finally gets to retirement age with their house finally paid for and a little nest egg put away for a rainy day, isn't it sad to see that person who **smokes this shit**, get struck down with any of the **many diseases** this **filth** brings at a time in their life when after years of hard grafting, they should be putting their feet up, enjoying some sunshine, travelling or spending time working in the garden or playing with their grandchildren.

The people of which I speak of, are the people of my father's age who have slaved for every possession they own and can have it taken from them quite literally in a heartbeat. Now that we live in the so called computer age, there are absolutely no excuses for the sins of our fathers and mothers to be repeated and for any **inhaler of this rotten shit to have to suffer unnecessarily**. It just doesn't have to happen. Why any person by todays standard would jeopardise being told they could have everything in life, or **lose everything including their life because of a filthy disgusting addiction to a drug like nicotine** is beyond my comprehension, but as an **ex addict of this filthy shit,** I understand how **it attempts to control you with cravings** so we'll continue our discussion. We live in a time of financial struggles for many. People today are under severe pressure to pay **household bills** such as **the electricity on time,** for fear of living in darkness and **some will still choose nicotine** over paying this bill if it came down to it. By repeating **this foolishness** of **feeding your addiction,** before basic bills are paid especially if you are someone who is finding their financial situation difficult, then it is **choosing a poison over a bill** (with the irony in this being that **it is nicotine** which has not only left you in darkness, but will eventually **put your lights out permanently).**

The **amount you have to lose** because of this **horrible addiction** far outweighs what you have to gain from it. Can you imagine any parent having to sit down their children to tell them that they have some **very bad news?** Nobody wants to imagine this but even as we speak, there are those at this moment in time preparing to give **this sad news** or explain to their loved ones that **time may not be on their side** any longer. How would any family react to receiving such **tragic** almost unbelievable and shocking news? As they would struggle to come to terms with the **cold hard fact** that a part of their **world is about to be taken away from them**, you also struggle with the gut wrenching decisions you now have to make, in preparations for **a needless funeral** and for the future they now face without you. Only those who have **suffered this terrible news** know the **heartbreak** that goes with it and will tell you that they wouldn't wish this **needless suffering** on anybody. To be diagnosed with any type of serious illness is tough for anyone but when it is a **self-inflicted illness** (to which you were aware was a possibility because of your lifestyle), then there are harder emotional mountains to climb. You are dealing with **a terminal disease** that up until now you played Russian roulette with and played the **"never happen to me"** card with **every drag you took of a carcinogenic (cancer causing) coffin nail.**

Even worse, is to get this news unintentionally as a person **who doesn't smoke this poisonous shit** except through **passive smoking.** To discover that either from working in a smoky environment or living day in and day out with a smoker (or number of smokers) is even more heart-breaking. The dreadful news of your **life changing** or **terminal illness** quite literally means you have been **killed** by some inconsiderate pricks **filthy disgusting addiction** inadvertently. This must be **a diagnosis** which is all the more **heart-breaking and frustrating.** When a smoker is told by the doctor that the preparations **for palliative care** should be arranged and all manner of words are used (which should be foreign to any person told that an **unavoidable premature death is inevitable),** then one can only imagine the feeling of **complete helplessness** and **loneliness.** Again, news all the more **heart breaking** when we know that all this **pain, suffering** and **misery** can be avoided if you just give yourself the opportunity to open your ears and eyes fully and truly and to genuinely make a heartfelt pledge to address the **filthy, disgusting addiction,** you are **forcing your fragile body to endure**. Your body, the vessel in which you reside, has more value than the bricks and mortar of the house or home you call you call your castle. The body is fragile, yet it can also be strong and resilient when the going gets tough and will help you to fight another day if you give it the opportunity. If our possessions are important to us then try to remember they mean fuck all when you're laid out in a wooden box.

"They had it all" is a term often used to describe someone who lost everything. The term can often be used in accordance with an addiction of some sort, be it drink, drugs, gambling or a combination of all of the above. The person who has lost it all is often spoken of in terms such as "didn't realise what they had till they lost it", and this can be true for many of us and not just those with **addictions.** 'You don't know what you've got till it's gone' as the song goes. We will all become aware of this at some stage of our lives. It can be as small as losing the car for two days to a repair to actually make you realise how difficult life can be when you need to drop the kids to school or carry bags home from a supermarket on foot when your usual mode of transport is out of action. Or it can be as big as **the loss of a loved one**, who either expected or unexpected **has departed this life** without you getting to say all the things that you wish you could have said **when they were alive**. It can be at this stage that the person who is mourning the **loss of a loved one** will look at a photograph and cry "I'd give anything to have you back".

I speak from my own personal experience and anyone who has **suffered the loss of someone** they considered to be a part of their world, will understand how **lonely** and **helpless** you feel. When any **person dies**, there is a sense of **tragedy** felt by those closest to them, but **when a death is completely preventable and avoidable,** it is all the more **heart breaking**. The person who has gone onto the next life is not the one left with all the **ifs** and **buts**. Hindsight is often used to describe a way of looking back at things and doing them differently. It is a shame when the word is used to talk about the **addictive personality to poisonous chemicals,** which may have caused the **premature death of their loved one**. 'Would of', 'could of', 'should of', are also words used to describe **regrets** and how things might have been and how different they may have turned out. It's a play on the word hindsight and someone might say, "I would have **given up smoking** if I had really known I was **killing myself**" or "I should have gave them up in my twenties" or " I would have given them up only for I was living with another smoker", all of which are **pathetic excuses**.

Change only happens when **the person who inhales 4000 poisonous chemicals** with every **cancer stick** they put to their lips accepts responsibility for their own actions and stops using **ridiculous excuses** such as blaming ignorance by today's media standards or peer pressure from another smoker.

If you were **ignorant** to the dangers back then, how could you be now? A **quality of life** better than you've ever known awaits any person who stops **polluting their body with poison** and **completely purifies it with air**. By any means necessary, you start doing this as soon as possible. If you feel the need to hammer both hands to the table in order to get you to stop (although I strongly advise against this as it can be quite dangerous, painful and tricky without assistance!) then do what you feel you have to do. If you're one of the many **addicted to poisonous nicotine** and the other many **thousand shitty chemicals**, ask yourself the following? First of all, why? We will all at some stage ask ourselves "**Why the fuck** did I even bother in the first place?" We often use this when we've tried to do something that doesn't have the desired effect we had hoped for. Ask yourself **why?** Why should I give up **my health** for the **small piece of poisonous paper** between my lips? **Why**, should I give my **hard earned money** for something which **controls the amount of time I spend on this planet?** Why should I have to face any **number of illnesses** and **cancers** that wouldn't even be a part of my vocabulary, only for the fact that **I'm addicted to a substance** which I know only causes **untold misery, grief** and **death?** Why should I take **a gamble** with the **precious time** I would like to spend with my family and friends? Why should **I work hard all my life** only to have all of this **taken away from me** in an instant just because I am too weak to **say no?**

It is when you start thinking this way that you begin to realise that the only one who is really in **control of your destiny** in regards to how your future begins is you. The buck stops with you and it stops not only when you realise this, but also when you incorporate your words and/or realisation into action. Use this new thought/action as the driving force to change not only your mind, but your body and its ability to overcome what you once saw as the impossible. Know that your **addiction to a disgusting chemical substance** which was responsible for **poisoning** every cell of your very existence with **tar, mucus** and **carbon monoxide**. If reading this you see yourself as a lone ranger or a private individual without any family or friends to be concerned about and who sees their **addiction** as the only comfort you have left in life, then the very fact that you have read the book this far shows **your desire to quit inhaling this shit.** There is much **more to life** than being alone with **nicotine** and **poisonous chemicals** to keep you company. If you happen to be reading this as some sort of **inconsiderate prick** whose family or friends has begged you to read it after many years of putting up with breathing in your **poisonous 1st, 2nd, and 3rd, hand shit**, and are sick to the teeth of your **ignorance**, then it is time for you to stop acting like a 15 year old rebellious teenager and to drop this "like it or lump it" attitude. Remember how your mother would grab you firmly by the hand as a child when crossing the road? That was to guide you safely across the road and keep you from **danger.** This is what your loved ones have done by **present**ing you with this book because that's what it is, a present of consideration, a gift, and if you read and heed what's written, and use what's written to **combat an addiction that's killing you,** then it will also be **the gift of life.** This is the life that is slipping away from you whether you realise it or not.

And if you do happen to be reading this because the **last piece of poisonous paper** has already been **stubbed out** (and you want it to **stay stubbed permanently)**, then you are the driving force behind the conquest of the written words you are now reading. Your decision, whenever it was made, should not for a moment be up for any kind of discussion that involves you becoming or even considering **becoming hooked or addicted to a poisonous piece of disgusting miserable paper** ever again. There should be no question about this when you see **this shit** for what it actually is. To allow yourself to even think about it again is to give credit to **this poisonous shit** and this you should not do, in the same way you would view or think about every **regretful** thing you've ever said or done in life. That's the only way that this **cancer causing, mucus filled piece of shit** should be given even one second of **your precious time**. Everything you now have in your life, regardless of your current status has been given to you because of your **health** up to this point. If you really think about it, **the health of your body** has allowed you to get this far. Whoever said that **your health is your wealth**, most certainly knew what they were talking about because it is everything. It is behind everything we achieve in this life and should be put before all else and alongside your family. The man or woman, who understands this, understands **the reason for our existence**. Healthy body, healthy mind. Our everyday appearance, our looks, our actions are all controlled by how well we look after the machine we call the body. Don't lose all life has given you, be it your home, your family or the body, the kingdom in which you have to live, just because you couldn't **refuse a poisonous addiction to smoking this filthy shit.**

QUIT THE SHIT AND THE BULLSHIT.

Earlier we spoke briefly about the many ways that shit is associated with this poisonous addictive substance and now we will elaborate more on the same filthy lies that stick to it like flies. If you **breathe poisonous shit** in through your mouth, then the chances are that you'll breathe out excuses in the form of **bullshit**, as to the many reasons why you won't or can't stop **breathing in and out poisonous chemicals.** This is where understanding the chapter titles words and/or meaning is very important to progress. When you are **tired of smoking this shit** and **you finally stop inhaling it**, you will look back and see how using the word **shit** in many sentences used daily when talking about **poisonous nicotine.** Sentences such as **"my skin looks like shit"**, **"I feel like shit"**, **"he was shit in bed"** **"her teeth looked like she was chewing shit"** **"I'm sick of smoking this shit",** actually go hand in hand. If you disagree or don't fully understand then try reading it like this; My skin really looks great since I started **smoking this shit,** my sex life has improved has really improved since I started **poisoning my bloodstream with 4000 chemicals**, Her teeth have never looked better since she **started inhaling tar**, I feel really healthy after **inhaling poisonous chemical shit.** They have the same meaning if you read it back again and if sarcasm is the lowest form of wit, then **nicotine is the lowest form of shit**.

All of the above is **shit talk,** but let's **discuss the bullshit** which is constantly used by **the smoker of this poison** when speaking to themselves or to others as to the reasons why they continue to **kill themselves,** or those around them. To allow those of you who continue to do so, I will again highlight the words **quit the shit** in order for your eyes to allow your brain to acknowledge what it is actually allowing your body to do. The words **inhaling shit** and anything else associated with this **shitty addiction** will continue to be **highlighted until the end** of this book to keep reinforcing **this filth** has no place in your body. Here are some of the reasons, (many as you will read are **bullshit excuses)** as to why those **who poison their bodies** can't, or won't stop doing so. Most commonly; the inhalation **of 4000 poisonous chemicals** in **every coffin nail** is used as a false coping mechanism for **many addicts**, with which to deal with the many issues they feel they have to contend with in their daily lives. I will remind these people that the native American Indians did not know what alcoholism was until they were introduced to whiskey or firewater by the white man. Point being, they didn't use alcohol to cope with how harsh life was before a coping mechanism, now used by many was introduced. If they smoked a traditional peace pipe or a ceremonial device, it was to symbolise a truce of a 10 year war between tribes and not because the stress of an electricity bill meant that **inhaling 4000 poisonous chemicals** would resolve paying the bill. They didn't walk around with peace pipes to cope, so don't look for justification here with a ridiculous argument.

Some, who **inhale this poison**, will say they do so because they enjoy it as if we were talking about playing football or jogging. What I have to say to this is to take the **cancer sticks** away from the **addict** for an hour and see how much fun it is then. You will see that there is nothing enjoyable about **this addiction** whatsoever as the mood of **the addict** quickly grows angry and agitated with the mood altering affects leaving the addict climbing the walls or "hanging for a smoke". Enjoyment and **addiction** are not friends and never get mistaken about this. You may use **a feeble excuse** to yourself that you actually like the whole **inhaling of poison** process, but again, this is the brain attempting to fool your body because the **poisonous nicotine injection** is in fact a **cruel mind fuck**. What has actually happened is that your body began to feel the withdrawal of **nicotine addiction** .You then **fed its addiction** or need, with a top up of **poison**, so is in actual fact, the shit you inhale, is to stop you **feeling like shit**. It is feeding **bullshit messages to your brain** that your body is enjoying being **pumped full of shit,** when in reality you feel and look like **shit with every poisonous piece of shit you force your body to endure**.

This is the shitty roundabout, your body has been struggling to stop going around, except you are not willing to jump off and give your body a break, because you are **feeding it shit,** in the form of an **addictive poison** and then **adding bullshit** excuses as to why you can't stop doing it. Again, the harmer of the self is harming the self, but everyone else is doing it so it's acceptable. Of course there are many such cases of **self-harm**, you could argue such as obesity but this is why I said one of the biggest cases of **self-harm** because the number of **nicotine addicts** globally is over **one Billion**. Out of this **one Billion**, there are very few who would ever see themselves as someone who **self-harms**. As we discussed previously, this is only what Goth teens do to seek attention or people with a mental health problem or someone who is chemically unbalanced, right?... Wrong...**self-harm** is to harm oneself intentionally as to a form of gratification or release. A way of stopping or controlling something with a rush or release, in the form of injuring oneself or with the knowledge that your actions are causing an injury to your body. Sound familiar? This may sound like **bullshit** to many **poisonous nicotine addicts,** but when you look at **what you do in your addiction to this poisonous shit** and how it **controls you**, it is then you will see how similar or how in actual fact, there is no difference between what you are doing and what a stereotypical **self-harmer** does**,** which is to **purposefully harm** the body as a way of release or relief. The stereotypical **self-harmer** will bear the scars or marks on their bodies, legs, arms or face in the form of cuts which many choose to cover up to hide the fact that they use to **self-harm,** or because they have fought their demons and no longer feel the need to inflict injury as a way to cope or as a release. A series of events in their lives, a chemical imbalance, depression or a combination of all three may have led them to believe that they were somehow less than they were actually worth, and by inflicting pain on themselves or by **self-harming,** it may have given them the relief or release they felt was the only way to make themselves feel better. Some wish that they could stop feeling like a piece of shit all the time and in order to do so, they harm the body for respite from the pain or anguish.

Now back to the **nicotine addict** who is no doubt offended by all this shit about being compared to **a self-harmer**. You like the **self-harmer** might use the events in your own life as to why you regularly place a **poisonous dried out piece of paper** to your mouth and set fire to it. But why do you think that you need to **poison your body** in order to cope with these events? Do you truly believe that the actions of **poisoning your bloodstream** is the best procedure for the situation you found or find yourself in? Even if many of you, like me, had been born into **nicotine addiction**, what type of crutch would you use if they had banned smoking from the planet on the day of your birth? Would you be an alcoholic in order to deal with your life, or the stress you now **poison** yourself about? Would you need a drink to destress from a simple argument or because an assignment had to be finished by a certain date? How would you get through the day, what would you do with your fingers and what would be your coping mechanism? And if you answered "alcohol I suppose", then take alcohol off the planet and what's left to use to help you cope with stress, or for any reason you choose to poison your body with nicotine? Would you turn to more drugs, cannabis, cocaine, or heroin maybe? Again, are you one of the many billions on this planet who has to be **addicted** to a **substance** in order to cope with real life?

Most of us are aware of the Amish people, the age old people in America, who live in very simple conditions in their own communities and without interference from the outside world. They work side by side as a large family unit to build homes, shelters, crops and farms to feed and house their own people as independently as possible. If the stress of a construction project becomes too much or if the crops fail or some elderly member of the community dies, can you see brother Jebidiah reaching for a **cancer stick** or found fast asleep on the porch with an empty bottle of whiskey in his hand? No, and why do you think this is? After all, he is a human being, just like you. He has emotions just like you, he feels pain, he suffers, feels sorrow, he celebrates joyous occasions also, so what is it about your lifestyle that sets you both apart? Why does he get on with acceptance after maybe finding peace in his holy book without turning to **a chemical substance,** whereas you feel the need to **inhale 4000 poisonous chemicals** to help you cope? And if you still haven't latched onto the fact that you are a **self-harmer** yet, then remember this; every day since you became **addicted** to **inhaling poison,** you have **harmed** every single part of your body inside and out, with over **4000 poisonous chemicals** at regular intervals and on a daily basis. The majority of this harm cannot be seen because the **sticky tar and chemicals you inhale** leave their mark in the **damage done** to every cell, **artery**, **capillary** and **organ of your body.** Some of the minor damage can be seen on your **yellow teeth, sagging skin,** and **weak thin hair** and if this is an indicator of what is visible on the outside, you must fully acknowledge at this stage the **damage** and **harm** you are causing to your insides.

It only takes two people, both the same age, one a **smoker** of **4000 poisonous chemicals** and one who **doesn't depend on poisons to cope,** in order to truly see **the harm that this shit does** with its **deadly harmful effects.** If both people stand side by side you will immediately be able to tell who is **a smoker** of **this poison** and who is not. You will see the **difference in the skin, hair, teeth,** and **nails** and see the **full effect of the damage caused to the outside of the smoker's body. The skin will look like shit,** **wrinkled** years before its time, and the **teeth and gums** can only take bleaching so many times before **bleeding gums** cause massive problems and will take no more. You still choose to use **bullshit excuses** all the time as to why you can't **quit the shit** even though you know in your own **tar filled heart** of hearts that **your poisonous addiction** is causing **not only self-harm,** but releasing **poisonous chemicals** which interact with your brains chemicals and function, by tricking you into believing you get a rush, and yet you still continue to purchase these **shitty, horrible** and **disgusting killers of human life.** When someone uses the expression which **many addicts** do saying "so what's the problem, the only person **I'm harming** is **myself?",** they fail to actually stop and listen to what they have actually just said, which is an acknowledgement of **self-harm,** is it not?

Think on this deeply for a moment. If we had a visit from another planet by an alien who decided to come here for a day trip and he stopped to ask a smoker what was this strange custom or contraption he or she put to their mouth, I'm sure the visitor would have a great story to tell about humanity on earth when he returned to his home planet. He would tell his alien friends that he asked this earthling what they were doing. The human explained to the alien that they were "having a smoke". The alien asked, "But, I thought humans were supposed to **breathe in air to survive?"** to which the human replied "Ah sure, the **only one I'm harming** is myself". This expression to me, never mind a visitor from another planet is fucked up and still accepted as a normal answer to a question about **harming** or **killing yourself** in today's societies. It is a **moronic** and **idiotic** answer used by far too many **idiots** the world over. It is as blatant to me as someone saying **"I am a self-harmer** and **I don't care about myself"**. Anyone who admits they are **self-harming** without putting the full extent of thought into what they are actually admitting to, should reconsider the choices they make in regards to how they treat their bodies. There is zero thought gone into this statement and although the statement itself may be **a bullshit** one to make, the content of the statement in regards to **harming the self**, is very **far from bullshit**. I see no difference as I've said from the person who uses **self-inflicted harm** (with a blade), as a release or as a rush and the person who uses **self-inflicted harm** (with poisonous chemicals) as a release or as a rush, as you can see, they both do the same thing. I believe that mental health plays a large part in both conditions. It has been established that mental health already is widely accepted in the case of stereotypical self-harming, but I firmly believe that an association between the mental health of a smoker and self-harming is on the way. Hitting your fingers with a hammer can get you signed in to an institution but blackening your lungs with poisons is accepted?? I see problems with this people.

The only difference it seems in society is that one is accepted while the other is deemed as unacceptable or requiring the help of a psychiatrist. Money talks and bullshit walks and so long as **you continue to pump your hard earned money into the pockets of the billion dollar poisonous tobacco companies pockets,** the bullshit will continue to walk. The simple truth is that if you continue to use the ups and downs of life as **feeble excuse** after **excuse** as to why you continue to fail at **inhaling poisonous chemicals** then be prepared to listen to this; life as glorious as it is, will constantly throw you ups and downs regardless of what part of the world you occupy. There will always be a death, a wedding, a birth, a break up, a 21st birthday party, a hen or stag do, bingo, work, stress, strains, bills, bankers and wankers! It is what it is. There is always going to be an event of some sort, be it good or bad, a trauma, a tribulation or any reason that makes you want to escape, let your hair down, or to just feel different. Every day most of us are taken outside of our comfort zones and it doesn't take me to explain any of this shit to you as you are already the expert on you. What sets those who decide they truly need to change apart from those who think they do, is that they are two entirely different individuals when it comes to **self-awareness** and focusing their **mind-sets**. You have a choice at deciding which of these individuals you wish to be, either one who talks about it or one who acts on it. Those who decide to talk about it will continue to do so even as they **waffle on about regrets** from their **premature death bed,** whereas those who act on it have already decided to **stop self-harming.** They will want to reinvent their lives and will use everything in their being to stick with it and to see it out fully, to reach the **new health** that awaits them. This is what separates the **strong** from the **weak** and those who are **sick of smoking shit**, from those who continue to **speak bullshit.** You can be any of the two. A person who stands by their word or a bullshitter. Your life is at stake. Choose wisely.

SMOKE AND MIRRORS.

This is a metaphor often used to explain a deceptive, fraudulent or insubstantial explanation or description. It is something that **distorts the truth**. Magicians often use mirrors to make something appear and **smoke** to make it is disappear in stage shows to wow the audience into believing the impossible is in fact very possible. The key word in all of this is **deception** and **deception** as we know or to **deceive a person** is to **hoodwink** somebody. Nobody likes to be **deceived** by somebody, especially if it is by someone they know. Nobody wants to be **hoodwinked** because it makes us feel **silly** or **foolish**, having fell for something that we trusted. It may be fine when **deception** is used by the magician to trick your mind into believing the illogical was logical, (this is after all harmless entertainment), but what if **smoke** and mirrors is used as a way to cover something **so sinister**, it is probably responsible for **every health issue you will ever face?** And what if I was to tell you, that the **deception** I speak of comes to you not as a stranger or even that of the **poisonous tobacco companies**, but is even closer to home than you may think. This person is **hoodwinking you** every hour of every day of every year and doesn't feel the need to stop whispering its poison into your ear. This person who you feel you can trust has left you down since the first **cancer stick** you lit and put to your lips and knows you better than anyone. That person (in case you haven't already guessed), **that deceiver**, the one who is **hoodwinking** you all the time is **you.**

You see, the odd **cancer stick** you played around with, that took on the form of a **nasty habit** and is now a **full blown filthy disgusting addiction** is all **you,** started by **you. It** now forces **you** into a false sense of security and what **you** now believe to be a coping mechanism for life's ups and downs. In actual fact, it is nothing but a **filthy disgusting addiction that is very far removed from what your body was born for and designed to do.** For years now as previously described, humanity has blamed several reasons for **inhaling poisonous toxic chemicals**. Take your pick, past time, hobby, stress, worry, peer pressure, social status, **addiction**, comfort, **ignorance, stupidity** or simply just not giving a fuck, the list is endless. What you will not find is someone who **inhales this poisonous shit** for health benefits or for **longevity of life.** Although we could go on about our worlds governments and the billions of dollars made per year from **pedalling their poisonous products**, they (the tobacco companies) have for the last number of years, followed the strict government laws (of each country they sell their **cancer sticks in),** and adhered to the laws set in place stating that writing and warnings, sometimes images must be available in print or picture in plain view on the box of **every pack of cancer sticks.**

Slogans such as **"smoking can cause a slow and painful death"** or **"smoking kills"** are now accompanied by **graphic images** (such as the image of **Bryan Curtis** inside this book) which show those who decided to **inhale this poisonous shit** instead of air, and **the damage caused to every organ of the body** with images of **cancerous lumps, amputations** and bodies laid out blue on a **mortuary slab**. 100 years ago, **smoking this filthy shit** was actually believed to have medicinal purposes with some doctors recommending it for asthma. As discussed earlier, only 50 years ago, it was marketed as being sexy. Today it is known and seen to be **dangerous, disgusting and deadly** to those who partake **in its misery**. I would love to point the full finger of blame at the **merchants of death**, the tobacco companies that supply **the poisons,** but what can I really say? They have played their part, in so far as playing by the rules to warn the users of their **poisons** worldwide of the deadly side effects of its **poisonous products**. They are abiding by the laws of the land and the rules of distribution and sale as set out by the world's governments as already stated. These companies, some will argue, employ many people worldwide and **the foolish addict** will say "how many people would lose their jobs if I gave up my **addiction to nicotine"**. This is a perfect example of your mind and your body **using smoke** and mirrors to **hoodwink you**. It is a **feeble and ridiculous attempt to lie to yourself** (which again, you cannot do!), and inside, you instinctively know this already. If we lived in a perfect world where people stopped using violence against one another, the gun makers and the bomb maker's would also be out of work but might quickly find jobs rebuilding the streets, cities, towns, and lives they have destroyed and work together to build a future for humanity instead of blowing it apart with weapons of mass destruction.

This sadly is not the world we live in, but we can be aware of our health to ensure life goes that bit easier. Those who are aware of the importance of **looking after** the bodies we possess and what's needed to maintain them as they were designed to be used, are already on that **level of awareness**. Smoke and mirrors is not used by these individuals. They won't **inhale poisonous chemicals** on purpose because they know the voice inside says **"don't do that to me, I need air, not poisonous nicotine"**. Because **addiction** has such a grip on those who require **nicotine** and its **chemical poisonous** buddies (**such as the other 3999 toxins**) it is worth looking at what it is in this big bad world that triggers you to place a **cancer stick** in your mouth. Only by reviewing the life/death of someone who has battled **a smoking related illness** or **succumbed to a smoking related cancer** can we analyse this respectfully. Again, the chances are that nearly every one of you will be aware of somebody who has gone through a **physical trauma or death** caused directly by **this filthy drug**. Look at that same person who has **lost their health or their life** and think about what you both have in common. What makes them different than you? What is it in your mentality that makes you think that **the suffering** they encountered does not await you? Did they also believe they were impenetrable when it came to **their illness or terminal diagnosis?** Did they plan on a **sudden heart attack** when they left their family that morning to go to work for the last time? Did they also play the **smoke** and mirrors game? Did they try to lie to themselves and convince themselves that what they were doing to their bodies was **just a habit** and that they would stop after Christmas, or after that wedding, or whatever other **bullshit excuse** they kept feeding themselves?

We said in our last chapter that you can feed yourself all the **bullshit excuses** you want because if and when (**and it is only a matter of time**), you get the **dreaded news** or **that sharp stabbing pain** that paralyses you before you **fall helplessly to the ground.** Only then will you realise (and for some, sadly far too late), that **you have been talking shit to yourself** for all these years and attempting to pull the wool over your own eyes. If you had listened to your body instead of covering it up with **excuse** after **excuse** as to the many reasons you felt you had to **poison your body**, then you may not have had **to suffer like this,** or had to explain to your family that you are going on **a permanent holiday.** There are those of you who will choose to use words such as casual use or light or social in an attempt to **hoodwink** yourself that you have a handle on your **intake of poison,** thus only advertising to others **on behalf of the poisonous tobacco companies.** These same people choose to **turn a blind eye** to facts and the facts are hard for these people to comprehend, even when these facts are presented at every opportunity to warn of the **dangers they represent**. For you to say, either to yourself or someone who questions **your addictions to poisonous addictions** "it's ok, I only smoke lights" or "occasionally" (or whatever is the equivalent of listening to an **addict** waffle on about how they have a handle on it), when asked about **their addiction to a poisonous drug. This is** smoke and mirrors at play. You can fool some people sometime, but you can't fool all the people all the time! How many times have you either heard or used the expression "a **sneaky cigarette**" or "a **sneaky smoke**", "I'll be back in five minutes, I'm just running out for a **sneaky smoke**". This expression is used when a person is doing something they know they **shouldn't be doing** because it's either forbidden or because they know **instinctively** that what they're doing is wrong.

Have you ever heard someone using the expression "I'll be back in five minutes I'm just running out for a sneaky glass of water or "a sneaky apple?" The reason being... that doing something that's considered right by the body is not considered sneaky whereas **polluting the body with poisonous chemicals is considered dirty,** wrong or sneaky and something that must be done slyly as its forbidden. I once saw small little miniature bottles of whiskey in a liquor store which read, "A sneaky little gem to straighten you out before you head into the office" Because it was a blatant attempt to market something that should not be done (such as drinking before going into the workplace) it was marked as sneaky. The idea of **smoke** and mirrors being used, whether by yourself to try and **"fool yourself"** or by the **poisonous tobacco merchants of death,** it still has all the elements of sneakiness no matter what way you look at it. Deception, lies and sneakiness, three negative aspects that accompany any form of **addiction.** The person **who is addicted**, be it food, alcohol, sex, gambling, drugs, or **poisonous nicotine**, will use all three, **deception,** lies and sneakiness as the tools of their trade to keep themselves in plentiful supply of the very thing that's doing them **more harm** than good. When it gets to the stage that the person is using all three on themselves and they start to **believe their own bullshit,** it is then that they are being lulled into a false belief that they are now at the point of no return. How do they do this you may ask?

Well, if you are one of these **type of addicts,** you will also know that as someone with an **addiction to poisonous nicotine**, you may have made an announcement at one point to everyone you know, or placed a bet with someone (who shares the same **filthy disgusting addiction** as you) that you are "finished, done", never to **pollute your body** ever again, and that you can't believe that you "ever started in the first place". Now, if whilst making this statement, you are already getting cravings and planning your next **toxic inhalation**, you were without maybe even realising it, pulling the wool over your own eyes. Your statement or intention may have seemed heartfelt, but by sticking with this word heartfelt, your own heart felt no emotions in your words whatsoever and is sadly at this stage well used to your empty promises. The truth can be seen here by the number of failed declarations you have made in the past and the number of times you're long suffering body has said **"yeah, I've heard it all before".** You truly are **fooling no one but yourself** if you resort to anything that goes against **being kind to your body** because it is you, who will **suffer the consequences** of your actions in the long run.

When you have reached the stage where **enough is truly enough** you will know and you will know for the following reasons. There will be no more lies and no more **deception.** You won't look at yourself as a dishonest person anymore in regards to a **bullshit excuse** or any **excuse** that you would have used in order to light up in the past. The words **"no thanks"** will become easier as time goes on and will be **heartfelt** when spoken. And please bear this in mind. As it stands today, the **poisonous addiction** you depend on **is killing millions of people** and will be responsible for the **deaths of billions worldwide** by the end of this century, if it is not extinguished for good. This is not fiction but fact. More people **globally have died in the last 200 years** than have **died** in both world wars. This number is rising every day and you are very possibly one of the **statistics** it claims in the future even as you read this.

We cannot allow ourselves in today's society to try for one moment blame ignorance to the dangers. If we try to **hoodwink** ourselves then it is only ourselves we have to blame because **our ignorance** takes on a completely different meaning. This is when those who **continue to poison themselves** do so because they choose to be ignorant. It's not because of **uneducated ignorance**; it's the "I don't really give a fuck" **ignorance** that is responsible for many of the **health problems** faced by the same people. It is only when a negative health aspect of this kind of **ignorance** affects them that the same "I don't really give a fuck" types of people start to give a fuck. There is nothing like being told by your doctor to "please sit down" to sadly hear the results of that **chest pain** that won't go away, or the cold you keep **getting on your lungs** to grab your attention and make you listen. If none of what you see in the papers, read on the internet, or watched on the television affects your frame of mind, then the chances are; that your brain cells are not incorporating your **health**, **vitality** and **mortality** in the equation where your bleak future is concerned. Ask yourself this, should I take a chance, **a 1 in 2 chance**, of a **heart attack, stroke,** or **cancer by poisoning my body?** Yes or no? Should I drink and drive? Should I **ingest rat poison**? Should I jump off this cliff? **No, No** and **No** is the obvious answer to all of the above and why is this? It's because of these **will lead to serious injury, death** or both and this of course includes **inhaling 4000 poisonous chemicals** on a regular daily basis.

Don't allow yourself to try bullshit yourself any further by allowing nicotine to control **your mind** and your **body**. Don't allow **ridiculous excuses** be responsible as to the reasons why you force your body to be **subjected to constant sickness** through **daily poisonous torture**. If you allow something as simple as a friend's birthday party as **an excuse to inhale shit**, then you are once again allowing **hoodwinking** take place by using a celebration of a friend's birthday as an excuse or **a reason to kill yourself with 4000 chemicals.** These **fraudulent circumstances** or **life's occurrences** (which you use to allow to make it ok **to inhale shit in your** foolish **addicted thought pattern**), will always be around and will always make it ok in your warped sense of fairness or entitlement/enjoyment as you see it, to inflict damage on your long suffering body. Even when you stop inhaling this shit there is still smoke and mirrors working hard to deceive. **Smoke** and mirrors are at play when you walk into a cloud of **toxic smoke;** where those around you are partaking in their **poisonous puff,** and making you feel unwelcome because you have made a choice that **you want to live** and have decided **not to partake.** When peer pressure or passive smoke attempts to bring you back with its stench or aroma to what you imagine to be a happy place, it is then, **smoke** and mirrors and its fakery is trying to work its dirty magic on you. If you allow yourself to give into peer pressure, then you have allowed **smoke** and mirrors to seduce you again into the one thing you are guaranteed to regret before **you meet your earthly demise**. You have allowed yourself to **distort the truth** in order for you to make **your addiction to poison** seem ok to use.

You will not be able to blame a insubstantial explanation or description anymore, because you have more than enough information about the **hazards** and **dangers** of what you are doing to yourself. If those you surround yourself with are being fooled or are allowing themselves to use **smoke** and mirrors to continue to **poison themselves** or even those around them, then don't be afraid to educate them on what you have learned yourself. **Your addiction to poisonous chemicals is killing every cell in your body** and **poisoning every part of your very being** and that's the **cold hard reality** or factual truth of the situation. Only a **fool**, an **idiot**, will as of today allow themselves to be told or to think differently. No more **deceit** and no more **hoodwinking**. Time to call a spade a spade. Never mind casual or social **smoking shit** by **breathing in poisonous light cancer sticks** or mint flavoured menthol **filth** or any other garbage that is thrown at you to make **this addiction** seem as though its ok to **inhale deeply into your lungs**. Don't allow any more **deception** to **hoodwink** you and **steal precious years** of **your life away from your family** and from yourselves. Take a stand. **Be honest** with yourself and with others. **Call your addiction out.** Call it what it is, **an addiction**. It is not a **dirty habit** in the same way as we might view throwing a used tea bag into the sink instead of the bin as a dirty habit. It's **a filthy disgusting addiction** that has for far too long now **controlled your body and your mind, but no more.** Be true to **yourself and your body.** Allow your declaration to gain control of your life be a bold statement filled with promise, meaning and truth. Move forward **without deceit.** No more **smoke** and mirrors, only fresh air and blue skies. This sounds, smells and tastes better. There is nothing dishonest about **fresh air** and blue skies until they become dangerously clouded with smoke and mirrors.

A FRIEND IN NEED AND AN ENEMY INDEED.

How many of you reading this has a true friend? What is it that qualifies a true friend? For me, the qualities of a true friend is a person who can read you like the alphabet, is aware of the joys in your life, is there in your darkest hour and has undying loyalty no matter the weather. Some people may be lucky to have many true friends while others may only have the one. A true friend can be your childhood friend, your partner, husband, wife, sister, brother or even your faithful Jack Russell dog! We may even depend on this true friend more often than we think and them on us, in this pairing of loyalty for loyalty. So where does nicotine come into this you may ask? Well…if the one you depend on in your time of need to comfort and reassure you, comes in the form of **a poisonous cancerous filtered piece of paper**, you already begin to realise that this friend comes bearing false gifts and is actually foe in disguise. This false friend has brought with it an agenda, a false loyalty. Its **intentions are harmful** and although you might think that you find their company reassuring, it is only because **you have been tricked** by this friend you trusted; using **a poisonous mind trick** called **addiction** with **nicotine** as its weapon. This is the friend who will stab you in the back and whose only indulgences it cares about are its own. They have been sent to you by the **poisonous tobacco companies** whose banks accounts you have been filling since you first allowed you're so called friends **poison into your lungs**. This friend in need is in actual fact **your worst enemy** and **unfortunately** for some, this only becomes clear when time is no longer on their side. Usually it finally reveals its true identity as **a black spot on the lung of a chest x-ray** or in the form of the words spoken as **"very bad news"** by your doctor.

Now when you turn to this friend for support financially, to **ask for a loan to pay for treatment**, you'll get no response, but they will always be good for a dose of **the poisonous shit** that put you in this position in the first place, as there is no shortage there. Now that **you are in distress**, a time that you need someone to count on, this **poisonous sneaky little shit** taps you on the shoulder sensing that you feel **under pressure** and could use a cruel crutch to help carry **your injured body**. Instead of offering help or coming to you like **a breath of fresh air**, it allows you to **inhale 4000 poisonous chemicals**. As we've already stated, **these chemicals are used to execute people** in **gas chambers** and **with lethal injections**. Your false friend is with you in all of the events throughout your life, including **the first time you inhaled this poisonous shit** right up until **you take your last breath, many years before your** time. Whether or not you like it, your friend will more than likely be responsible for **every health issue** you've ever had. It has in fact contributed somehow to **the unhealthiest** you've ever been in life. This friend, as well as **giving you cancer** would actually follow you up to **your dying bed** to **get into your lungs with your last breath** if it wasn't for the hospitals "no smoking" policies. This is because; just like **the poisonous tobacco companies** you're so called friend works for, it is absolutely **ruthless**.

Once, on my travels, I came across a meeting with a known drug dealer and asked him "why do you sell that shit to kids, **you're poisoning people** around here and ruining their lives". These were people he had grown up around on the street and many of them would have seen him as a friend. He told me very bluntly that **"if animals want to be fed, then I'll feed them**. That's all I do, is **feed the animals"**. I now realise that although I didn't agree with his lifestyle and what he was doing, it was quite apparent from a business or money perspective, that this drug dealer had seen a gap in the market that he believed needed to be filled and he was filling it. Drug addicts wanted drugs and a drug dealer was supplying them with the drug they demanded, and that's how easy this transaction took place. For as long as there is **demand** there will be **supply**. If the demand for a product stops, the supplier is out of business. This piece of shit treated his customers as if they were his best friend when he was really only laughing at what he saw as their **stupidity** and becoming **rich off their misery and suffering**. On a much larger scale this is what the **cancer stick companies** are doing every day, and have done for well over a hundred years now. The man who sells **dope** is committing a crime by **spreading his misery** in an illegal fashion and will be penalised by a custodial sentence if caught. He takes **his products** and he passes it around the towns and cities **addicts**, be it crack, cocaine, heroin and he allows those with dependency issues (regardless of age, race, or background) try out **his products** at vulnerable episodes of their lives, until they **become familiar with the drug**. This drug when used again, brings **a false comfort** that starts with **casual use** and quickly develops into **habit** and that habit as we know turns to **dependency** and eventually turns to **addiction** in a very short period of time. The dealer now has **the hook** stuck firmly in. He has his customer base and it will be extremely hard for the addict to pull this **addictive hook** back out and walk away from the substance that the dealer **now has them hooked on**. Not all of **his customers** are going to have happy endings and many of them because of their **addiction** are quickly going to see changes in regard to **their health.** Some will come from the poorest of a pauper's background and others will be princes of kings but that doesn't matter to **the dealer** as long as they both use the same cash to buy the **same addictive substance.** When some of **these addicts meet an early demise,** this is no skin off the dealers nose because for every **addict** that goes **6 foot under the clay**, there's another **young addict** needing a drug to deal with real life, lining up to **take the dead addicts place**. When the dealer is finally jailed (as is often the inevitable outcome in **this horrible trade**), his shoes will also be filled by the next street dealer who sees the **demand** he needs to **supply.** He now has the task of **"feeding the animals"** and such is the life of narcotics and **drug addiction.**

The only difference between the common **drug pusher** or street hoodlum, and the owners of **the poisonous tobacco companies** is this; one is selling his drugs legally and the other illegally. Again, ridiculous social acceptance. But again this is the only difference. Both sell drugs that are **poisonous** and **deadly dangerous** to a person who is **addicted** to such a **shitty product** and both have **customers** who become **agitated** if they go for a short period of time without their **addictive poisonous** fix. **Death, pain, suffering** and **misery** are spread by both. In an ideal society or in a perfect world, both would be frowned upon, outlawed, illegal but the world we live in as we know is far from perfect or ideal. Again, we sadly continue to have a warped view in our society of what we deem to be normal or acceptable. I am not, I should point out yet again, trying to draw comparisons with a crack addict who sells her body to feed her **addiction,** but merely the comparisons between the need to feed the **cravings** to a **poisonous chemical** the addicts have to pay to use. What I'm saying is that just like the person **hooked on drugs**, you too are **an addict** and just **like the addict**, you need **your fix** to get through the day. **Your dealer,** also a **dealer in death** can also be found in various street corners, be it vending machines, garages, supermarkets or corner shops and just like the **junkies fix,** is good to go into your hand at any time during the day or night once you have the **hard earned cash** to pay for it. The junkie's hands shake when they've been kept away from **their addictive poison** or made to wait around for it. How often have your own hands shook in anticipation whilst tearing the plastic film from a **pack of cancer sticks?** How often has your mood been altered when you've had to go longer than an hour **without a smoke** or when **you've made a serious attempt to quit?**

When we look at **addictive substances,** we understand the grip it can take on a person's existence and how it controls everything they do. Cocaine, for example, **a highly addictive substance** is shipped across the world from countries like Columbia or heroin from Afghanistan and deployed across every country in the world. Again, not possible to supply **such poisonous shit** if there is **no demand**. This is how peddlers of any **poisonous substance** including **nicotine** make their money; from **repeat prescriptions of the helpless addict.** Any **addiction** works in this **supply** and **demand** and it all boils down to **the**

dealer understanding that he has **the hook stuck in** you and that you now pay a **daily subscription**. Money for them, **misery for you**, it's that simple. Our entire planet uses this model of economics for much of its barter and trade and again it's quite simple to understand; I provide a service and you pay me for that service. If that service like the drug trade is illegal, then it's going to be that bit more difficult to do business, but the drugs trade is still a billion dollar industry because money talks and **demand** is high. If that service is legal like the **nicotine** trade, then business is booming, with **addicts** being born into and **dying** from **addiction** every day. Again one trade is acceptable to society and one is deemed unacceptable. Globally, narcotics are unaccepted because of **the misery, pain, suffering** and **death** it carries with it. There is not one single positive outcome or event for an individual who has become **addicted** to a drug such as crack cocaine or heroin. Who can we blame for **this misery**, for **this addiction?** Do we blame the poppy field farmer in Afghanistan for harvesting his crop or the workers who take his harvest and turn it into a **poisonous addictive substance?** Is the small time drug dealer who struggles to make ends meet to blame, or can we blame the governments for not doing enough to keep this **filthy poison** off the streets? Does the **blame of addiction** fall at the feet of **the addict**, remember **"the animals need to be fed"**, or has society failed the **addict** by allowing them to become **addicted** in the first place?

I hold addiction to any substance, cocaine, heroin or nicotine, solely on the person who keeps the demand alive. The expression that **money talks** and **bullshit walks** is perfect in describing the entire **poisonous tobacco industry**. Usually though with addiction, it is your money that walks. Cash is king in the world we live in and as long as the **poisoned addict** keeps feeding themselves **lies** and **excuses** as to not doing themselves "real damage" or such bullshit as "I'll quit the week after the week after", then your money will walk and their **bullshit** will talk. The tobacco company's owners for far too long now have been **laughing all the way to the bank** and **living off the misery** of the billions of people who have spent their **hard earned money** on their **poisonous product**, (some before they buy food) and continue in doing so. These same **merchants of misery or dealers in death**, cannot believe how lucky they have been (even when the governments of the world have intervened by making images such as **Bryan Curtis's dying** photo available on the front of these **poisonous packs**), and that people are **still stupid** and **ignorant** enough to allow these **disgusting tobacco companies** excel in their annual sales every year. The companies are scratching their heads laughing and must be saying to themselves "either we are extremely lucky or **these addicts are really stupid"**. The tobacco companies have abided by the laws and have said to **the worlds addicts** "ok, look, fair enough, we give in, have a look, this is **what our prod-**

uct contains and this is what it will do to you, **your children, your lungs, your heart, your skin, your body, your unborn child.**" And it is ignored! They turn to the governments of the world and say "well, we told them, we showed them, we did what you asked, what more can we do?" To which the governments whose taxing of these companies comes to billions per annum say "well, you did your best, that's all for now". Money talk's folks, remember this. We live in a time where this "greed is good" concept seems to be the way **forward in life** and "health is wealth" seems to be an expression not properly understood or practised. I remember reading an old Cree Indian expression which states "only when the last tree has died, the last of the fruit has withered and the last river runs dry, will man realise that we cannot eat money". Again health is wealth seems to come second, with fragility of the body forgotten over the dollar and we wonder why the majority of people on the planet struggle to cope with stress..

Sometimes when a person is **agitated**, nervous or feeling a bit overwhelmed, light headed, or faint, a stranger, friend, workmate or doctor may offer the person a glass of water to calm them down or to ease their anxiety. A glass of water will hydrate the person on edge and a person's body will react with **a pleasant acceptance** which soothes the nervousness of the person as it has long been **a natural remedy** to any **discomfort the body feels** when calm needs to be restored. **The body reacts this way** because its **nature working in harmony with nature.** Our bodies which are made up mostly of water require this element of the earth for **survival.** Men and women can and have **survived** without food for months at a time, but we can only survive a couple of days without drinking water (or fluids containing water). Now to offer a person who is anxious or nervous a **poisonous chemical laced cancer stick** to help calm them down or soothe their woes, is not a kind act or an act of friendship. What you consider to be a friendly gesture has just pitted **nature** against something so **unnatural that it is designed to kill, poison and nothing else.** What you see as a kind gesture is a foolish one and will send your friends body into overdrive to help it cope with the **thousands of poisonous chemicals** it now **struggles to endure.** This is far from a friendly gesture or an act of kindness. A true friend will never do anything that they know will amount to **the suffering, pain or death** of another friend. An enemy however will specialise in it. Because of this, we should never allow ourselves to get caught up in the false thought pattern that a person or persons needs **inhaling poisonous shit in their lungs or bloodstream** in order to cope. It is the other way around and it's **this poison that needs them.** Read that again; smoking needs them, does this make sense? If not, keep reading until it does.

If we tried to look at it this way, if every person on the planet who is **addicted to**

this poisonous shit for whatever their reason decided tomorrow that **enough is enough, no more poisonous shitty nicotine in our bodies**, where would that leave the tobacco companies? What would they do with **the millions of gallons of chemical poisons** they have purchased to use in **their deadly addictive products**? Would they sell these **poisons** back to **the chemical factories** and laboratories where they were made? Would they sell these **poisons** to those who would actually use them for what they were designed to do, such as the **manufacturers of bleach, cleaning fluids and fertilizers**? Would you even care now that **you are free from being one of the slaves of their addictive poisons**? No, you would not, and the reason is that for the first time since **you became an addict**, you would **feel the freedom, health** you were born with and even the wealth, that you were up until this point **spending on poisonous addictive shit**. You would begin to see **how foolish** you have been by treating **this poisonous chemical** like a friend in need when it truly is **an enemy** indeed. You will soon begin to realise that you have never needed **this poison** to cope or to **survive** in the first place and that it is the other way around and that it is **this poison** that depended on you to survive and to thrive. **Its poisonous business depends on you** and on **every other addict** it has coerced to keep its bank balance overflowing with **your hard earned cash**. You will see how ironic the word **survival** is in all of this because in order for the tobacco companies to survive they have to **take an addicts health and eventually life**.

The irony is that the **survival** of **the addict** is at stake to allow the **survival of the poisonous tobacco companies** and **the addict fails** to acknowledge this **grave reality**. They want you to **live for as long as possible** while **poisoning you're airways** even though **you're survival rate is greatly diminished with every single drag of poisonous shit**. They warn what **damage their product does to your body** and your health and **how they are killing you**, yet **you refuse to take notice**. These companies also realise that their **unevolved clientele** are **dropping like flies** because of all manner of **biological catastrophic injuries, diseases** and **deaths** due to the **small boxes of misery they produce** which some see as more important than air, and this makes no difference to them because as was already stated, "if the animals want to be fed". If a person feels **that a cancer stick** is the one comfort they have left in **their life**, then they need to **have a serious think about their mental health**. If your **dependence on a cancer causing addiction** is all you have to look forward to, then there are **several wrong roads** you have taken in **your life** and you must try to understand that there is nothing right about **using a statement where poison is all you live for in life**. This just isn't right **in any walk of life**, no matter how you've lived up until this point. The person who sees **a cancer stick** as their only friend in a time of need or as a thing of comfort, **has gone wrong** somewhere and needs to get their life back on track. It is **sad** to think that someone may see a **1 in 2 chance of a cancerous disease** or **premature death** as the only alternative to coping in their life. **To think in this way is to think very lowly of yourself.** You are missing the point of what **we as humans were designed for, and that is to live and to breathe.** There is so **much more in life** that you have to **look forward to** if you cleared **the smoke of this poisonous shit** out of your eyes and out of your body. The false relationship you feel **you can't live** without has kept you **bound with illness** for too long. Your enemy is staring you straight in the face. All you have to do is to look into a mirror and ask yourself **whether you want to live healthy or die of an avoidable cancer or disease**. If you sit back down and light up, you have just made **a fatal error** quite literally. If you have decided you want to **change your life** and do what you were **designed to do, which again is to live and breathe**, then please read on…..

WHO OR WHAT THE FUCK IS WILLPOWER?

The first misconception about **Willpower** is that someone will usually choose to remark that it doesn't exist, they don't have it or that they have very little of it, if it does exist. The very reading of this book is definitive proof that it exists in the person who has chosen to read it. Reading **takes Willpower** for some of us. The fact that you are **breathing and alive**, is also proof of this somewhat elusive **Willpower** and shows that it's actually **much stronger** than you are giving it credit for. I spoke at the start of this book of how the race for sperm to reach an egg at the time of conception involves 300 million other contestants. Well you and I, and anyone else who is walking, crawling, sitting or standing were the victors in this gruelling marathon for the top prize of a fertile egg. You did not trip over and fall into that egg, you competed for it and in competing for it you raced and won the equivalent of a grown human being swimming **4000 miles** or **6500 kilometres** in one day. It would take a jumbo jet **8 hours** to do this so to even doubt yourself and your ability in **Willpower** is to underestimate a person who is **more capable** than you **give yourself credit** for. **Faith in the self** is required to do anything in this life and it only diminishes if you allow it to happen. Some like to refer to **Willpower** as the human spirit and maybe that's what it is. All I can tell you is that I personally know it to be something **very real** and once summoned; can **push you forward** in ways and with **strengths** which you didn't imagine to be possible. It is a part of who we are and is as real as what you see when you look into the mirror. It doesn't go when you get older or all grown up and is always there whenever a person makes **a conscious decision** to do something in life and to stick with it, (this time for good). This isn't some Peter Pan, live forever, magical fairy, wizardry, motivational bullshit pep talk... it simply is what it is.

I only began to realise this myself after many failed attempts to **conquer addiction**. I eventually discovered that to acknowledge to either myself or to somebody else, that I had absolutely no **Willpower** was **nicotine's** way of **whispering poisonous lies** into my ear, lungs, throat or any other organ I allowed it to. There is a huge difference between "I might give them up next week", "**I will give them up tomorrow**" and "**I will give these up now**". Which one sounds as though it's spoken with **Willpowers** back up? When I, on numerous occasions said to myself or others that "I have made a **decision to give them up** next Monday", I knew like many of you that really, in my heart of **poisoned**

hearts, my statement was one of lack or that there was as much sincerity in my statement as a politicians speech. When I finally came to my senses (this by the way, took many years because of **my bullshit excuses**) and **made a conscious decision** and a statement to myself, (and not to anyone else) by saying **"I will give these up now"**, not tomorrow but now because "I'm **sick of feeling like shit all the time"**. Only then, did I fuck the **box of cancer** as far away from me as I could. Now at this point, I want to reiterate; that this most certainly wasn't the last time I thought about **my cancerous poison** or that I didn't pine for it, because I did as soon as the box hit the ground, but it was **Willpower** that gave me **the strength** to do so, and was there from this moment on to make sure I never reached for a box again. This was a very important lesson for me in the existence and the **strength of Willpower** and showed me how real **this inner strength** actually is. This inner **strength or power** can be mighty or weak (depending on how it's harnessed) and it is the individual who controls it by one of two things, either love or hate. You must begin to **love your life** and begin to hate the idea of losing it and to realise and reinforce the truth, that this could very easily be a reality **if you continue poisoning yourself.**

Like many of you, in my previous attempts to **quit the shit;** the reason I found that I kept going back for a bite of the **poisonous** apple was that I was confused, **poisoned by addictive chemicals** and not educated enough on the reality of what can be achieved by harnessing or summoning the **inner strength** which I now understand is as powerful and **as real as the heart and lungs** that **keep us alive. Willpower** is present all the time and it is not a matter of you climbing a mountain to shout for it or clicking your sparkly red heels together and making a wish. You do however; need to learn how to **summon it** in order to see it working to its full capacity. If you are still at this point experiencing difficulty in understanding or failing completely to understand how a person can **harness, summon** and use **Willpower,** then here are a few simple examples of it being used on a daily basis. Little tasks such as when you hear "Cut that fucking grass" and stop talking about it…takes **Willpower.** You may not want to, but you do it anyway. Holding your temper takes inner strength. Going to a gym and not buying the chocolate you crave or not eating that piece of cake whilst on that diet all take **Willpower.** Keeping our mouths shut and our opinions to ourselves or biting your tongue in certain circumstances takes **Willpower** whereas allowing our opinions be known or to voice our concerns (or for some), a talk, a lecture or speech, also takes **Willpower.** Pushing yourself that extra mile, going the distance as they say or going that little bit extra for somebody else is another example of **Willpower.** When you say you will do something and see it through, this all takes **Willpower.** I bet that every one of you can relate to this

To have your **Willpower** (the inner strength we are all born with), work for you, there can be absolutely no doubt, not a single moment when you can even consider or use the words "I think I'll just have the one". When you start to play around with this thought, you haven't implemented the full use of your **Willpower**. It means that you have only scratched the surface of its potential, and that means you haven't even allowed **Willpower** to play a part in your game plan. **Willpower** must be used and not talked about and this is very important. Your game plan should be to live, to breathe fresh air by whatever means necessary. You will have your moment of absolute clarity at a stage when you least expect it; and will realise that to breathe air, is the only thing your mind (quite correctly) will allow you to think about doing. **This is when Willpower will raise its head to support you fully** and cover you from every angle, to guide you through the dark times of the come down. Remember, if you don't make a clear concise decision, you are only fooling yourself and you will struggle to find **Willpower** coming into your being, without full commitment. This is not possible until you make it abundantly clear to yourself that this is what you want. More importantly; realise this is the step you need to take so that you climb towards freedom from addiction and not to be stuck on the same rung of the ladder controlled by poisonous chemicals. Procrastination in this sense is killing you like the chemicals you are addicted to, so make haste. You will find that if you are at the stage where you are well and truly sick of this poisonous shit being fed into your body, that the eureka or lightbulb moment you've had, will be followed by a realisation of many of the things in life you have missed out on, such as health and wellbeing and I suppose that extra financial cash bonus. These things come to you quickly once you've gotten over the initial withdrawal of poisons from your body. **Willpower** will pop up before during and after when it is summoned and over your shoulder will whisper reminders of the misery involved in this poisonous addiction and messages of support at all times.

To give you an account of how my own victory over **addictive nicotine** and how **Willpower was a key factor**, I will begin by telling you my thought pattern and how I began using **Willpower** as the primary tool over every other method I had tried up until this point. After spending many years as a **born again smoker**, I began to realise that whilst my **health was suffering,** so were many other aspects of my life. Many of you will be all too familiar with this. I didn't like being **breathless** all the time. This involved being **breathless** whilst running for a short period of time, sometimes walking or even mundane little things such as walking up and down a flight of stairs made me **breathless** if I had to exert myself by going up and down several times. To be considered a young man and to dread walking into a building where the elevator was out of service is a very bad thing. I didn't like the fact that **my teeth were yellow and stained**. I didn't like the fact that it was hard to **scrub the brown tar from in between my fingers** after **chain smoking** on a night out. I didn't like the fact that **I wheezed after sex, and sometimes during**. I didn't like my **lungs** being **congested** with **poisonous tar** and **phlegm**, which all those who **inhale this poisonous shit** are familiar with trying to shift. I didn't like that **my breath smelled like shit** (and again, if someone tells you that your breath smells like roses, then they are being polite, sarcastic or are lying to you). I didn't like that I was always struggling to **pay for a poisonous product** that had me **addicted to a chemical** which had a very high chance of **giving me cancer**. My **medical bills** were always high and my bank balance always low. Friends who **didn't inhale this poisonous shit** holidayed twice a year and I didn't have money for a weekend away, (REMEMBER some spend 5000 grand a year on this shit). I didn't like **standing out in the rain like a drowned rat** just so I could partake in a **poisonous pull** only to walk back into a club or bar **smelling like stale shit** and soaked if there was no smoking area outside. I was young but still aware from personal experience, of the **devastation** that this **scourge** causes by **ending the life** of a young person and **destroying families** forever. I didn't **want to die 15 years before my time** for doing something that looking back on it now, I never really enjoyed in the first place. These are just some of the reasons I said **"fuck it, enough"**, and made the **conscious decision** that I was done. Because I had tried many different ways and techniques, my light bulb moment, or epiphany came to me in the same way it has come to you, as a realisation of how you have **wasted time**, **money** and most importantly **your health** to something **so poisonous** that it should be made an offence to sell or to purchase them.

Whilst sitting down with a friend one day, it was maybe a week after my **decision to quit inhaling shit**, we started to try and calculate how much money we had spent between us **purchasing poisonous chemical laced heart stopping cancer sticks,** since we had both picked **this filthy addiction** up The answer we came up with was so shocking we had to recalculate but again got the same answer. My **Willpower** had been kept **quite strong** up until this point but when I calculated the amount I had spent on **shortening my lifespan** and giving me a **1 in 2 chance of getting cancer**, my **Willpower** became **reinforced** to an extent where there would be **no going back** ever. It became not only **reinforced** but unbreakable. I had already said **never again** and this was absolute reconfirmation if any doubt attempted to penetrate my **Willpower**.

To add **insult to injury**, my mind began to wander further only **strengthening** my **Willpower** at an almost supernatural level. I began to analyse things in life which I now felt I had missed out on such as not having a deposit for my first house up front, borrowing money from lenders and banks, settling for second best because this is what I only seemed to get when I allowed **my health** second place over **nicotine**, not being able to use my body to its full potential by working out more, or treating my body with the respect I should have. The financial side of it annoyed me but it was the time I thought I had wasted and the **health** I had affected that irritated me the most. Although these thoughts **reinforced my Willpower**, they also allowed me to think of myself in a very **negative** and **unhealthy way**. By this I mean beating myself up over things that cannot be undone. To counteract this, even today, I push myself to do things in everyday life to the best of my ability, not to breaking point mind you, but to a point where I only allow myself to do or feel whatever makes me feel happy both mentally, physically or I suppose, inside and out. When you begin to have these thoughts and believe me you will, just remember to keep your eyes on the prize. That prize is the **health, wealth** and **wellbeing** all rolled into **one from the day you decide you want to live and not die prematurely from inhaling addictive poisonous shit.** The greatest thing about **willpower** assisting you through all of this is that it **costs nothing**. You don't pay for a **box of nicotine** chewing gum, a hypnotherapy session, a patch, an e-cigarette, a counsellor, a con artist or a magician because no costly gimmicks are needed whatsoever only **common sense** and **Willpower**. You may of course use any of the above if you believe it will help you achieve your permanent goal but please bear in mind that any product which claims to help or assist you to **get clean of nicotine addiction** will always **contain nicotine** with a warning about it **affecting your health** and will also have "may require **Willpower** to work" or "may require **Willpower**".

Some of the makers of these products like to write it very small so that you are led into a false sense of purchasing something that guarantees you fuck all, only a lighter wallet and **poisonous nicotine** in a vapour patch or gum form (nicotine is nicotine by any other name). Tough love, common sense and **Willpower**. Use this as your mantra from the moment you **make your conscious decision.** If you have **punished your body** by saying yes for all these years, then you can show your body some kindness and respect by allowing your **Willpower** to say no. Again, the chances are if you are reading this book, you have already tried all or some of the gimmicks readily available. Because many of these products **contain nicotine** to help you with your **withdrawal**, isn't it interesting to think that the very **poisonous product** that got you **addicted** in the first place now asks you for more of **your hard earned money** to literally **buy your life back?** It's like when someone is bitten by a cobra or a venomous spider and has to extract the anti-venom in the form of **more poison** in order to help them recover. If you feel the need to do so to help your cause, I will again say by all means go ahead, but I am advising against it, because the fact of the matter is that you have to come down from your **poisonous** buzz at some stage and that means **no nicotine** involved whatsoever; so tough love and tackling **this addiction** head on, means you won't be supplementing your **addiction** to **cancer sticks** with these **ridiculous and dangerous e cig devices** or **chewing poisonous gum** for the rest of your life. When your **Willpower** is at its **strongest** and you have reached that **"enough is enough"** stage where you actually mean it, (not just by using words or making false declarations), then you will instinctively know that you will never put **a lighting cancer stick** near your body ever again.

I have seen this first hand and not just in my own case. It was my first experience of witnessing **continued Willpower** and how strong it actually is. I can recall on the day my grandmother **died from cancer,** I saw **Willpower** at its finest hour but didn't realise it until many years later. My family, having just received the news of my grandmother's **untimely death** were sitting around the kitchen table in shock. Everyone was silent, smoking and I remember her son, my uncle, getting up, putting his **box of cancer sticks** in his jacket pocket, grabbing the dogs lead from the coat hanger in the kitchen and walking out the front door without saying a word. I sat around with my siblings and listened to the unfortunate sobs and wails of disbelief and **sorrow** at the **loss** of a family matriarch **so young to cancer.** Less than an hour had passed when my uncle returned in through the front door with **a cancer stick** hanging from his mouth. He said nothing, only walked past us all in silence and hung the dogs lead back up on the coat hanger. He then walked over to the table where everyone had gathered around smoking and paused for a moment. I remember my aunt asking him if he was alright and without answering her he took the **cancer stick** from his mouth, looked at it and said these words which I can still clearly hear and see him saying even now, **"that's it, I'm done"** before he took **one last pull of poison** almost as if he was poetically saying goodbye to something that he believed he needed up until this point, but also I think, he blamed for playing a part in the sorrow he now felt he was experiencing. With that, in a gesture I suppose of finality, he stubbed the half smoked **cancer stick** roughly in amongst the other **poisonous butts** in the overflowing ashtray. He didn't finish the cancer stick and this is what I remember most. Amongst all the thoughts that went on in his head, whatever way he communicated with himself when he walked out the door, he somehow managed to walk out with an **addiction that was killing him** and walk back in **with Willpower so strong**, it was saving his life in supporting the **conscious decision** he would stick to this very day.

That was in 1995. He is today a relatively young man in his early 60s and is as fit as a fiddle. I would be blessed several years later by taking what I had witnessed and using it to conquer **my own poisonous addiction.** Sometimes to witness, hear, or even to read of an event can lead you to **take control** of something that has consumed you and like my uncle, myself and those who are or **were addicted to poisonous nicotine,** sometimes a shock to the system or **a life changing event** or fright, is what's needed for you to take control of the thing that's consumed you, in order to have the strength to **take your life back.** As I have already said, this is something which may affect some people while others may ask for one last drag as they **lay on their bed** of demise, so strong (they wrongly believe) is **their addiction**. Only you choose. When **Willpower** is harnessed and used correctly, it overrides this urge completely and **the will to survive and stay alive** becomes much stronger than the urge to **kill yourself** either slowly or **prematurely** from the inhalation of **4000 chemicals** which are used to **kill** any type of biological living creature. The **will to live** usually only surfaces when we find ourselves faced with uncertainty of the future. We understand that the will to do something makes the difference between doing and not doing. **Use Willpower** today so that you do not face an uncertain future. If you have the will to stand out in the rain inhaling poisonous chemicals into your lungs, then you most certainly have **the Willpower** to walk down a beach taking in large breaths of fresh air. No excuses and stop being so weak. **Summon your Willpower, harness your Willpower** and **use your Willpower**. It is built into you and it will not let you down if you use it to its fullest potential. Remember the following just to sum up this chapter…

Willpower is the driving force built into every human being. It is used by men and women who want to succeed in the very act of living itself. It pushes us forward and gives those who know how to harness it the advantage or the upper hand to deal with situations that others find hard to cope with. It is these men and women that are willing to go the extra mile, to not give up and not quit, to have the courage to say no in any given situation that they realise is harmful or that will prove a grievance to themselves. They have the will to succeed in what they set out to do. If any person sets out to do anything they wish to achieve with iron Will and conviction, they stand a greater chance of success in reaching their goals if they harness the **Willpower they were born with.** Every person regardless of age, has the ability to do amazing things with their lives. Do not allow a poisonous addictive piece of paper make the decisions that have caused you so much misery any longer. Those who have the confidence and **the Willpower to walk away** from poisonous shit that has held them back can now look forward to a new found freedom. Confidence in living life is more appealing than arrogance about one's life and unnecessary demise. **This is Willpower speaking.**

NO IFS OR BUTTS.

This in short means under no circumstances whatsoever. If an **ex-nicotine addict** allows themselves to make a pact with the devil and says to themselves "If I can stay off them for the month then I'll have the one sneaky smoke to celebrate" or "If I give them up on the week days, I'll only have a few at the weekend to relax", then they may as well put down this book and calculate your life span minus the 15 years **this poisonous shit** is going to take from you. Also try to bear in mind that there is fuck all relaxing with a **cancer stick** that **poisons you** with **4000 deadly chemicals** and the only celebrating you should be doing is when it turns your stomach to even look at one. Do not allow yourself to give as much as one second of **your precious time** to entertain the thought of putting a **cancerous, mucus causing, lung clogging coffin nail** anywhere near your mouth. If there are any **butts** that creep into your mind such as "but I have a wedding coming up or that night out with the girls" or "I'll never make it over that stag do without a smoke", then replace that but with "but **I want to live**" or "but **I want to grow old** and watch my grandkids play and have fun". Use the word **but** as a positive word when encountered with a negative thought as **butts** try to sneak back in. **Butts** are the **cancerous poisonous** stubs you will be looking at in a **disgusting smelly ashtray** if you give into their **filthy addictive shit** any time they enter your thought pattern. If you have made the decision or are waiting until you finish this book, I can tell you now, there can be absolutely no **ifs** or **butts** whatsoever involved.

If you must, summon every fibre in your being to give you **the strength** to not even consider **bumming a cancer stick** or getting into the car and driving to that shop or garage. If this is how weak you are to give into **ifs** or **butts,** then again, the book up until this point has been of no good to you because of your **weakness** and **lack of self-respect** and **self-belief. Your Willpower** is the only **strength** required combined with common sense and you must remember this. The voice of reason is spoken by **Willpower** saying **"fuck this poisonous shit**, I'm not being controlled **like a slave to this shit** any longer" and shows that you are in charge with **Willpower** standing right behind you. When you are at this stage (and it is only a decision away for any of you), you are able to reason and talk to yourself in a **logical** and controlled fashion and I would like you to remember this; in order to get rid of a craving you have to **master it**. Use the word **master** as often as you like and as often as you need to drum it into your head that "In order for me to be **the master** of my urges, **I must control my thoughts"**. Once a person can **master** their thoughts, **they can control their actions.** Bearing in mind, that **the master** is the one in control all the time. You as an **addict** at this stage resemble the creature Gollum from the lord of the rings, seeking to hold "the precious". Take "the precious" (meaning **your cancer sticks** obviously!) and fuck them into a river, bin or nearest fire and become **the master** (quite literally) of your own destiny. **Control your thoughts** means controlling your actions and to help, here is a list of the **ifs** and **butts** you must avoid at all costs and a way to deal with them if they seem somewhat unavoidable.

IF…you get **cravings for nicotine**, remember that it is one of **4000 poisonous chemicals** that has created **sickness** and **misery** in your body. You may associate them with good times but the inside of your body; **heart, lungs, blood** etc. beg to differ and is still trying to cope with **the damage these poisons** have **inflicted**. Cravings, as physical as the symptoms may be, are just that, cravings. They pass very quickly and are basically **a cruel mind fuck** where **your brain tricks your body** into believing it will suffer if you don't give into them whereas the complete opposite happens to be the truth. You, the individual who understands that the eureka moment they experienced will allow this craving to pass, knowing that only a **complete moron** would even consider letting a **ridiculous urge** get in the way of their **health** and **wellbeing**. **IF**….I do fall back into my **addiction**, what does that mean? Am I **doomed** to **inhale this poisonous shit** for ever? Let me just say that if you have managed to get this far into the book and agreed with what you've read up to this point, you will not be **inhaling poisonous chemicals** after reading it. That is to say if you've truly read every word and absorbed the meanings in each chapter. How any person could read a book on the dangers and the **stupidity** involved in **inhaling a poisonous addictive substance** that can give them any number of **life threatening conditions or cancers** and agree with what's written, only to continue to keep doing what they do, has me doubting human evolution.

Even if you choose to agree with only one paragraph in this book and continue to **pollute the lungs** of yourself or others around you, then not only are you completely **brainless** and **ignorant**, but as **unintelligent** and as **careless**, and on a different **level of awareness** (with your Neanderthal **ignorance**) compared to those who are finally beginning to realise that we are more than just flesh bone and water. We were **born to live, to breathe**, and to **thrive**. Remember this, **the air we breathe is our fuel** and the food we put in our bodies is the energy that drives us. When this all makes perfect sense to you then "eureka" will have all the more significance to you. Speaking of Neanderthals…. although I can't remember back as far as the day of the cave people, I'm sure if we could have watched one stick its fingers in a fire when they first discovered it, it would pull its burnt fingers back out because the natural reaction his body would signal to it is to "get your fingers out of there asap because they aint supposed to go into the fire" The natural reaction felt by the cave person thousands of years ago was the instinct of the body letting the cave person know through the feeling of pain, that it would be in its best interest to take out those fingers because they needed them to hunt food, make food, make tools etc. Our ancestor lived or walked this planet many thousand years ago and even though could they not speak a language, they could still communicate with those around them, but most importantly with itself. And this communication through instinct and pain told the cave person that it would be in your best interest to keep those fingers away from the fire as it's not something you should be doing, with the cave person probably nodding his hairy skull in agreement, as it made sense to them.

Fast forward to many thousand years later and we have "you" the direct descendants of the cave person only for you are supposedly far more advanced, a bit more evolved and less hairy than your ancestor. You are the technological wonder of today that can eat food without wrestling a woolly mammoth to the ground to feed your family, and unlike your hairy predecessor; you aren't stupid enough to poke your fingers into fire….or are you? If the cave man is stupid enough to put his fingers into the fire and learn not to do so, then why thousands of years later, are you putting black smoke in lungs that were born pink in colour **to inhale air?** There is no evolution in **stupidity** as it goes against something which you also go against with **your filthy disgusting addiction,** and that is nature. **Stupid** doesn't **survive** unless it learns. This sets apart those of you who are **aware** and those of you who are not. Only you can choose which of these you want to be.

IF… you say, I am finding that as time goes on, that I am starting to think more and more about **my poisonous addiction** and find myself in situations of temptations, what should I do? First off, I'd say snap the fuck out of it. **Get a grip and stop talking shit.** While you're at it, why not **try smoking crack** or **shooting up some heroin?** Just because society accepts **inhaling poisons** as normal, whilst injecting it is illegal or frowned upon, doesn't give you the right to put any form of **shit in your body.** We live in a world where unfortunately cash is king. The governments of our world are always going to attempt to do what looks right to the people or what looks right by the people, but the truth of the matter is that if there was a way of bagging up heroin that could be taxed and deemed to pass safety standards, then the same governments would have it advertised as a way for the people to relax and would be seen on billboards and televisions across the globe. This is the world we live in unfortunately for the time being. The **poisonous tobacco companies**, money and our governments **don't give a fuck about you,** I, or anyone else and the very allowing of **this poisonous shit** to be packaged and sold is a testament to this. If **people accepted heroin** as the social norm tomorrow, it could be purchased in corner shops the following day. It's not viewed as acceptable so we have **cancer sticks** in their place which are, but hopefully for not too much longer. These same governments launch their statistics of **global deaths** from **this horrible poisonous shit** with plans of tackling **this scourge** such as raising prices or different packaging or whatever bullshit they concoct to appease the concerned masses. The final solution to **this deadly hazard** can only be resolved by a total ban on smoking by the world's governments or a total awakening or awareness in those using **this poisonous addictive shit.** If you are **idiotic** enough to feel the need to become another of the **many millions of global statistics** whose **early demise** involved **inhaling poisonous chemicals** then by all means, keep handing **your cash, which you worked hard to collect** day in and day out, to those who laugh all the way to the bank while **you're struggling family cry all the way to the morgue** to view **your corpse**. This can only change for you when excuses stop and **ifs and butts** become words of the past just like your **poisonous addiction. BUTT** …you add….. "even though I've had my eureka moment, I'm still in an environment where **I'm forced to inhale the poisonous chemicals** of the other **inconsiderate addicts** who either know or don't care that I've decided **I want to live and to breathe air**. What can I possibly do to avoid this situation?" Thankfully in most parts of the world today, the same governments have been forced to implement laws that make it forbidden in most workplaces and public buildings or areas where people have **to breathe the same air.** Because of this, there is an opportunity for you if you are an employee who is forced to **inhale the shitty poisonous fumes from the cancer stick of another** worker to report the **damage caused to your breathing space and body**. This should be dealt with by the relevant authorities who in turn should refrain or restrain you from head butting the same **ignoramus**. If the situation has arisen where a get together or a night out is unavoidable and you are concerned then don't be. Embrace it and as I've said before, walk in with your head held high and if **poisonous fumes** become an issue to the extent that all around you seem to **light up their poison and engulf you**, then just leave the equation. Move out of the plume of **toxic fumes** and find yourself **some fresh breathing space**, even if that **breathing space** is an outdoor toilet (which may indeed smell unpleasant but **won't wrinkle your skin and blacken your lungs**).

If you're eureka moment is in full effect and you still have to suffer the consequences of **another person's idiotic choice to inhale poisonous chemicals** (like your other half, husband/wife) in the same air space as you, then you have several options. You can sit down and talk to them and read from this book. Point out some very obvious common sense parts that cannot be argued or refuted (basically the whole book). Tell them that not even the president of a

poison tobacco company could argue with what's written. It also helps if you ask them to just listen carefully, as you tell them that you need their support 100% on this one thing. If you have to plead with them to come on board and let them know **the benefits** you both have to look forward to and how you can depend on each other for moral support **instead of counting on poison** to give you no **end of misery**, then do just that. Let them know that this is a very **positive step forward.** If you are unfortunate enough to have your eureka moment counteracted by a negative person who either doesn't care about your decision and continues **to inhale poison** at every given opportunity in a **stupid** show of **defiance**, then do your damndest to spend as little time as possible around this person or these people. Just because they are not on the same wavelength as you doesn't mean you have to fall from the path you have chosen to walk on. They will soon begin to realise that you will only share the same air as them once they are **not polluting it with their poisonous chemicals**. Never for a moment allow them to make you think that what you are doing is **wrong**. It is right to want to **live a healthy life** and it is right to **want to breathe the air** that **your lungs** and **your body** need to **thrive and survive**. Do not be swayed by their **ignorance** and **stupidity**. I can guarantee that when you stick it out and these people see the changes in **your health** and **the glow** you will have within weeks; it is they, who will start looking to change and lose the **disgusting addiction** you have had **the strength** to **conquer** and **overcome**, and it is you; they will eventually beg to help them.

BUTT.... Inhaling poisonous chemicals seems to be the only way that I can cope with everything that's going on in my life at the moment. Could I just keep doing it until I get that stressful bank loan paid back or can I just wait until I get over my long term break up before I decide to **quit the shit for good?** The real answer to this if I'm being totally honest, is that at this stage of the book, if you are still asking such questions, then you **have learned fuck all**. Your levels of **self-indulgence** and **self-pitying** are completely magnified by your **addiction to inhaling poisonous shitty chemicals**. You may have read the book so far but you have not observed and absorbed the words written down. You haven't soaked up each chapter and its meaning. **Cravings for poisons** have drowned out the inner voice that **screams at you for mercy**. This is your body **begging you to stop poisoning it over and over again**. You are one of the many people who will hear the good news and not believe it to be true. The expression "sounds too good to be true means that it usually is" will be an expression you are either familiar with or use yourself whenever the occasion arises. You probably also use the expression "I don't believe it". Well believe it. In **this dangerous game of life and death**, a game you have been playing with your body for far too long now. There are no winners, only **the dealers in death**

from which you **purchase your addictive poison** every day. There is a voice inside you that if you listen carefully enough, will scream **"enough is enough"** every time you **force poison upon it**. It is when this faint voice becomes louder and louder and eventually becomes so loud that it takes a stand and bravely drowns out the voice of the craving and **the sneaky whispers** of the **addiction** that you will now stand and declare to anyone who cares to listen that **"enough is enough, I'm finished for good with this poisonous shit"**. When you are at this stage, then absolutely **no ifs or butts** will become as clear as your reflection in the mirror and **the strongest** realisation that there will be **no excuses** any more, **no ifs or butts!** I'm not saying that if you ever have a moment of doubt you should look at yourself in the mirror and make a declaration but if it helps, then why not. It may even make your declaration more personal to you. While you're at it, have a good look at **some of the damage inhaling this poisonous shit** may have already caused to your **face, teeth, gums, hair, wrinkles, skin, yellow fingers**, or **bleeding gums** and make a vow of "never again" with every issue you can point out. Starting fresh, make a promise to yourself or to your reflection that if you don't like what you see looking back, you are going to dedicate yourself to change. Not only **physically** but **mentally** by **becoming stronger** than the **poisonous addictive substance** that has up to this point controlled many aspects of your life. Promise yourself that **you will not live in regret** for what damage has been done but will **live working to repair that damage**. **Promise** to put back in what you have spent so long taking out.

Finally, make **a declaration** that under no circumstances regardless of how you view any **ifs or butts** that enter your mind, will you give a moment's thought to returning to **the poison** or the person you used to, (but no longer) wish to be. Usually when something is deemed "too good to be true" people are always waiting for the **"but"** and will say "there has to be **a but** somewhere", whilst waiting to hear the catch or negative twist to the good news being given. People seem to think that there has to be terms and conditions with all good news or that good news can't last forever. In this regard, the good news about the good news is that when **you decide to quit inhaling poisonous chemicals,** it is **good news** all the way. You are no longer sliding down the snake in life but climbing up the ladder. At the top of this ladder waits **a new life**, the life you were **born to live and to breathe.** It promises good things in regards **to your health** and with every step you climb, you move closer to **a breath of fresh air** and a welcome home to your long lost **fitness levels. Tar** no longer keeps you stuck to the floor and **nicotine** no longer is the **disgusting poison** which controls you but merely a word you no longer wish to use or to have a relationship with. There are **no ifs or butts** you have from now on in your life, only what's next in your new adventure?

wish to be anymore, i.e. **a filthy disgusting nicotine addict**, get me? Go to the pub, just not the smoking area, go to the barbeque, just choose **not to inhale the poisonous chemicals** of others **who don't give a fuck about themselves** or others. Remember…don't change who you are, change who you no longer wish to be. Don't become a hermit, don't avoid situations or events, yet challenge yourself by showing up and making a healthy heartfelt declaration. Even if you decide to keep this to yourself, that's fine because you **quitting the shit** is all that matters here. A **"no thanks"** should suffice any time that someone tries to be kind by **offering you cancer**. Even if there are those insistent annoying element of **yes men** and **women** who persist and insist with "you will, go on", or start a debate or argument about the statistics that show that "you're more likely to be hit by a Boeing jet while standing in a red phone box at 3 o clock on a Saturday afternoon than you are **dying from smoking"**, just nod your head in agreement, smile politely, and walk away without **engaging in bullshit conversation** or debates **not worthy of your time.**

These **idiots** will sadly learn **the hard way.** You have to **do what you are doing for yourself** and fuck any of these **idiots** who want to chastise or criticise you because you are trying to **improve your quality of life** and are now at a higher state of **awareness** than they are. There are those of you who may wish to react differently by giving those statistics and arguing your side and that's entirely up to you. Do whatever works for you. When I say that, I say it with firm conviction and not as a loose statement. "Whatever works" means **not inhaling this poisonous shit** ever again. Having the occasional **sneaky cancer stick** is **failing miserably** and not working whatsoever but **working against you.** There can be absolutely no slip ups when you **make your decision,** or no going back. Remember all the attempts you have made over your lifetime to **put an end to this filthy disgusting addiction.** All the **wasted time**, effort, **money** and **health** over the years. Do not allow yourself to become a **yes man** or a **yes woman as a feeble excuse,** just so you can **allow cancer causing poisons into your bloodstream.** You have come a long way, even by reading this book and it's obvious that you now have **determination** to succeed this time and go all the way to the finish. To even consider **inhaling 4000 poisonous chemicals** now, should make you feel **idiotic**, for only a complete **moron** with **no self-respect** or feelings for their loved ones could be overpowered by an imaginary **craving for a toxic cancer causing poison.** If you fancied a big mac and McDonalds was closed, the craving you thought was going to drive you over the edge would very quickly pass, so stick with it. You have **strength** and **nicotine is a poison** whose strength is **taking people's lives through addiction** and **you are much stronger** than this **horrible shit.** Remember **your Willpower** can be summoned with a thought and herein lies the only **strength** you require. **Take a stand against poison and addiction** so that you stand out for the right reasons and not because you look **weak.** Smokers look weak and I don't care if you're a Mr Universe or a Miss World winner who begs to differ because I'm not talking about size or beauty or physical strength.

Those **addicted to this poisonous shit** are weak in ways that those who **don't depend on nicotine** are strong. If you have the **strength in life** to **say no** to anything you believe is not for your **greater good,** then you stand out because you **stand up for yourself.** Whether or not you stand out from the crowd for the wrong reasons is up to you, **it's your choice.** Remember that standing out in the wrong way would be getting noticed or remembered for your yellow or green teeth or brown fingers. To stand out because you cough more than others around you are because **you get breathless** climbing the stairs is **your choice.** To stand **beside the grave of someone who has died prematurely** because of a **filthy disgusting addiction** and to continue sucking the **same poison** is for fucking **idiots** and **your choice** to ignore such a **senseless waste of life.** Those who stand out from the crowd because they **look younger** than their 60 years or because they want to be there for their grandchild's wedding day are the ones who have had **the strength** to **say no** to the **yes men** and **women.** They have learned and now understand how to **harness their Willpower** to work with them and not against them. Finding it yourself means finding strength you doubted (but as we said earlier), have always had.

It is with this new found **strength** that **the yes men** or **women** you encounter should be treated like a piece of string you find hanging off your t shirt or jumper. If they begin to annoy you, just like the piece of string that you pull off and throw away, do the exact same. Discard them, walk away or tell them in whichever way you find suitable that you don't or won't ever jeopardise your **health** or **life** by **inhaling poisonous shit again.** And this doesn't mean you have to get big headed or turn into a monster just because you have made a choice to live differently in **respects to your body.** If you have decided to no longer be a part of a club where the only benefits are **cancer, illness** and **death,** then by all means walk with your **head held high.** If they decide to make fun of you, then let them. Chances are as I've already stated when they themselves try to find their own lightbulb moment, it will only be after they see how great you look and how happy you are with the new you. And it will be you they approach for guidance on **overcoming a vile addiction they continue to struggle with.** When you have finally **made your decision** or if you managed to make it before you even picked this book up, always bear in mind **the burden of responsibility** that this entails. Burden is bad in this case but only if you allow the word burden to actually come to life, by taking on burden instead of owning it. We do this by remembering that anything or anyone we up

SAYING NO TO THE YES MEN.

You don't need to be wealthy in any way shape or form to be surrounded by **yes men** and **women**. Any person who has ever **made a decision to quit** any particular addiction encounters these morons at any given time or event. If someone says for example that they have had enough of alcohol and wants a night out without alcohol or some sobriety, there is always the one person who will skit and laugh and give the occasional jeer to make the person who is trying to abstain feel as though they're missing out, when in actual fact waking up without a hangover with the memories of a great night out still intact, is very far from missing out. Although the **yes men** or **women** may not think they are doing any **harm** by offering, badgering, pressurising or even laughing at the person trying to abstain, they are in fact at times, planting a seed of doubt in the person allowing them to question their positive motives, which leaves them wondering as to whether or not abstinence is the right thing to be doing. This can be **harmful** if the person trying to abstain gives in and says "Ah fuck it, why not" if their decision to get started at stopping for good doesn't have the strongest resolve. To these people, the **yes men** and **women** who pressure or force their selfish thoughtless suggestions on someone trying to get their **health**, **body** and **mind** back in working order, I say shame on you. You are taking your own **habits** or **addictions** that you either don't feel the need to change (or don't have the courage or commitment to address yourself), and passing them onto someone who's trying to deal with changes they've made in their own life. Big thanks for the support. For future reference, I would ask any persons who have in the past or who continue to infect others with their negative opinions or comments to refrain from doing so and to stop spreading your **misery** and **show some respect** for the person who is struggling to get their **life back on track**. If any individual is attempting to **quit something** that affects **their health**, be it food, **poisonous nicotine**, alcohol or drugs, there should be a level of support and any person who is on this level and that aids them in some way in returning to **the old poisonous ways** is not fully supportive and should keep their distance.

Don't get me wrong, I am well aware that there are people who like to interact and enjoy themselves on a social level with a few drinks to relax and unwind and those people I applaud and say keep doing what you're doing if you can abstain from **your poisonous addiction**. What makes a **yes man** or **woman** a real **yes man** or **woman** is that they are well aware that their colleague, friend, partner or significant other is doing their damndest in an attempt to **finally**

kick the addiction that has up until this point **held them back,** and they show little or no restraint or regard when it comes to **supporting this persons decision.** This may involve lighting up in the same room, airspace or offering them **a cancer stick** laughing and telling them "you know you want one". A person who is mindful of the struggle of the person who is **abstaining** and leaves the area to continue their own **filthy disgusting addiction** (whilst still **suffering** themselves) may at a later stage be rewarded, when the person who wins **their health** back, returns the favour by giving them this book or advice on how to stick with it.

The **yes men** and **women** at times don't even realise that this is what they actually are, that is to say, those who **through ignorance** will offer a person a **cancer stick** because they have not read a book, listened to advice or simply through pleading bullshit **ignorance.** There are still those who claim they don't genuinely realise the effects that **4000 poisonous chemicals** have on the human body. They are the same people who smile when **cancer** and **smoking** are used in the same sentence ("it will never happen to me" syndrome), and are usually dim in most aspects of their lives. These particular people or group of **yes men** or **women** can be found everywhere in the **ex addicts** daily lives. They can be hard to avoid and are extremely generous when handing out their **offers of this cancerous poison.** This is where the **ex-smoker** has to **take responsibility** and **a stand** if need be, in all aspects of dealing with **yes men** and **women.** If you have decided to **gain control of your life** and **desire to be free** from any negative **thing that binds you,** then you must have the **courage to say no** to the **yes men** and **women** at any given time and hold your head high when calling yourself **an ex-smoker** with an air of **pride**, from the moment **you stub out your last cancerous piece of poisonous shit.** This remember, takes **Willpower** and **strength** but as you now know, is there in abundance and grows every time you tell someone **"no thanks"** or to even **"fuck off"** if needed when or if they persist. Many people will try to avoid situations and occasions or times of stress or anything that may make them want to pick up where they left off and while I say again, if this works for you, then by all means, stick with it but remember, you must have the resolve to stick with it or your attempts and hard work were wasted on fuck all, and you are back to square one. Again, the chances are that if you are reading a book called **Stop Fucking Smoking,** then you haven't had the most success with this, so I would approach this with the following advice; Sometimes in life, I truly believe, that in order to face up to something, fear for example, you should put yourself in a situation that creates fear. This is when you really take the bull by the horns. What I'm saying here, for those who don't understand is that; if you are the social sort, don't change who you are just because you are trying to change a part of who you no longer until this point blamed for **our addiction**, goes out the window and we **take full responsibility** from here on out for **every cancer stick** we have ever placed between our lips. You are the one in charge and **in your state of awareness;** you should comply only with the strongest opinion that **your Willpower** has to offer you. **The yes men** and **women** have their own **miserable** paths to walk and the only weapons they possess at the moment is their persuasion of others to try **poison,** but not an ounce of determination to tackle or convince themselves to **choose life. The misery they inhale** is entirely up to them and please note that any offer made to you as we've already acknowledged is through chosen **ignorance** and/or **stupidity.**

When you are in an environment and you find some of these **yes men** and **women** and they politely or forcefully try to ply their poisonous wares on you, they may say "do you want a smoke?" or "here, have a smoke", but what you should hear coming out of their mouths is **"do you want cancer?"** and say **"no thanks, I'll stick with the fresh air"** before walking away from the **plume of poisonous chemicals.** When you not only say, but feel it loud and clear; that all these people have to offer you is **sickness, poison** and **death**, and you can confidently decline their offer, (or if you feel in a generous mood), offer them some of **your own life saving advice** and experience, it is then **you have mastered the art of refusal** to **an addiction.** This symbolises that you have finally cut the **shackles** that **bound you** for years. To be able to walk with your **head held high** and to take in **deep breaths of fresh air** is a wonderful thing. It is in fact priceless and yet it costs nothing. I recently spoke with a man who is in his sixties and had gone back on the **cancer sticks** after he was off them for a number of years. He had spent most of his adult life running in marathons and when I asked him what his reasons where for going back on them, he told me that he didn't know. He just said "no particular reason, a bit **stupid** of me really", as carefree as if he was talking about ham in a sandwich. If the same man I speak of knew how much he meant to his family and that they wanted him around for as long as possible so they could watch him play with his grandchildren and see them grow, then his casual statement indicates that **like many inhalers of this poisonous shit** they live in the **"it'll never happen to me bubble".** A **logical person** aware of the love of their family would **never jeopardise their health** in such a casual manner and remember I said **"logical"** which is something not found in the abundance of those **addicted** to a substance like **nicotine.** Whether this same man was **weak** enough to be coerced by **yes men** or **women** or whether it was of his own **free will**, his decision to return to **inhaling this shit** was his own choice and his burden. But this burden like a heavy debt could very soon be easily passed on to the ones **he claims he would die for.** If any one of **the cancers** or **illnesses** attributed to

inhaling this shit decides to **invade his body**, then it is the family who cares for this man who will be left to **pick up the pieces**, bury them, and carry the burden of **grief around with them for the rest of their lives.** This same individual should know that it is never too late to **stop inhaling this shit permanently** and we now know this scientifically and medically. He needs to realise that he has a family that love him much more than his very own **addiction to this poison,** and it is time for him to reciprocate the feelings. Their desire for him to stay is far more powerful than any craving he'll ever know. When he realises this, he will have stepped back into a **higher level of awareness**. To stay at this level is the key to his **survival** and **longevity of life.** Saying yes is easy with this **horrible addiction** and saying no can at times feel like the hardest thing you'll ever have to do, but the reality of the situation is that all it truly takes is the ability to **say no** and to **mean no.**

I WANT TO LIVE.

This is the most basic, most simple form of instructions; in order for you to **detox your lungs and airwaves** and to start using them again **for what they were designed to do**. There is absolutely no complication involved aside from the craving which is where **Willpower** takes charge. As we have already learned in our chapter on **Willpower,** we are more than equipped to deal with the **poisonous cravings** that tempt us (with **bullshit unrealistic needs** and **realistic cancers**), than we realise. This is the most inexpensive way for you to **quit inhaling shit** and is also guaranteed to work if you take what you've learned and applied it to the fact that you **wish to live** and not to **die prematurely or suddenly**. There are no gimmicks, no medications, no meditations, no doctors' visits or outside interference required. This is about you, for you and for your family, who should be behind your decision **to quit the shit 100%** with total support. All that you need here is a pen and paper and a piece of sticky tape. Start by writing the number 1 and keep writing until you get to 21. Do this on the day you **decide you want to live** (hopefully today!) and it doesn't matter whether it's 7 in the morning or 11 in the night because the time of day is irrelevant to when a person decides **that they want to live**. If you have already made this decision, then go ahead and make a declaration. Again, do this how you wish, either silently to yourself or from the rooftops; it doesn't really matter because there is no going back now anyhow. You have decided and **your Willpower** has got your back, so let's do this shit! If you have the support of loved ones who up until this point have grown sick and tired of your **excuses** and failed attempts, walk into the kitchen and tell them with conviction **"no more fucking smoking this poisonous shit"** and tell them as they raise their "here we go again eyebrows" that you are **doing it for them** and this time there is no going back. **Tell them that you love them more than nicotine** so that you further cement your promise to **quit inhaling this shit.**

I should at this stage point out that you should not be deterred from telling other people in your life for fear of ridicule, just because you expect this reaction based on your many previous failed attempts. Again, this is about you **wanting to live** and to **recover from addiction to a poisonous chemical** which has controlled your life up to this point. This decision will not affect them (unless they passively inhale your poison), only you. This decision to stop is far more important than what people think. You are now giving yourself a chance to go back in time and say **"no thanks"**. There is probably no point in giving you an in depth biology lesson at this point or to go through all the ins and outs of cravings and **addictions** because I'm sure that those reading this are almost experts with the first-hand experience of many previous attempts. If this is your very first attempt or your first and final shot at this target **then failure is not an option. Craving nicotine is all in the mind** and as bad or as hard as it may feel, **it is all in your head** and after a day (probably the most **critical stage**, craving wise), the physical symptoms have passed and then your body begins its **long awaited recovery.** This is when the body which has become **hooked on the poison you forced it to endure,** cries out through craving because it believes it needs and that it misses **chemical poisonous toxins.** In actual fact; all it is looking to do is to get a **temporary fix of poison** with which to satisfy this **false lust.** We are told all of our lives to **listen carefully to the body** but it is at this point you must put the body in its place with a polite "no fucking way" if you must, and **replace that need for poison with a need to live.** Swapping lust with life, if you will! Remember how we talked about **Willpower** and how it is as real as the face we see in the mirror. **Willpower** will receive a message via your **distress call**, summoning it to step forward and support you more than ever for the time it's required and this includes any time it's needed in the near or distant future. **Willpower** is as we've already stated, **your body's representative**, and on behalf of your body, it pledges its full support in this war on **self-inflicted terror.** This close ally will never leave your side. Although it is constantly present, all you need to do is summon it to see how **strong** of an Ally it truly is.

Now to explain what some may see as sounding crazy, silly or whatever. All I know is that it worked for me. For whatever reason possessed me in my **battle against poisonous nicotine**, I decided in my own logic to replace the habits I had acquired associated with **inhaling shit**, (such as using my fingers to hold a **cancer stick** and carrying a box in my hand). To do this I took note of when I smoked most during the day and quickly realised that I would smoke 2 to 3 **cancer sticks** whilst drinking tea and because of this I drank up to between 10 and 15 sugary cups of tea a day. In my mind I saw that a cup of tea was a good **excuse to inhale a cancer stick** and **a cancer stick** was a good reason to have another cup of tea, (again any excuse). I can speak from experience and personally tell you that this amount of sugary tea or coffee along with **20 or 30 cancer sticks** isn't the healthiest of diets and how it leaves a person's **teeth and gums** I will leave to your own imagination. Needless to say, you couldn't use Hollywood smile in the same breath or sentence as tea, sugar, caffeine and nicotine combined. Of course I wanted **health** and **my life back,** but a **clean set of teeth** was an added bonus, so I decided to kill many birds with one stone and replaced sugary tea and **cancer sticks** with what many of you will find odd but as you already know, **ended my addiction to the horrible shit which is nicotine.** This is the somewhat odd and temporary approach I took in order to **beat my battle with addiction to poisonous chemicals.** This was very simple and if you want to **beat your addiction** in the same fashion all you need to do is stock up on the following; water and **Weetabix**, the diet of a monk. If you can't stomach **Weetabix,** then porridge or a pack of dry digestives/cream crackers. And this is how I did it; every day I drank a 2 litre of water, and it didn't matter if it came from an outside tap, a well, a bottle or the kitchen sink. Be sure to carry a 2 litre of water and drink at least two litres before you head to bed, even leaving a glass or bottle beside the bed. This will flush your system out and we don't need a medical opinion on **the benefits of water to the body** so I won't give one.

Now as for the **Weetabix.** When you buy a pack of **Weetabix,** you can buy them in packs of 24, which is not too far off a **20 box of cancer sticks**. This may sound quite strange but I want you to look at it this way. One biscuit alone contains 18grams of whole wheat which also contains fibre. **One cancer stick contains over 4000 poisonous chemicals** each of which are designed to **kill biological life** and contains many **carcinogenic (cancer causing) toxins**. A **packet of this shit** will cost over 10 dollars and a box of Weetabix will set you back 3 dollars. Remember that **this is temporary** and is used until your cravings stop which believe me will be very fast if you follow this correctly. At the start I decided that every time I was thirsty and craved **a cancer stick** at the same time, I would take a **single Weetabix biscuit** out of the box and put it in a bowl and pour water over it like you would do with milk whilst making breakfast but this wasn't very feasible with work and driving and the like (and it tasted like shit), so I just carried a pack of **Weetabix** with me wherever I went. Anytime I was thirsty, I drank from my water bottle and any time I craved **nicotine,** I ate one of the **Weetabix** dry or raw as if it were a normal biscuit and tried to wash it down with water. Anyone who has ever attempted this knows only too well how difficult it is to chew, how long this takes and how dry and **unpleasant** it tastes. In my head I was thinking that if I could get my mind to associate the **craving for poison** answered by a dry **Weetabix,** then the **craving would soon subside. This conditioning** worked for me in less than 3 days. The physical ache lasted just over a day but I knew that anything I felt after this was out of habit, so my packet of **Weetabix** was a substitute to the **pack of cancer sticks** and the bottle of water was all I held in my hands when they got fidgety. There is nothing pleasant about this technique but there is also nothing difficult about it.

I'm not suggesting anyone should try this but it has worked for me and for everyone, (not some, but everyone) I know, who has used it to its full extent. That means doing this **until you no longer inhale poisonous chemicals** to get through the day. If anyone finds the idea of dry **Weetabix** abhorrent or "just wrong" then you should research **the poisonous cancerous product** you place between your lips. I could understand if I was asking you to eat a couple of oysters at the very moment you woke up, or to chew on a squid instead of nicotine gum. This indeed, you may struggle with to get such items down the hatch! I can guarantee you that your **salvation from this addictive shit** is found using this technique but only if you **condition yourself correctly**. This by the way is not a diet. If you usually eat like a horse then continue to do so. This book is about **quitting inhaling poisonous chemicals** and not weight loss. The **Weetabix** should replace your intake of **cancer sticks** and the water and your everyday diet should help with any constipation or stomach troubles anyone is concerned about. Because your body is used to **being bombarded with poisons** all the time it would welcome such tender treatment and will not struggle or reject **Weetabix** and water. I can remember how I mentioned what I had planned on doing to **beat this horrible addiction** to a work mate (another nicotine addict) and his hilarious reaction.

Getting into his car after work one day he asked "how's the miracle cure coming along?" whilst he flicked his **poison** ash out through the window laughing. I told him it was going great and that almost a week had passed and that not even as much as a tiny urge had made me feel like **putting poison** back in my system. "I don't know where you got this crazy idea from" he said, "but surely all this **Weetabix** can't be good for you", he joked, looking puzzled. I told him that "I'd prefer to overdose on the healthy ingredients found in **Weetabix** and water any day, over **the shit I've forced my body to endure** for the last 13 years". He laughed and called me "a crazy bastard", before he added, "Well maybe there's something in it, keep it up, I hope it works out for you". "I will do", I told him, stepping away from the **poisonous fumes** he was **breathing in and out,** because the all too **familiar toxic stench** was attempting to climb into my nostrils also. As he reversed out past me, he shouted at me, his arm outstretched with half a **cancer stick** between his fingers hanging out the window and held it up as he offered it to me asking "are you sure you won't come over to the dark side?", motioning at me to step forward and take it. "I won't, you can keep it", I laughed back and got into my car. "Your missing out" he shouted, "Beats the shit out of **Weetabix** any day", before he flicked it up in the air and drove off, driving over the **lighting butt of the cancer stick.**

The reason I can remember this with such clarity is for several reasons. One reason was that my colleague was a jester, witty and always clowning around and his comments drove me to stick with what I had been doing. The second reason was that ironically; the same man would remind me of this story every time we met, and right up until he **passed away** from **throat cancer at only 58 years of age**. Chain smoking was almost a part of his character. This is the truth and again; is not a violins story and designed for heartstrings to be tugged at. It's told as it happened. The same man when diagnosed was a good friend and a very brave individual, and although his diagnosis was an unexpected shock to him when he first received it, he dealt with it using typical black humor and joked that "maybe I should try the **Weetabix** and water" right up until my last conversation with him **two days before his death.** I will say one last thing about this man and it is that I can honestly say after years of working and **inhaling poisonous shit together**, we had never discussed the dangers associated with our **addiction to nicotine.** He would never, not in a million years, have thought that he would get **cancer** or **become a death** now **registered as a smoking related statistic.** It just so happens that he, **like myself and billions of other addicts of this poisonous shit**, liked to live on our **bubble of unawareness** or unreality to **the complete devastation we force our bodies to endure with relentless and repetitive poisoning.** R.I.P. Gene.

I continued with my mission to **beat my addiction** and here is **the logic** or the thought pattern I continued to hold fast in my mind. Every time that I craved a **cancer stick** or I became anxious or fidgety, I would reach for my packet of **Weetabix** and take one biscuit out and take a bite out of it. I can say hand on heart that I am a massive fan of **Weetabix,** especially with cold milk (great for energy, full of protein and very tasty) but as I said, tastes like shit when eaten with water. Every bite was tasteless and dry and hard to manoeuvre around your mouth, tongue, gums, and throat. The only relent from it sticking to the roof of your mouth and in between your teeth was to take a swig from the bottle of water. This may seem like a prison diet but it was allowing me to be free from the **poisonous manacles** that **nicotine** had forced me to endure through **poisonous addiction** for far too long. At first (like any other **suffering addict** (who understands the sorrows associated with trying to **quit this shit**), I went through the initial stage of allowing the last of the **nicotine** to leave my system. This stage which only lasts a couple of hours is when addiction kicks in and habit tends to try and back addiction up. **Willpower;** when summoned here is one tough fucker to beat when it's at its most **powerful** and most **willing.** This is the confrontation where **habit** and **addiction** square up with you and **your Willpower** in its final act of desperate defiance. Bearing in mind at this stage that **habit** and **addiction** are the ones who will depend on your failure in order for them to succeed and will scream with cravings to try and "pull you back in again" as they say in the godfather movie. When several hours go by after your conscious decision to never look back has been made, **the urges to inhale poison** for many will seem like a natural urge. Remember that it is a craving **through addiction** and is a highly **unnatural want**. A natural urge is someone bursting to use the bathroom or even breathing so don't get this confused with forcing your body to **ingest nicotine** or **inhaling poisonous shit.** Whenever these feelings arise and you feel that urge or craving becomes too much to bear, then reach for your **Weetabix** packet, take out a biscuit and begin to munch.

Trust me; you won't be writing letters home about it but you will manage to get through it, so keep munching. Now about two hours will pass and you'll begin to allow your mind to wander and will become fidgety again. The thoughts of **poisonous addiction** which seems like a lifetime ago (even though it has only been a matter of hours) will call to you, beckoning you to bum a **cancer stick** or get into the car and drive to the nearest place for a **purchase of poison** and this is where your **Willpower** will instruct you to open your packet of **Weetabix** and again, start munching. **Willpower** against **craving for cancer**, who will you allow to speak louder? Do this again and again and for as long as you have to. It doesn't matter if it's at home, in work, picking up the kids from school or even keeping a pack of 3 or 4 **Weetabix** in your handbag on a night out or at the dinner table if you must. Do not be concerned about how anyone views what you are doing and asks have you mental health issues! The chances are that in your first few hours or for some days of come down from **nicotine addiction**, you'll probably be so agitated that you'll tell anyone who attempts to scoff or laugh at you to "fuck off and mind their own business". After a time you will adjust and eating these **Weetabix** will become almost second nature. This doesn't mean it becomes pleasant,(oh no, still a chore) but very bearable and not approached with such a feeling of dread every time you knew craving meant you had to indulge in one.

Within a two week period, I had gradually regained my **sense of smell** and **taste** and although I wasn't fit enough to run (or walk) a marathon, I was beginning to feel a lot better. The urge to light up seemed to dwindle less frequently. I think my brain seemed to now recognise that every time a craving or urge caused me to get fidgety; I was satisfying this craving by feeding it dry cereal. My brain seemed to begin to recognise this as the only substitute it was going to receive no matter how much **it cried out for nicotine**. It seemed my cravings only appeared when I found myself in a position or situation like a social gathering or function, where those around me where still **inhaling poisonous chemicals.** Because my cravings began to diminish, so did the need to pump 12 **Weetabix** (yes 12! and some days more) into my body. To be honest, I don't know if it was the **Weetabix** and water or just my body getting **back to normal** but I had **a feeling of energy** and **strength** that I hadn't felt for a long time. I decided that even though my cravings had almost gone after week 2, that I would continue with **my 21 day programme**. I remember reading that as far back as 200 thousand years ago; people have left records which show that they spent long periods of time **detoxing their bodies.** Some of our religious figures even quote drinking plenty of water and fasting in a desert to rid the body of **poisonous** and **excessive toxins**. This is what I want you, the reader, who has made this very **important decision to live** for themselves and their **loved ones** to understand. When **you decide you want to quit inhaling shit** for any particular reason, be it family, health, longevity of life or all of the above, then do whatever it takes and again **stick with it** until **you no longer inhale this poisonous addictive shit**. If you decide to challenge yourself to try the water and **Weetabix** technique, then the rules, if any, are very simple; Do not attempt unless **you have made a conscious decision** to **quit for good** and **not a half assed new year resolution type empty promise**, and that you have truly **had enough of breathing in shit**, and **breathing out bullshit excuses**. Do not attempt this until you are fully prepared to go to the very end of **21 days**, if you feel this is necessary. Remember, this doesn't mean that you have to live off **Weetabix** for **21 days**, eat what you wish but keep the **Weetabix** at hand in case of cravings. Don't hide the fact that you've made **a decision to live** and don't be afraid to tell people where to go if you get strange looks. You are after all, only eating cereal dry and **not inhaling 4000 poisonous chemicals into your body** which (as we know!) should in actual fact be something frowned upon by society. Make sure (if needed) that even if its two weeks **after you've quit;** to incorporate one or two dried **Weetabix** into your meal times or in-between as a snack so that your mind is **focused on your goal.**

You'll soon begin to see that even though you're brain registers that **you're filling your time with something other than poison,** it will tell your body that **you're sick of eating this shit.** It won't do that with **nicotine** because **nicotine is as highly addictive** as heroin, so the **endorphins** (or happy chemicals) that **nicotine** tricks into jumping for joy won't get the same excitement for a dry breakfast biscuit, without any **addictive properties or poisons.** You will not become addicted to Weetabix, I think is a fair statement and if you do then what harm! It's at this stage that you can almost call yourself a **non-smoker.** When you get to the end of the **21 days** you will reflect on the time that has passed. You should look at how you feel with more energy and even how your appearance has changed. Look into a mirror and say to yourself "Ok; I've put myself through hell for the last **21 days** in order to **conquer my addiction"**. I **haven't lit up once, I feel good** and **I look so much better".** Then try asking yourself; **"Will I ever inhale this poisonous shit again?** The strong person will remember not only the **21 days of hell** but the **21 years of poison** they **forced upon their bodies.** If any person tries this challenge and fails, then it can only be through **weakness, self-loathing** and **idiotic stupidity** and that's just it, nothing else can be said. Those who look into the mirror and still feel an urge, but who realise it will pass are the ones who deserve to say **they are ex-smokers** and are overwhelmed by **a desire to live** a healthy existence and

not overwhelmed by an addictive poison. These two groups will separate **who it is that cares for their body** and for **valued time with family** and **who is weak** enough to not **give a fuck** and give **into a false sense of comfort,** because they are **willing to throw it all away for their inability to say no to a cancer stick.** If you want to live then stop talking about it. If you think you can trade dry Weetabix and water with poisonous chemical shit for 21 days then start today. Don't be weak and whinge for your fix like a baby crying for milk. Living starts when dying unnaturally and needlessly is taken out of the equation. **If you give a fuck about your family** and your life then do this today. **I want to live** means **wanting to live.** This shouldn't be just some of the time but all of the time.

THE 10 COMMANDMENTS OF THE EX SMOKER.

If you have got this far in the book and if you have already stopped **inhaling poisonous shitty addictive chemicals**, then I salute you and I take my hat off to you. What you are doing is exactly that; **DOING and not talking about it.** You may be doing or have done it for any number of reasons described in this book, either because it made you **wake up** and **smell the much needed fresh air,** or simply because it just **makes sense to inhale air instead of cancerous poison.** Whatever the reasons; it is **all you're doing** and **is your decision.** This leaves the **responsibility to stick with it** now **entirely up to you. Only you have the final say** on how the pages in the book of your life will turn out. It's time for you to write your own story, your own future and whether it's a fairy-tale ending or again, written like a Greek tragedy is **entirely up to you.** The chapters of your future should be bright and long if the decisions you make are **the right ones.** Here are the 10 commandments of the ex-smoker to reflect upon whenever **poison creeps in** or around **your healthy new life** and attempts to build a **poisonous** bridge. Tear out this page or write the following down. Leave them anywhere you think you may need reminding at all times of the **misery** and **unhappiness, nicotine** and **poisonous chemicals** have brought to you over the years. Put them on fridge, a mirror or even a pocket, wallet or handbag as a constant reminder of how **healthy and happy** you have been since **you stopped inhaling these cancerous poisonous fumes.** The **10 commandments** of **the ex-smoker** are as follows;

1. **I refuse to pollute my heart, lungs, arteries and skin with 4000 poisonous chemicals any more. Those days are gone.**

2. **Whenever I breathe from now on, it will be deep breaths of air doing exactly what my lungs were designed to do. If I can manage to do this whilst out walking on a beach, through a field of freshly cut grass or on a crisp frosty morning, then even better.**

3. **I will take any hard earned money that I would usually have spent on my cancerous addiction and save it or spend it wisely on bene fitting myself, my health and my children/ family.**

4. **I will walk, jog, run or push myself to do whatever it takes for me to clear my body of the poisons I have forced upon it for far too**

long. I will get my lungs and my heart back to the function I was born with.

5. I will not listen to the yes men and women, whom I encounter on a daily basis, nor will I accept the poisonous chemicals they offer me, nor will I allow myself to stand in the same toxic airspace as these careless individuals.

6. I will accept that every human being including myself, has what we call ups and downs of life and will not use any excuse, either a positive or a negative event to reach for a filthy cancer stick to help or assist me as I understand that these pieces of poisonous paper are the equivalent of cancer, calamity and death.

7. I realise that as a smoker with a filthy disgusting addiction, I was doing untold damage and harm to both myself and anyone I inflicted it upon by making them inhale my poisonous fumes. I know understand fully the damage I have done and vow to never again repeat my mistakes.

8. I will use my own bad experiences of inhaling 4000 different types of poisonous chemicals and relate how they have had a profound and negative impact on my life to my friends, family, loved ones or anyone who will listen in order to impact their own decision to stop poisoning themselves with this poisonous shit or not to start in the first place.

9. I will not give a seconds thought to regrets, to not doing this sooner, or when I was younger; because I now realise that we are all on borrowed time and that time is the most valuable asset we possess along with our health and wellbeing. Stopping a filthy addiction means that the clocks hands now run in my favour.

10. I promise myself that I will live. I will do the things that I was put here to do and that this doesn't involve breathing in poisonous fumes from cancer sticks. I will give my body all that it needs to thrive, as it gives me all that I need to survive. I will fight to stay fit instead of fighting to breathe I will look forward to my healthy future and not back at my poisonous past. I am doing this for my family and for myself. I will never repeat the mistakes I have made in the past regarding my health. I love being able to taste, smell, and breathe properly. I love my new life and I want to live. This I promise myself, I will do.

And there you have it. Now is the time for you to reflect and if need be, start reading this book again. You may be feeling as though someone has been shouting in your ears through some or maybe all of these chapters and you're probably right. If you found it vocal then you were hearing your own voice throughout, speaking on behalf of your body, begging you to listen and to take notice. There is no such thing as giving up when the time is right in regards to **a filthy disgusting addiction.** There is only the now, this minute, this second, and this instant. We have learned in our chapters that each one of us is made up with different genetics, with some of us prone to different elements than others, leaving us exposed to the elements of the world that surrounds us. We all have different **strengths** and **weaknesses**. One person's strong points can be another's weaknesses and vice versa. What we do know is (as of the times we now live in), that **inhaling chemicals (designed to kill)** into the lungs which are **designed to breathe air** is for **idiots** and is **unacceptable.** Those who have decided to walk tall and **breathe in the fresh air** have seen the error of their ways and should realise that anything else is just not good enough. For you, **good times are coming.** For those of you who read the words and did not or refused to believe them, I would say to read this book again and again and again if needed until what's written does make sense. If you don't, then listen out for the next **cough, splutter,** or **wheeze** that your **chest and lungs** make when you attempt to scale a long flight of stairs or run after your child's football. Listen for **the rasp** that the **phlegm** makes as it tries to **escape your arteries** which are **constantly blocked.** If you won't listen to my voice, then **listen to your bodies**. There are enough signals for you to listen to. The signs will be there for you to read in **your slow movements, snoring, and shortness of breath** and sadly if not heeded, **premature death**. The constant colds and flus you suffer caused by your low **immune system** right through to **the stains on your teeth** when you look in the mirror will let you know that there is an **addiction** responsible for **the misery** which **keeps reoccurring**. Your body is **shouting at you to stop killing it** and it is time for you to listen. Take notice before you **run out of time.** I will take some time now before I run out of it myself to say that as an **ex-smoker** I am very aware of the traps that allow a person **to fall from grace** when it comes to attempting to pick back up a **poisonous addiction.**

I have had all manners of the tests we know as life's ups and downs thrown at me since I've quit and I have passed every one of them with flying colours. This is not because I am **stronger** than anyone reading this or because **my Willpower** is of superhuman capacity. I have failed in many areas of my life as like many of you, I am a **weak human being**. I am fragile like we all are when it comes to our biology and realise that to error is human. What makes both the **determined** reader and I the exact same is our **willingness** to admit that **we were wrong** and to **acknowledge** our **mistakes.** Only when we **own these mistakes** can we no longer **be in denial.** Be ready to accept **the past faults** which allow us the closure needed to move into the future and to **keep pushing forward** towards **our goal of freedom from addiction** to **poison in order to cope**. To move forward is to advance and this means not looking back and to embrace **new things in life** instead of clinging to things of the past that held us back where we were. Anytime a situation has arisen where I've seen a person lighting up a **poisonous cancer stick**, I move away instinctively and if needed, completely out of that airspace. There is always going to be that part of you that at first feels anger towards that person, for not taking the people **who want to breathe air into consideration.** When I move away; that anger subsides and as I watch the person from a distance, the emotion of anger turns I suppose to… **pity**, would be the right word. I feel **pity** for **their ignorance**, their **stupidity** and **pity** for those who I see as **innocents,** if they are **forced against their will** to share the same airspace of these **uneducated** and **uncaring idiots.** Although there are those who will say "I don't ask them to stand there, why don't they move if they don't like it?" I would say "fuck you and anyone who resembles you". These **sub human beings** are the **DIE HARDS** (I used this expression and highlighted it again because it is truly fitting), who will stand outside the hospital doors and **inhale their poisonous shit** in the presence of the **young old or infirm** who have to walk in or out of the building. The same **ignorant shitbags** of **inconsiderate degenerates**, who are **uneducated**, carefree or careless about the damage **passive smoking** causes to other human beings, will stand outside of a hospital entrance **looking like shit** which has been dragged backwards through a ditch and will have a negative outlook about all aspects of life. I don't give a fuck about stereotyping because anyone who has **self-respect** or is **concerned about the welfare of other human beings** doesn't stand outside a hospital door **where sick people have to walk in and out and blow poisonous shit into their faces. These same filthy fuckers will whine and piss and moan about everybody else and how hard the world is for them**. When they finally do get a **smoking related illness** or **cancer** they will complain about the treatment they receive **until the last drag on the cancer stick** that caused the **disease**. These same **idiots** are not by any means **a breath of fresh air** and if you find yourself in company with those **inconsiderate pricks** that don't give a fuck for their health and **yours**, then move the fuck away and leave them do the fake **poisonous little ritual** they feel they have to do in order to socialise **or survive.**

You are no longer a part of **club 50/50** and nor do you wish to be. As you are now all aware, I have no qualms in allowing my feelings be known and on the planet we live in neither should you. I'm not for one moment suggesting that any person should become a vigilante that targets **weaker inconsiderates** who are **too stupid** to realise they are **poisoning themselves and those around them**. What I am saying is to have the **courage** and the **strength** to say "no" or **"not in front of me or my children"** or elderly relative or whoever the case may be and to walk away from the situation if that's what's required. You are on a different wavelength to these people. **They choose to pollute their bodies with poison while you choose to treat yours with respect.** They don't care how long they remain on the planet or don't realise they are **on borrowed time,** while you remain grateful for all that you have and understand that **time is a limited and precious commodity**. Most will never get to meet their grandkids while you want to see yours get married. This is the difference between you and them. Different wavelengths, different frequencies and different lives completely. **You at last have a quality of life**. They, because of **their filthy disgusting addiction** will never have a life full with **healthy potential** and **will endure endless** and **needless illnesses**. Now that **you have decided on a better quality of life**, take some time to allow all of the **happy, positive and healthy things** you now have to look forward to sink in. Start to make plans that you probably never would have made, **if you were still addicted to inhaling this poisonous addictive shit.** Never allow your age to become an issue where the health is concerned and never allow **disability** or **illness,** to mean you cannot achieve what you set out to do. If, like **Bryan Curtis**, you are a person who is **terminally ill** from **a smoking related illness** and **living on borrowed time,** I would ask that if you had the **strength** left in your body to speak and to spread the word to anyone who will listen about **your pain** and **suffering**. Let them know and make them aware of the **misery that inhaling this poisonous shit has needlessly caused you** and your **loved ones**. As I hate to see another human being in **distress,** I hope **your passing** is made somewhat easy for you and I'd like to thank you for **having the courage** to leave those who continue to **poison themselves with a message of inspiration.**

As **sad** as this may be; it is as we all know a **very sad reality** which is going on around us every day. We spoke throughout about the bubble smokers like to live and breathe in. Far too many people are walking around even now in the **"it will never happen to me bubble"**. This bubble they live in, must be burst before they (through smoke signals) take heed and by then as we know it is often too late. The world has to start to take notice and act on **this socially acceptable killer of men, women, children and the unborn**. Life and all it represents is **far too precious** to be thrown away by the use of **addictive poi-**

sons. Life can be hard at even the best of times and **to add 4000 poisonous chemicals 20** or **30** times a day doesn't make it any easier, no matter what the **addict of nicotine** thinks. Perception of life's problems is often resolved with health, (healthy body-healthy mind) so make life as easy or as hard as you want. An electricity or gas bill doesn't have to be worried about when you stop spending 120 dollars a week on an addictive poison for example.

It is never too late to leave a mark on this earth. Even, as I've said, like the late **Bryan Curtis** on the picture in this book. With **your last breath** you can leave a legacy. Whether or not your legacy is about **a life cut down in its prime, or way before its time because of a self-inflicted addiction is entirely up to you**. You should at this stage have your own little **ex-smokers** account where you stick your saved money on a daily basis from the **poisonous shit you used to** purchase. This **10/20 dollars** a day should quickly gather momentum as you start to see dollars quickly **turning from hundreds** to **thousands** in a matter of months. Make sure to circle the day **you quit inhaling shit** on a calendar which can be seen regularly, to watch how the **70 dollars a week** is very soon going to be **multiplied by 52 weeks** as the first year passes faster than you can blink. The only difference is that at the end of this calendar year, you will be healthier and **3640 dollars better off** and with **7280 dollars** to add to the household if both you and your partner are **ex addicts of this poisonous shit.** This is **nice money** to play around with at the end of the year for a holiday, towards a car or to get a kitchen or bathroom refurbished. If you do your best not to dip into your nest egg until a year or two has passed and when the right amount is saved up after a year or two, look at what you have **achieved health wise,** as well as adding to the **longevity of your life** and your pocket. Keep saving to your ever growing wallet where you now have money for an extension on the house or a worldwide luxury cruise. If you were wealthy or abundant starting off then I don't know? Maybe give your money to a charity or cancer research fund and if you're a tightwad, then hold it tight, it doesn't really matter.

What does matter is **you have decided to give your body the chance it deserves** and this is the real wealth. I'm not going to go on about this whole "health is your wealth" thing again, but when you start to feel differently in regards to your wellbeing, then the rewards are worth more than you could ever save up. **I haven't inhaled poison in the self-inflicted sense in over 13 years now and since then; I've regained my physical strength** and have more energy than I ever had as a smoker. Today, **when I look at my filthy smoky past history**, I have no regrets and mainly because of how I viewed it back then and because **I was ignorant** (often through choice) to the **harm** I caused to my body. I realise this is part of the problem for **some addicts** today, many of whom are brought into this world through **nicotine's horrible poisonous** baptism of smoke. I again say that it is only when our societies start to see that the **inhalation of poisonous chemicals and toxins into a human's lungs is abnormal and unacceptable**, that this can ever possibly change. Massive changes are needed on our planet in regards to what we now take as "the norm".

We are still developing slowly as a species and although our technologies are racing forward at an alarming rate, our **treatment of our bodies** is dwindling and forcing us backwards. Several hundred years ago a woman could be burned at the stake for having a wart on her nose or a birthmark on her cheek if she was found guilty of being a witch. What was considered the norm back then would be viewed as barbaric today. Not so long ago in the last century, limbs where removed on the battlefield by allowing some poor bastard bite down hard on a piece of leather or a stick while the injured appendage was removed using a saw, with whiskey to dull the pain because there was no anaesthetic or painkiller to render the patient unconscious. This would be unheard of today or unaccepted in today's cultures and societies. In this regard, I'll finish by saying I hope our offspring of the future react in a similar fashion with complete shock and awe when they hear about how their fellow men and women suffered many moons ago, and all because of a **lack of self-awareness**, **ignorance** or **self-harm,** whilst they are looking at a **cancer stick** inside the glass case of a history museum, where it belongs.

Remember that fish were born to survive in the sea with water and humans on the land with air. It's that simple. Lungs, air, survival!

You should bear these 10 things in mind to keep it short and sweet as a sour reminder

A little list of reality checks.

1.Black lungs**, 2.**shit breath**, 3.** Yellow/brown/green teeth**, 4.** Premature death**, 5.** Heart attack/Stroke**, 6.**Cancer **7.** Shit skin**, 8.** Limp dick**, 9.** Brown/black/green/red tarry phlegm**, 10.** Filthy brown fingers. These and more are the main ingredients to this filthy addiction. Live the life you were meant to live and follow the 10 commandments of the ex-smoker. The 10 shit stains I mentioned above are only the tip of the iceberg when it comes to the filth you no longer wish to be part of. You were born to live and this in itself is a commandment from the body. **Be strong and breathe as you were born to do.** Get that fresh air deep into your pipes. This is freedom and this is what it means to be alive!

JOE VERSUS THE VOLCANO.

For any of you reading, especially those who are pissed off, angry, offended, itching to break my neck or itching to light up a **cancer stick** to blow it right into my face, then this my smoky old chums is where we get to have it out on paper. As someone who was once addicted to the same **poisonous chemicals** as you wish to defend, please allow me to write this chapter on your behalf and put forward some opinions and comments of which I am well aware many of you feel is your absolute right to be made known. To help, I am going to create a scenario. We will time travel for this set up and journey a couple or so years into the future. It is at a time when our world's governments have set up a high commission that plans not only to ban tobacco from our streets but also to make it completely illegal, so that it is never again sold or used for any purpose whatsoever. Because I am an **ex nicotine addict** and a normal Joe soap who understands that I would have campaigned for my right to smoke, I will play your part and represent smokers everywhere on this planet who feel that this new law is an outrageous proposal and is a blatant disregard of your rights not only as an adult, but as a human being. As I take my seat at this summit meeting, I am informed by the head speaker, that I and several others will be called at various intervals throughout the session to allow our voices be heard. Some will be for and others against; but to please show respect for all opinions on this matter. I only plan on letting these people know that they are taking away my rights and the rights of hundreds of millions worldwide who can do with their bodies as they damn well please. I am feeling confident that my words will be heard as I prepare to hear the government official give his reasons for this **ridiculous abuse** of human rights.

This idiot gives the following plan of action by outlining his world's government's policies and how he'd like to see them enforced within five years. These plans include a complete cessation of the production of any form of tobacco, which can be used for the purpose of inhalation with prosecution for non-compliance. To have smoking recognised, not only as a **deadly health hazard** but also registered as a **form of self-harm** or **self-mutilation**, which should be treated using proper and correct medical and mental health intervention. To allow our schools globally to set up a health awareness initiative as part of the school curriculum focusing on the importance of cell growth and its stimulation by **the inhalation of pure oxygen in order to thrive and survive**. To take unemployment faced by those in the tobacco industry and tackle it head on with the employment in the redistribution of felled trees in the forestry sector.

He finishes to a massive encore from his supporters. I listen to the deafening applause from the modern day hippies in the gallery before I'm called and I'm told to stand, give my name, who I represent and why I'm here. Knowing that my voice is for every living person whose freedom I am here to represent, I address the congress by telling them that my name is not important but that I am the voice of the many millions on this planet who feels it is their god given right to do with their bodies as they please. I am here today to defend that right and using the freedom of speech I wish to say the following.

Standing, feeling confident and gutsy, I tell these dictators that since the first day **I took a breath of fresh air**, I was the one in control. From day one, I made the decisions about how my life went and I'll be damned if I'm going to let some suit dictate to me what I can and cannot do in regards to my body and my health. I've been working hard all my life and since I've been old enough to pay taxes, I've done so every week without relent or complaint. If I decide that I want to spend my hard earned money on tobacco, whiskey or cocaine, then that's my business. If I'm not hurting anyone else, then who are you or anybody else to tell me any differently? I work eight days a week and a cigarette is the only thing that I look forward to during lunch to break up the day and even this pleasure you have interfered with by forcing us smokers to go outside like drowned rats to have a quick drag. If I decide on my time off or any of the few weekends I get off to take a break or to smoke myself silly, then that's entirely my business and no one else's. How can you possibly believe that your proposed plans on taking away the one thing that so many people depend on and enjoy is ever going to work out and be accepted? Its absolute craziness to even entertain such nonsense. If you think that the millions of those I represent will take this lying down then you are sadly mistaken. This is no better than communism or absolute state control. If I work hard and pay my taxes, then what right has someone to tell me what I can and cannot do in regards to my health? My family was raised to believe in the many freedoms and entitlements we have as humans, so why do you feel the need to tell them what they can or cannot do in regards to their health also? If I feel like inhaling tobacco smoke, then that's my right. If I feel like jumping off a bridge or putting an end to my life tomorrow, what's to stop me, so why do you think you have or should have control over what I do with my health? Next you'll be banning the sale and supply of alcohol for damaging the liver and kidneys, or closing down all the fast food restaurants for clogging up people's arteries. When will it stop? , When it's the law for people to walk on treadmills before they go to work in the mornings? Your plans are ridiculous and the policies you wish to implement are not going to work. And where may I ask do you get this self-harm nonsense or self-mutilation bullshit from? I don't cut myself, I'm not depressed and my mental health is fine. I have a job, I have a family and there is fuck all wrong with my mental health and anything to the contrary is downright offensive. What you are trying to do is to completely control people whose only bit of comfort or joy is a pack of smokes and you're looking to take that away as some sort of ridiculous conquest to change the world or to save the planet. You are ignorant as non-smokers id imagine, to the comfort that a cigarette gives to a grieving mother or an old man whose been smoking all their life and is now forced outside a bar or restaurant to smoke in the cold or the rain. You are taking away the basic right of any person affected by the bullshit laws you wish to introduce and enforce complete control over an individual's right to treat their own body whichever way they bloody well decide. You also speak of educating our children on health when my own kids go to the best schools and with the best education system money can buy. Why attempt to change an education system that's been working for hundreds of years? Sure, I don't want my own children to pick up my smoking habit but if they decide that this is the road they want to go down when they become an adult, then who am I , you, or anyone to try and change their minds? They should be allowed make up their own minds and not told how to live their lives. What you are proposing is complete control and is wrong. You may have millions who agree with what you are trying to do but those of us who feel it's our rights to do what we feel with our bodies also number in the millions possibly billions and I speak here today for them also, when I tell you now that we totally disagree with your Ludacris sabotage of a person's rights. You have stopped us from smoking in the workplace and we have adhered to it. You have forced us to socialise outside of bars, clubs and restaurants and we have put up little or no resistance. You have even put an end to advertising the cigarettes we use to try to keep us from doing something we feel entitled to do and all the while we have taken this lying down, but I can honestly say that speaking for every single person on this planet who chooses to smoke, that you are facing a revolution and a force of rejection with large volumes of non-compliance worldwide if you allow your proposals to come into force as law. I hope my words here today will have an effect as they are spoken with as much passion as possible in the hope that you may seriously reconsider the conclusions you have come to, in what you see as fixing something that's not broken. I think I have said all that I feel needs to be said on the matter, so please, if anyone needs to put an argument forward or thinks they have the ability to change the minds of the many millions of smokers globally, then feel free, as we are all ears.

A large round of applause deafens the entire audience of the high commission as the cheers and whistling of your fellow smokers and supporters drown out the boos and hisses of those who object to your speeches contents. As silence is called for, a man stands up and steps forward to introduce himself as the next speaker to answer your questions and to voice his own opinions on the plans of the high commission. He tells the commission that his job is the surgeon general, whose job it is to warn society of the dangers of products we use to digest, inhale, ingest or inject. 'If it comes with a health warning' he tells the audience, then he is the man responsible for putting it there. After giving a short introduction and a brief rundown of his credentials, he turns to me and tells me that although he doesn't applaud or agree with the colourful language I've chosen to use, he does applaud the vigour and passion I feel for my rights to smoke and the courage to speak on the behalf of the many millions globally who feel the same way. This bubble of praise is short lived and quickly bursts when he then follows with "If only your passion to stay alive was as strong, then I'm certain that many of the issues humanity faces could be addressed here today. When I gasp and mumble the words "excuse me?" he sharply hits back by telling me that I had finished my speech by saying I was all ears which he then adds "is the very problem with the millions of smokers on the planet, including yourself". Intrigued and a bit shocked and offended, I let him speak. "I'm all ears" he continues," is an expression that you have probably been using since the first day you started smoking. These 3 words I'm all ears is for you, a statement of lack. They are words that you use which are of no significance or meaning to you and any individual who chooses to smoke. It is the very same when you use the expression, "I see, I see", to a thing being explained to you, to which you actually see nothing. You also say ridiculous things such as "oh I get it", when in actual fact, you don't get it at all. Your addiction to a substance plus stubborn refusal to hear, see or use your brain, can also be used as the false bravado by which to ignore the thing that is coming and believe me, that thing is coming. That thing I speak of has more than one title. Sexy, cool, smart, rebellious, are not words I would associate with this thing whereas grief, pain, death, suffering, loss and misery are. You may say that you do not care for government policies or your rights being interfered with, but this is as clearly spoken as an addict refusing the help of someone who wishes to see them flourish instead of falter. Take a bottle from an alcoholic or a syringe from a user of heroin, are you doing so to save their lives or do you hand them back the substance which is killing them to stand back and watch them die slowly? You and the millions of others on this planet are of the opinion that just because something is considered to be acceptable in society and is legally allowed by all governments to be sold, that it is somewhat ok to use. You claim to listen and when told that your addiction is taking 15 years off your lifespan, you choose to ignore the facts and live in fiction and refuse to absorb the spoken words. You have seen the warnings, the graphic illustrations, even those who have succumbed to the horrible dangers of inhaling poisonous chemicals dying slow painful deaths and yet you choose to turn a blind eye. You have also been more than educated with every media outlet available worldwide allowing your brain to pick up and calculate the simple maths, that one in two smokers will die because of addiction and this goes in one ear and out the other. There is no one, especially not me, going to dictate to you. What you are doing is getting dictation confused with genuine concern. The fact that you have made several comments which I see as contradictions are the very reasons I would like you to heed the dangers you enforce upon yourself so willingly. If you have paid your taxes all your life, then you have no doubt worked very hard. If you have taken your hard earned money and spent it on a multi billion dollar company whose products are designed to allow you to become addicted, both physically and mentally to poisonous chemicals and you do so because you believe that it is by choice, then you are foolishly spending the money you have worked so hard to obtain. You say this is your free will as if you are choosing to ingest poisonous chemicals and not through addiction and I beg to differ. You also claim that if it is your choice to drink or smoke and that if you are not hurting anyone else, then who's to tell you any differently? This very statement is an admission that you are hurting yourself and the clues are in the words as clear as the day. Can you not see how hurting oneself and harming oneself are done here with mis-intention? If you also fail to see yourself as someone who mutilates themselves, then every cell in your body disagrees. You only need to use the internet and view medical studies to look at the cells of a smokers lungs compared to that of a non-smoker to see the difference. You point out that partaking in a cigarette is an entitlement and something to look forward to, without realising it is merely a relief from nicotine withdrawal and will continue for as long as you allow yourself to be controlled. You and millions of other addicts can do this tomorrow, to no longer be controlled, just by making a decision not to purchase a small box which contains an addictive poison designed specifically towards addiction and death. The freedoms and entitlements you speak of so passionately should be replaced by the freedom to breathe air and the entitlement to live a long healthy life. Freedom and entitlements are not words I believe should be associated with smoking or inhaling chemicals on purpose. As for jumping off bridges or putting an end to your life tomorrow, then you are right; just like smoking, there are laws and procedures in place to control or help such situations, but unfortunately this cannot always be avoided and people often make decisions regardless of guidance or advice. What I can say on this matter is while it would be foolish to say that no person is free from thoughts on one's mortality, life, death and all that lies in between, it is shocking to know that there are people like yourself who can claim to use cigarettes in the firm acknowledgement that they realise cancer, emphysema, a slow painful death or a heart attack or stroke is inevitable and continue to poison themselves. This speaks volumes on choices and suicide to claim to understand that premature death is an inevitable reality because of an addiction and to continue to do so. This to me is the very frightening reality of this particular addiction. As for comments made in regards to banning the sale and supply or purchase of alcohol or stopping people from eating fattening foods, then we happen to be lucky in this regard as more and more people are starting to realise the value of their health and this is very much welcomed in any society. It is wonderful to see that more people are becoming aware at every level that the secrets of longevity of the human body is all about how the body is treated and that the correct fuel powers it to its full potential. At this stage, I would like to talk about a reference you made about your health and mental health in regard to smoking. I have no doubt that you are in good mental health like many of those who choose to smoke cigarettes. My own opinions on this are exactly that, my own and may not be welcome, but I'll continue. Any element of a person's life or any decision made by or through addiction to a substance is not a decision or action made by the person in the right frame of mind. To constantly think about your next fix and to not be able to concentrate properly because of a craving clouds a person's judgment and your inability to make a decision about an event in life normally revolves around trying to include a cigarette in there somewhere. This may be fine if you are a man or woman of leisure but may affect a person who has to make important executive or crucial decisions and who need to be clear, present, lucid and level headed at all times. This interruption of the thought process is interference in our mental capacity to give a particular situation our undivided attention, so to this extent, I believe that smoking can interfere with a combination of craving, addiction and withdrawal if not fed with more chemicals to maintain a feeling of mental stability or normality. These views are based on my own research and what I believe to be a common sense approach to the effects of addiction which can be observed whilst watching a smoker chewing their nails or pacing in anticipation or anxiety when left for too long in between a cigarette. As they are my own opinions they may not be viewed by everyone as valid and I will allow the guests here today to reserve their own thoughts and judgments on these opinions. What I do believe to have real validity however, is the world governments attempts to truly start fresh. I believe once this poisonous addiction has been eradicated fully from our society, then the government's plans on teaching the importance of our bodies and our health is a stepping stone which will allow the future generations to focus on healthy bodies, healthy minds and a future where humans understand that in order for us to flourish and to thrive, to work to the best of our ability, we must learn that our first and last actions on this planet involves breathing in and out fresh air. It is what we are designed to do. We take our first breath on our arrival to this planet and we take our last breath when we leave it. Whether or not the smokers of this planet choose to do this naturally, prematurely or through a machine that helps them to do so is entirely up to them. We should teach our children to leave a mark on our societies and not a brown stain. Nicotine and the chemicals in every cigarette are deadly dangerous and I truly believe that they are a scourge on not only society but on the lungs of any humans who sees it as a right to destroy their bodies. We are very simply put; biological creatures that fall apart when mixed with chemicals. Tobacco costs a fortune to kill whereas the air that keeps you alive costs nothing and only a society that sees this and understands it collectively, can move on in proper sociological evolution. And now to those who continue to die from the countless cancers this cacogenic chemical causes, I will finish by wishing you the very best in your uncertain future. You may believe you are securing freedom here today but you are all blinded by the slavery of addiction and there are only two ways to secure your freedom. One is by walking away from this addiction and the other is in a box. We are all born with choice but it is what you do with that choice which separates the strong from the weak. With that he walks down to whistles claps and shouts from his supportive party. He passes you as he takes his seat and smiles. You don't say anything because he has grabbed your attention and as you look around, you notice that your nicotine addicted supporters are no longer making noise and looking at each other shrugging their shoulders in an almost defiant agreement. What more can be said from both sides? Nothing… everyone has said all there is to say and now just like in real life, it all comes down to choice…have you made your decision and more importantly will you stick to it?

21 days of hell for a lifetime of heavenly health.

We touched on this 21 days thing throughout and like the rest of this book; its simple common sense and straight forward. Some of you may want a little guidance on this 21 days so here is a little recap. We talked earlier about the bullshit that is the fad. Anytime there is a fad or trend or diet that promises you instant results or overnight success is a load of bullshit. The National Lottery is about the only thing that can give you money or success overnight and anything else in life has to be chased or worked hard for. This chapter is going to be short and sweet and if followed correctly will yield lifelong **benefits for the person who sticks with it**. It's very simple. **You stop putting shit in your body for 21 days and that's it**. We have all heard of 21 day detox programmes. Even ancient civilizations used this so we won't complicate it and keep it nice and simple. And here is the method to the madness. **If you don't inhale poisonous shit** for 24 hours and you move into hour 25 then, hour 26 and so on, with **solid determination never to smoke nicotine again**, then after **21 days**, you never will. And here's why; any person who has the ability to **abstain for 21 days from an addiction** that they have battled for years, has not only **determination to live** but the **strength** to follow through on their pledge of taking a stand, without backing down **or kneeling in defeat** to a **substance that is killing them**. Think about yourself when you read this. If you can **detox your body** and put yourself through climbing the walls and manage to do so for **21 days** or 3 weeks of what you perceive to be hell, why would you then consider **inhaling a poison which takes 15 years off your life?** Only a **fucking idiot** would make **this fatal mistake**.

The chances are that some of you in the past may have spent weeks, months or even years without this **poisonous drug** only to return after an event or upset of some kind came knocking or maybe it was just a social thing or because you were bored. This is only because your perception of what you were doing was only viewed as **habit** and not **addiction**. It was then that you were **weak** and lived with chosen **ignorance**. After reading this far, you have shown that you can take a bit of tough love and your resolve is obviously **stronger** than those who didn't get past the first chapter. Taking an ear bashing and acknowledging the truth even if it's **devastating** to listen to, shows that you have **the determination** to **quit inhaling shit permanently.** This time you **won't fail** because you realise exactly what is at stake. **Failure cannot be an option** in a

dangerous game where the odds of losing are **1 in 2**, so you understand that you must stick this out and **stub this poison out for good**. Those who have got this far in the book should **not doubt their ability** or use past experiences of failure as a guideline. Remember that this was when you were **unprepared** and **weak**. You should look at the attempts made by an **alcoholic** or a **heroin addict** and compare their drug of choice to your drug of choice. I ask you? How many times have you commented on an alcoholic or a junkie (maybe a celebrity if you don't know any) and said "I bet they don't last a week?" Again, not comparing any particular drugs only the **addiction.** If an alcoholic stays sober for **21 days** and then relapses you will normally hear "there they go again, **such a waste".**

What could be the reason for that relapse? Usually they will do so because an event in life will throw them an obstacle where risking their health or a **certain death** is the only way to resolve the same issue, whereas a person without dependency or addiction issues can handle this issue without resorting to **self-harm.** The inevitable being the alcohol used as a crutch, will always be around just like life's ups and downs. It's a substance of comfort for an **addict.** Get yourself into this **frame of mind** when you ever question or doubt **your ability** to deal with any issue be it a birth, death, bill or a marriage! Remember ;these are everyday events that you will partake in up until you eventually kick the bucket yourself, so to use a **poisonous substance** as a reason to celebrate, commiserate or deal with any of life's everyday occurrences is only the **weak** and **feeble** solution of an **addict**. Some people face their trials in life by going out for some **fresh air** to clear the head and this is how you approach a time you may find stressful. Others light **a cancer stick** that some billion dollar company **pumps addictive poisonous chemicals in** to keep them **hooked** and the issue they faced still doesn't change one bit, but the cells and organs in their bodies most certainly do. If this is all making sense to you then good. All I would like to see for anyone who **decides that they have had enough of inhaling poisonous shit** is that they learn to **breathe deeply** and enjoy life because it was meant to be lived and enjoyed and not bound by **addiction to nicotine.**

After **21 days of abstinence**, you have two choices to make… Either keep going and never look back or you can celebrate **not inhaling shit for 21 days** by **inhaling shit.** Only a **fucking fool** can make **a fools decision** because anyone who **stays detoxed** for so long and returns to **poisoning their body with chemical cancer causing shit is a waster of time**, **energy** and **life**. What would anyone say about a heroin **addict** who did the same? Again they would say, "I told you so" or "It was obviously bound to happen". If somebody wishes to treat their body this way then it is hard for anyone to feel sympathy for them. When a person's body works hard to help them **detox the shit from every organ** and they thank it by **poisoning it** all over again, it is only a matter of time before the body says **"fuck you, I'm outta here"**. It is the benefits that people will feel as time progresses which makes all the **detox suffering** worthwhile, because every day that you **fill your lungs and bloodstream** with **oxygen** can only mean **you will feel and look physically** and **even mentally stronger**. This is not **shit talk**, it's from experience. I remember thinking after a month or two that I felt **sick** or **ill** and thought I was never going to be as fit as I was before I picked **this filthy addiction** up, but **I was wrong**. I started slow and got myself back walking and training and eventually started running. The running didn't agree with my legs so I just joined a gym and before I knew it, I was training 5 days a week and loving every minute of it. Of course there is such a thing as overdoing it with anything in life as we know, but I have now found my routine and it is an addiction I never thought I would have but I truly love working out and cardiovascular exercising. Please understand that this comes from the mouth of a **previously, nicotine addicted** couch potato, who always had a remote control in one hand and a **cancer stick** in the other. I feel fitter now than I did as a teenager and that is not some bullshit cliché. I am **physically and mentally stronger than I have ever been**. It is what it is, I'm **as fit as a fiddle** and it is something I could never have done had I continued to **inhale poisonous addictive shit**. This applies to all of you **regardless of age**. I would like to have played professional football or competed in an event at the Olympics, but being realistic about it, both due to age and other circumstances, the chances of both are either slim or none, but as I said, **I'm fit, I'm active, I'm healthy** and **most importantly I'm happy**.

So for anyone of any age group, **give up this poisonous shit** and **stay the fuck away from it**. If youth is on your side then use it to your advantage and start fresh in the literal sense. If like myself you are getting that bit older, then take back the years with a **healthy passionate force**. If you happen to be in the twilight years then I salute your tenacity and your **passion for life**. It is **never too late to want to start living**. Your body wants to live so much so that even on our **death beds** our bodies fight to stay alive, so **embrace life** and get **as much air**, (the **very essence of life** itself **into your lungs**) and **breathe deeply**. The **initial 21 day period** will fly by in no time and **after 21 days** take a long long walk on a beach or up a road or out the countryside and keep walking until you are fit to fall down. This is your victory dance and a **tribute to your body**. When you fall asleep from exhaustion that night, your body will do what it does best and that is to go to work repairing your tired and aching bones and muscles. For the first time in years, it will no longer have to work overtime to **cleanse your blood** and your **organs of the poisonous shit** it once endured in the past. Every day after you wake up you will start to notice the colour coming back into your skin as proper circulation comes back into the blood vessels and pigmentation of your face and body. **The greyish appearance** of **a smoker** is not seen on everyone as females tend to cover up with make up a lot of the time but in men it is very apparent. This grey appearance goes with circulation firing back up as the **toxins leave the body** and you can be guaranteed someone will comment on **how good you look**.

Remember that life can only improve when the body is fed **what it needs to survive** so get onto a proper diet right away. I'm not a dietician and everyone has different needs and we come in all shapes and sizes, so just stick to what works for you and I'm not talking about greasy fries and pizzas! We all know the whole vegetable, protein, wholegrain, fibre type stuff that the body requires to function at its best so talk to someone in the know and get this stuff into you. Any good gym will sort you out with a programme and most gyms are affordable for anyone these days so there can be no excuses. Turn your life around 360 degrees and say fuck off to anyone who said you couldn't do it. This is about you and your health and not about what others think so do what you have to do for you and not them. Get fit, start living and start breathing deeply because after many many attempts, you have finally managed to **stop fucking smoking.**

A CONVERSATION ON A POISONOUS PAST.

When I think back on many aspects of my life, there are very few regrets. There are things I maybe would have done differently perhaps but I have come to understand that every event in my life whether I perceived it at the time to be good, bad or indifferent has given me a little lesson on this journey I'm on. I never understood the expression "adventures in life" as a younger man but I have come to realise what it means. Everything we do in life has meaning and we never know what's around the corner, and this is where adventure comes into it. If I was to take anything back, it would have to be the years I spent and the money I spent inhaling an addictive poison through ignorance, but because I can't change this I have learned to accept it and move on. This is not to say there are other things I did to and with my body that I should not have, but this is part of growing up and I also accept these circumstances and events and allow them to fade to memories. The reason the smoking aspect of my past sticks out so much is the time wasted sitting around and inhaling 4000 poisonous chemicals, when others of my age were out living. I used to laugh at people who didn't smoke as if they were the ones who had a problem, or were somehow odd because they could socialise without having a smoke in their hand. Of course when you are raised in a house full of smokers it seems the norm or the natural order of things to start as you mean to go on. It is now many years later, that I see how abnormal it actually was, and I think my frustration in regards to watching others act without consideration for non-smokers, stems from this ignorant approach to what someone is actually doing to their health, and to the health of those around them. That annoyance (as you can probably tell by now!), follows me to this day and I don't argue the fact that a good counselling session may be in order. I have lost many family and friends and missed out on many events in life because of inhaling this addictive shit and it is eye opening for me to think back on it now as I write this. The story of Bryan Curtis should hit home with anyone addicted to nicotine and not only me, because he was also talking to you and about you and to anyone who needs to stop this filthy addiction. His story, my story and the story of anyone who inhales this toxic filth is only different when you make a decision to quit permanently. We are all Bryan Curtis and cancer is always hanging over the head of anyone who wants to play its cruel Russian roulette with cancer sticks. The sooner our societies take a stance on educating its children on the horrors associated with inhaling this shit, will be a day that can't come too soon. There is not enough emphasis on it as it stands and the global cancer deaths annually is a testament to this sad figure. I have no doubt that many of you may feel the same way, but realistically we are the lucky ones. There are still those who haven't seen the error of their ways or refuse to believe the news that there is hope for anyone who is determined to live a long healthy life. Bryan Curtis like millions on this planet have met their needless demise for absolutely nothing other than a horrible addiction to a legally sold poison. Sadly for them it is too late, but now you understand what it is you have to do. The addiction which once controlled you, controls you no more and it must remain this way. Don't ever be foolish enough to view life through the "it will never happen to me" goggles. Again, these are usually worn by those with addictions who stick their heads in the sand like an ostrich and pretend everything is ok when in fact it never really is. In my own case, I began to see changes in my body, appearance and health and I saw the world with these goggles on for many years, refusing to believe that cancer or heart attacks were possible, even though my grandfather had died a young man from a belt in the chest. My grandmother then passed away from cancer and it was an event which still didn't register because I was blinded by addiction, ignorance, carelessness and I suppose youth. The fragility of life can usually only be felt by those who have faced their mortality head on but a person should never have to have to experience a brush with death to give them an appreciation for breathing and for being alive. When death is avoidable, you should stay on this path. With inhaling this shitty poisonous addictive chemical, it is not avoidable, so stay the fuck away from it and avoid it at all costs because it is going to end badly, even if it doesn't kill you with cancer. The only positive I can take from this horrible addiction is the chance I got to read the Bryan Curtis story and to write this book which has allowed me to rant and rave on a personal hate. Bryan said that even if his story changed one life then his death wasn't in vain and I hope that if this book helped you, then you can help someone else by passing it on. Bryan Curtis did not die in vain. If anyone has been affected by his illness or inspired by his story it is me. I didn't know him and if I had, I would probably have sat at his bedside and been ignorant or stupid enough to have a cancer stick hanging out from my lips. I often think to myself, "I wonder what he would have said to me?"

The words…**"STOP FUCKING SMOKING"** … Always springs to mind.

ACKNOWLEDGEMENTS.

This book would not be possible if it wasn't for Bryan Curtis and his brutally honest message. Some saw a graphic image and turned away. I saw a man in distress with a message that he needed to pass on. Thank you to Sue Landry for her brave and open reporting. To V Jane Windsor for her kind words and powerful and moving photography. Tim Rozgonyi of the Tampa Bay Times FL. for his guidance and advice and permission. All of the above were wonderful in assisting me in some way before publication. A man who told me to get this book published was Dr Chris Mulhall. He explained that words have no power if not translated correctly and for this I am eternally grateful. This man is the definition of literature and of the spoken word! Thank you Chris for the friendship encouragement and for your time. You have changed my train of thought and I am better for it. Thank you to John Loftus for your guidance and your wonderful graphic design. I enjoy our conversations and your advice on our many discussions over the years have been golden. A thank you to Barry's tea, for keeping me topped up throughout this writing! I firmly recommend that anyone who decides to write a book should start with a cup of Barry's tea before the pen touches the page. To brother Liam 'Golden Eagle' Maher, thank you for being born, much respect my friend. A special thank you to my editor, proof reader, friend, counsellor, companion and wife Rachael. Through the chaos as it swirls x…My words to you shall eternally remain private. Finally I'd like to thank those who have read this book and used it to make a decision to live. I wish you fresh air and a healthy life from this moment on. Please do not doubt your ability for one moment. You are on the way to a new and better you, so keep moving forward.

NOTES.

NOTES.

NOTES.

NOTES.

Printed in Great Britain
by Amazon